AS SHADOWS FALL

To Dan & Nancy -
Thank you and I
hope you enjoy
the rest of the story -
Grace Anne
Schaefer

People of the Frozen Earth

Book Two

AS SHADOWS FALL

GRACE ANNE SCHAEFER

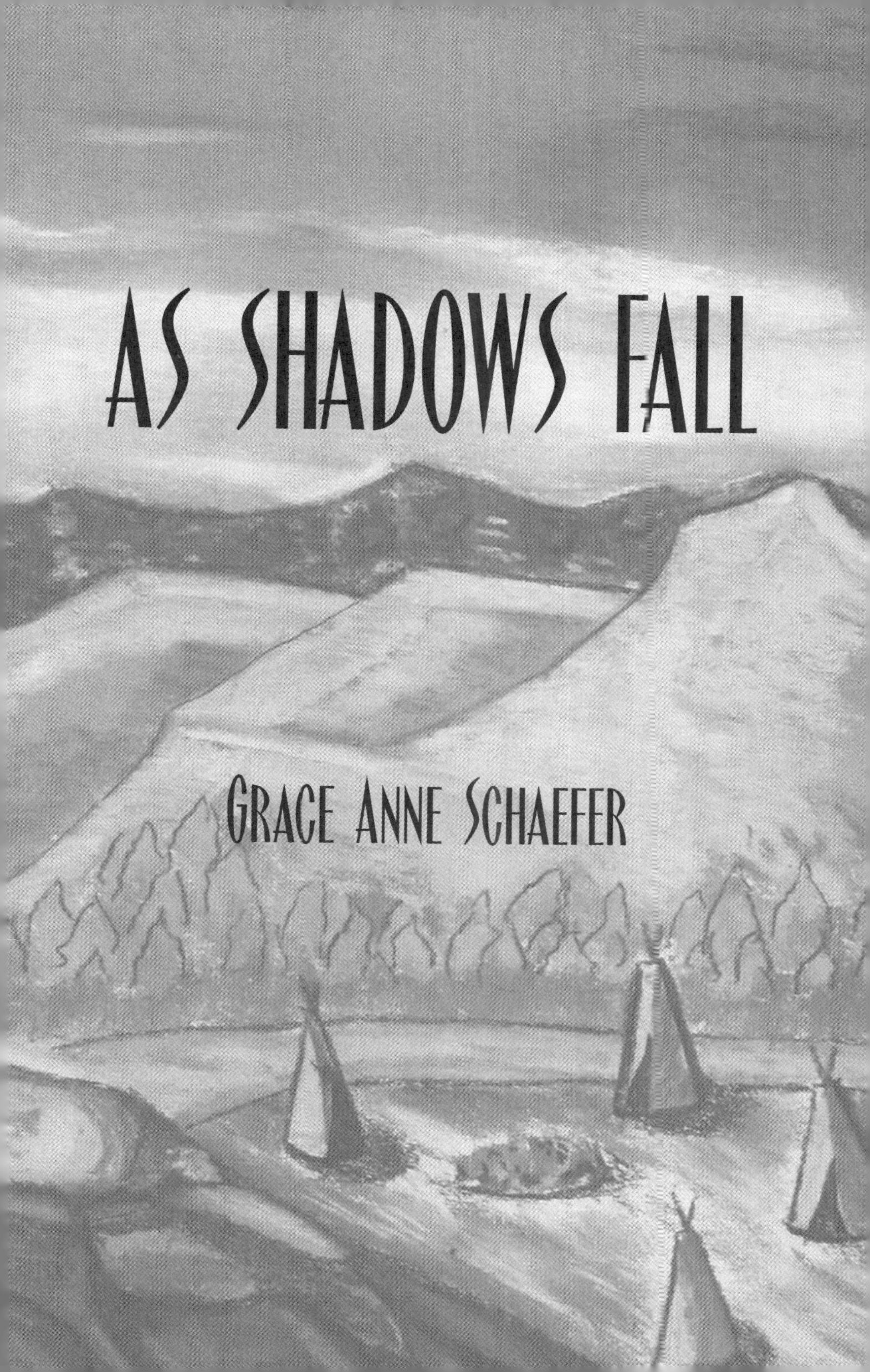

GASLight Publishing
512-528-1727
PO Box 1025
Leander, TX 78646
orders@gaslightpublishing.com
www.gaslightpublishing.com

ISBN 13:
e-book: 978-0-9754796-9-8
paperback: 978-0-9754796-5-0

ISBN 10:
e-book: 0-9754796-9-5
paperback: 0-9754796-5-2

Library of Congress Control Number: 2007925220

Printed in the United States of America

Other books by Grace Anne Schaefer

THE NEW DAY DAWNS

Also available from GASLight Publishing

The Last Boat Out
by Truong-Nhu Dinh and Tran Thi Truong Nga

Stroke of Luck
by Lillie Ammann

Patchwork Trail
by Janet Kaderli

2006 Native American Art Calendar
by David Eveningthunder

visit us at:
gaslightpublishing.com

Dedication

To Eileen Brooks who cared about me and my books. She made me feel special as a teenager, and she continued all the way to the end of her life. I miss her.

To Aunt Sis and Nannie who stood behind me last year while I recovered. I don't know if I would have made it without you.

To Johnny Schaefer who waited as long as he could for me to finish this book. I'm sorry I was so slow.

To all the people who made the first book happen. I know you know your names.

And finally always to Kenn and Granny who make me believe because they believe I can and push me until I do.

Dear Readers,

Welcome back to my world of the People of the Frozen Earth. Many things have happened to me during the time between the first and second books, but I am pleased to continue the story for you.

I would love the opportunity to meet with your reading groups and book clubs. I enjoy sharing my experiences—both writing and researching the books as well as life experiences that include thirty-two years of teaching school, cancer, heart failure, and lap banding.

I learned a long time ago that it is much nicer to laugh than to cry so I try to always find the humorous side of everything that happens to me.

Please feel free to contact me if you'd like to have me speak with your book club or reading group. My personal e-mail is graceanne@peopleofthefrozenearth.com.

I look forward to meeting you farther on down the road.

><> Grace Anne Schaefer

ACKNOWLEDGMENTS

My thanks to all of you who took the time to write to me to tell me you like my stories. I cannot begin to tell you what a thrill it is to know that I have in some way touched people — some of whom I have never met, and others with whom I had not had contact in forty years. Thank you and I love you all.

More importantly, I owe a tremendous debt of gratitude to Bobby, Frank, Chris, Belva, Kathie and Selene who took the time to read this manuscript and make suggestions – the improvements are from their help, but any problems that remain are my own because sometimes I didn't listen. Thanks again. I would never have made it without you.

Chapter 1

SHOCK FLASHED THROUGH HORDA, making her fingers tingle. *The Council doesn't do such things. My father wouldn't do such a thing to me. Would he?* Squeezing her eyes shut, she drew deep breaths until her anger trickled away. *Oh, please, Mother Life, wake me from this nightmare.*

She peeked through her eyelashes and found herself still in the midst of the Gathering assembly. The midday sun still beat down on the high mountains to the west casting small puddles of shadow on the brown grasses of the plains. The lazy breeze tweaked her nose and gently swirled the smoke from the assembly fire on its way to the other world. The crisp smells of pine, cedar, and sage mingled with the tart odor of grasses trampled beneath the feet of the People.

Opening her eyes, she looked up at her mate, Mach. The sun's golden rays cast red and blue highlights in his waist-length ebony hair and glistened on his shoulders. His scars from the Dance of the Sun had faded to pale circles on his pectoral muscles. Her fingers itched to trace the lines of his chest — anything to make her father's words go away. *I was dreaming*. She tried to pretend she hadn't heard the words that would change her life forever.

She watched Mach whisper some comment to Thuro, his taller, but thinner, darker, and quieter best friend. Their eyes snapped and sparked like children who have just been given more camas molasses candy than they can hold in both hands. Her father Zaaco's words hadn't upset them.

"Did you know anything about this?" Thuro's voice betrayed his awe.

Mach shook his head. "Just what I told you yesterday. That the People are forming a new band — mostly of younger warriors. I had no idea they were naming us the leaders. I can't believe it."

Thuro grinned. "I hinted to Elko that Wilda and I would like to be in the new band if we could. He said he didn't have anything to do with the formation of bands."

"I came out and told Zaaco that Horda and I would like to belong to the young band if it was possible." Mach chuckled and shook his head. "He told me to be careful listening to gossip. Said I could get in a lot of trouble that way."

Thuro slapped Mach on the back. "After all these years, we finally belong to the same band."

Mach sobered. "Thuro, we're in charge of the same band."

Thuro shuddered while terror warred with the delight dancing in his dark eyes. "They must be crazy," he said, shaking his head.

"I'm afraid they've made a mistake." Mach's bright smile wobbled just a little bit as a puffy cloud shadowed the sun.

"Do we know enough for this?"

"The Council thinks we do."

"I'm afraid the new band's in trouble if I'm one of the leaders," said Thuro with a grimace.

Copper-skinned Wilda, tiny with a flat, almost bridgeless nose and round moon-shaped face, jingled the shells and beads adorning her smooth, black braids and glared at her mate before she stomped her bead-encrusted moccasin. "Don't even say such things, Thuro. I don't understand you. You will never amount to anything if you don't quit telling everyone your own faults."

Thuro hugged her. "And if I listen to you, I'll be the most conceited warrior in the People of the Frozen Earth." He laughed. "I have to keep a happy medium."

She sniffed and continued to glare but didn't say anything else.

Watching the exchange, Horda pushed at the golden brown wisps of hair curling around her lighter face. *Why do I have to deal with Wilda who looks exactly like everyone else when I am so different? Why can't I at least deal with someone more like me?* Mentally she shrugged. There really wasn't anyone else like her in the tribe.

Her father, the old chief Zaaco, once had thick brown hair with golden highlights, but it had always been coarse and straight like everybody else's. Only Challa, the spoiled daughter of Khollo, had brown, curling hair with gold and copper highlights like Horda's. Everyone else in the tribe had dark hair that never curled.

Only Horda and Challa of all the People of the Frozen Earth had amber eyes although Challa's were several shades darker than Horda's. Both the young woman and the child had light honey-colored skin — no one else shared the golden tones they did. Only Horda had a delicate upturned nose; even Challa's nose looked more like the rest of the People's. All the others had dark, dark eyes ranging from brown to maroon to almost black, and everyone else's skin had dark bronzy-copper tones.

Mach often told Horda she was beautiful; and when she looked into his eyes, she felt beautiful. But his love and admiration couldn't quite drown the echoes of the taunts she had heard through her childhood. *No matter how hard I pretended otherwise, they had hurt — a lot.* Even as an adult, she still wished she looked more like everyone else.

She watched the tiny Wilda and fought the urge to slump, but slumping wouldn't make her shorter. She'd still be taller than everyone in the tribe except Mach, Thuro, and her father's second chief, Elko. *Some of the young People seem to be growing taller. Maybe they'll catch me someday.*

A small puffy cloud cast smudgy shadows, and a breeze wafted the mouth-watering smells of the Final Feast across the assembly. Horda's stomach growled, and Mach grinned at her. She ignored him and stared at the Council sitting on the raised platform around the Circle of Light. *If I don't admit it, my world won't be upside down, and my stomach won't have made that rude noise.*

Zaaco said, "We also want to recognize another of our able warriors who has chosen to join this new band. Zhrul, please stand."

The short, stocky warrior grinned and waved to the People who applauded. Zaaco smiled. "Will his mates Lucza and Urscia stand?" Horda's mind wandered as the women climbed to their feet.

"And another fine warrior who has shown his wisdom

and skills many times has asked to be a part of our newest band." Zaaco's voice rose cutting through his daughter's inconsequential thoughts. "Zeek, will you and your mates Lena, Dita, and Reeme please stand?" Horda felt a smile curve her lips. She and Mach owed their lives to Zeek. If they had to be in this new band, it would be good to have him to help them.

Help us? Anger fluttered in her stomach. If Mach was to be one of the leaders of the new band, then she, as his number one mate, would also be one of the leaders. *Mother Life! My father can't be serious about turning us loose to guide a band. We are too young, and we don't begin to know enough.*

She stared at Zaaco standing in the Circle of Light. "You adults may be seated," he said and waited for silence to fall once more. He smiled as he waited, but the undertone of sadness in his voice had touched a chord in her. Then he said, "Now, we recognize the most important members of any band — the children. I want all the little ones who belong to the new band to stand. If they're too young to stand on their own, someone please hold them up so we can all see them and give them our applause."

And Horda knew without a doubt he thought of Selah, his last and youngest mate. She had been breeding when Bear Claw stole Horda and the others. Zaaco, her father, had left his mates to search for her and the other women, and when he returned — Selah and their little one walked the Frozen Wilds. Neither Nuroo nor Norlon could explain what had happened.

One day Selah had seemed to be fine, but the next day she began to vomit uncontrollably, and then the waters had come. Nuroo knew it was too soon. Hardly a hand of moons had passed, but nothing he tried stopped the wracking pains or even slowed them. The little one was born quickly — too quickly. The tiny warrior could hardly breathe and lay quietly like a little leather doll on his mother's breast. With tears in her eyes Selah said, "I wish Zaaco was here." Then like wisps of smoke on the gentle breezes both she and her little one were gone.

Zaaco seldom mentioned them, but at this Gathering Horda had noticed he often wore the tunics Selah had made for him. Sometimes he would touch the fringe or a sleeve almost as if he could feel her hand on his arm. He wore a faraway look in his eyes that had not been there before. Horda remembered how much he had loved the lively and spirited young woman. *Oh, Fa, I miss her too.*

Zaaco shifted the weight off his right leg. Anguish pierced her heart. *That's the leg he injured saving us from Bear Claw. Two turnings of the seasons and still it pains him.* The old chief's thin braids gleamed silver in the sun. *Mother Life! My father's an old man. He will never take another mate. He will never have another little one. Soon ... too soon ... he will walk the Frozen Wilds himself. Oh, Mother Life, help me bear this pain!* Lowering her eyes she swallowed hard against the hot lump of tears growing in her throat.

She forced herself to count the children standing around the assembly. One finger less than a hand plus one hands. *My! I had no idea there were so many.*

Rain Drop and Storm Cloud stood solemnly beside the seated Unna until Zaaco called their names. Then bright smiles lighted their faces, and they waved both arms above their heads. The quiet little wraiths they had found when the kidnapped women arrived at Bear Claw's camp had been replaced by sturdy laughing children.

The little boy and girl each had a hand of winters according to Unna, the old medicine woman who had helped the Women of the Frozen Earth through their captivity. The oldest and youngest were the only surviving remnant of the People of the Tall Grass. Rain Drop and Storm Cloud had attached themselves to Horda and Suka when they had entered their camp.

Unconsciously, she cupped her hands around her flat stomach while Bear Claw's scarred face and angry words pushed their ways into her memory. Tears streamed once more as she remembered the pain shooting through her body.

"Because — I — was — not — your — first — man." Bear Claw had punctuated each word with another punch.

Remembered pain ripped through her stomach. *Mother Life, save me. I don't want to walk the Frozen Wilds. I want to go home. I want Mach. I rolled myself protectively around my stomach while Bear Claw continued to hit and kick me. The pain's fiery fingers wrapped around me and squeezed more tightly. My little one was departing …*

A different kind of pain came roaring back. Horda swayed and leaned against Mach's solid warmth. "Are you all right?" He placed his arm around her shoulders.

She blinked and looked around, surprised to find herself at Gathering when she had been back in the nightmare of her kidnapping. "Yes."

Mach hugged her, but his attention had already returned to Thuro. She shook her head to dispel the memories, but they wouldn't go. That little one would be a toddler entering his second winter now. Grief clutched her heart and twisted.

She bit down on the inside of her mouth to keep from crying out.

Bear Claw's dead. He can't hurt me anymore. Nuroo and Unna say there's no reason I can't have more little ones — someday. It will be all right. Just like when we faced the council. It will be all right. Horda squared her shoulders and raised her head. *The hurt will go away. Mother Life gave me Rain Drop and Storm Cloud to love. I will be all right.*

"... the challenges of the new band?" Suka, a short, stocky woman with a hand's hands plus two hands of winters, waist-length raven-colored hair accented with a few strands of grey, and snapping brown eyes looked expectantly at her friend.

Horda blinked. *Oh, my. When did my father finish speaking?* "Suka, I'm sorry I didn't hear you."

Suka, the second chief Elko's mate, laughed and shook her head. "I know it's a little daunting to suddenly find yourself the first mate of a leader, but I didn't expect *you* to be speechless."

"It was quite ... unexpected," Horda said softly.

Suddenly serious, Suka said, "But?"

"But what?"

"I sense you're not as excited as Mach and Thuro about their appointments. What's wrong?"

Horda looked toward Wilda who was still tapping the toe of her moccasin and jingling the decorations in her hair.

"I really didn't need to ask." Suka grinned. "Come walk with me. I have things to tell you."

Memories swirled in Horda's head as she silently followed Suka away from the assembly.

"Oh, Suka, I'm sorry."

"Sorry?"

"I've put you in a bad position. I didn't think anyone would ever know. But now they do."

"I do not believe you deserve to taste the Wrath of Fire."

"Oh, Suka, I don't think so either, but I can't just pretend this didn't happen. I'm sorry. I just can't. The fear of what will happen if anyone else speaks of it to the Council festers inside me like a wound."

"I think you're wrong. I hope you find it in your hearts to forgive yourselves and go forward from this time. You and Mach have a great deal to offer the People of the Frozen Earth I pray you do not choose to throw all that you are away because you mated a few days before the Mating Ceremony, but I cannot make the choice for you."

Suka will listen to my anger, but what if I lose her respect ... Horda swallowed an ironic smile. *If my unsanctified pregnancy didn't cost me her respect, why do I worry about such a little thing?*

Because it is such a little thing, a voice deep inside her whispered. *You and Wilda are adults. Your mates are going to share the leadership of a new band. Nobody says you have to like each other, but you have to get along.* Horda muttered, "I'd have a better chance of getting along with a wounded grizzly."

Suka smiled knowingly. "You must be speaking of wonderful Wilda."

Horda felt her face flush. "I didn't mean to speak aloud."

"You should be ashamed for saying such an unseemly thing though it was an apt comparison." Suka's dark eyes twinkled in her stern face.

"Suka, I don't know what to do," wailed Horda. "She doesn't like me. She has never liked me. Even when we were children, she talked about my hair and eyes and made sure everyone noticed I was bigger and clumsier than she was."

"That was a long time ago, Horda. You're adults now," said Suka.

"I know. I've told myself that. I try to get along with her, but she ignores me and acts like I smell bad. She blames me because Thuro joined the party to save us."

"I sometimes wonder what she would have done if she'd been one of Bear Claw's captives." Tears glistened in Suka's eyes.

Memories flooded Horda once more. Bear Claw's icy silver eyes glittered in his scarred face while his big fists smashed into her body, and his mirthless laughter echoed in her ears. Remembered helplessness twisted through her.

Horda felt tears running down her face and reminded herself Bear Claw was dead. Mach had killed him. She reached out and clasped Suka's hand. No one who had not experienced the horror of Bear Claw's encampment could truly understand it. Nor could those who experienced it forget it.

Suka shook her head then glanced around to be sure no one else was near. Her lips curved into a smile. "Elko told me he wished Bear Claw had wanted Wilda. Then we wouldn't have been in that camp."

"Mach would have helped Thuro get Wilda back just like Thuro helped him." Horda shivered thinking of what might have been. A fat tear hung on her lower lash before it dripped to her cheek. "Then I would have been alone ..."

"I'm sorry, Horda. That's over," Suka squeezed her cold hand and smiled. "I told Elko somebody would have been there if it wasn't us. But he said Bear Claw could have had

Wilda, and he and Zaaco would have given prime furs to be sure he kept her."

Horda's mouth fell open. "Suka, that's awful."

"I know," said Suka solemnly, "but doesn't it make you feel better to know you aren't the only one who doesn't like Princess I'm Prettier than You?"

"You're terrible."

Suka hung her head and pursed her lips in a perfect expression of dismay, but her dancing eyes spoiled the effect. "The Council would have a fit if they could hear the number one mate of the second Chief now."

"What would they do?" Horda asked.

Suka furrowed her brow, then smiled. "Scold, I imagine. Then grin behind their hands because they secretly agree with me though they're much too polite to admit it."

Horda nodded. Her father thought little of Wilda. She remembered his anger when Wilda suggested Thuro be appointed to the Inner Band as a reward for saving Mach and a small boy from drowning. *Wilda's like my mother, Meiran.* Horda tried to dismiss that thought, but it kept nibbling at the corner of her mind.

Zaaco had tempered Meiran's thirst for power with his quiet strength. He listened to her schemes and seldom raised his voice, though he teased, cajoled, or ignored her until she abandoned her more outrageous ideas and pleas for power.

Horda prayed silently. *Mother Life, help Thuro learn to control Wilda. If he doesn't, he's going to suffer just like Zaaco predicted.*

Suka frowned. "Did you ever stop to think she might be jealous of you?"

Horda squawked, "Jealous? Of me? What makes you say

such a thing?"

"Look at you." Suka made a show of looking Horda up and down. "You've grown into a very special young woman."

Horda rolled her eyes. "My hair won't stay smooth for anything, and I'm too ta—"

"I know all the things you tell yourself to keep from admitting how beautiful you are," snapped Suka, "but I have eyes." She pointed to them. "I can see. Anyway, I'm not exactly talking about your looks. You have an air about—"

"Perhaps I need a bath," joked Horda.

"You draw people to you," Suka said as if Horda hadn't interrupted. "They trust you and know you'll help them if they need it even at great cost to yourself. Horrible though it was, our captivity taught you to relate to people. You really helped us."

"I was hanging on by my fingernails just trying to get through it."

Suka stared at her. "Maybe so, but the others didn't realize it. All they knew was you protected them — and me — from Bear Claw by taking his wrath on yourself."

"I didn't do a very good job of it." Horda smiled sadly. "Besides, Wilda doesn't know anything about that."

Suka seemed to ignore Horda's words. "Mach loves you very much. You're truly mates of the heart."

"Thuro loves her."

"Oh, yes, he loves her and carries her around on a fawn skin pillow," Suka sniffed and leaned closer to Horda, "but he doesn't trust her."

"What do you mean?"

"I believe Thuro realizes she is a grasping, power-hungry woman. He knows he must watch her. Her thoughtless actions could cost him everything he's gained on his own."

Suka shook her head. "This wouldn't be a first offense. Zaaco won't be so tolerant a second time."

Horda felt her mouth drop open. Suka chuckled and pushed it shut with her right index finger. "Zaaco told Elko how she tried to get into the Inner Band. They're afraid she'll do something else stupid."

Horda frowned. "Since everyone seems to know how bad Wilda is, why was her mate chosen to be one of the leaders?"

"Because he deserves the honor. He's smart and a natural leader," Suka said.

Horda shook her head. "I don't see how he can be happy with her."

Suka shrugged. "Just because he realizes how bad she is doesn't mean he has accepted it."

"Why did he choose her?"

Suka grinned. "Men often think with other parts of their bodies besides their heads."

"Suka!" Horda felt her face flame.

"Well, they do," said Suka defensively. "Oh, I almost forgot. Zaaco asked me to explain why the Council named Mach and Thuro co-leaders of the new band."

Horda shook her head. "I was wondering. They're awfully young."

"That's one reason. Stop interrupting." Suka smiled to take the sting out of her rebuke. "Wilda has the same temperament as Meiran."

A cold fist clenched in the pit of Horda's stomach, and she felt the blood drain from her face.

"I don't mean to hurt your feelings, Horda. But when

Meiran was young, she didn't always act kindly."

Horda bit her lip, but her honesty forced her to reply. "I know. It was a struggle even to the end of her life."

"Anyway, you and Zaaco did a good job of," Suka paused searching for a tactful word, "calming her."

"Zaaco did it."

Suka arched an eyebrow. "He did, but not alone. You helped him from the time you could talk."

"He said that?" Tears threatened as memories of Meiran rushed back. Totally different from Meiran in both looks and temperament, Horda had loved her dearly, but she had not realized until the end of her mother's life that Meiran had loved her as well.

"No," said Suka. "Not exactly. I watched you from the time you were a little girl try to help her be more kind and gentle."

Horda wouldn't meet Suka's eyes. "So you want me to try to tame Wilda?"

Suka nodded.

"Why don't you give me something easy to do? Like stopping the wind from blowing? Or making it rain? It's awfully dry, you know."

"I knew you'd understand." Suka touched her shoulder gently.

Horda wailed. "You didn't even ask before you volunteered me for the worst job in the entire tribe."

"I didn't volunteer you." Suka waited for Horda to look her in the eyes. "Zaaco did."

Horda glared at her friend. "He wouldn't do such a thing to me."

Suka smiled. "Together we did."

"Mother Life, deliver me from my friends and father."

"I told you I'm only explaining one reason the council chose Mach and Thuro," said Suka. "And that's because you can help Thuro with Wilda."

Horda rolled her eyes.

"Stop that," said Suka. "The other reason they were chosen is they're the best men for the job — and you're the best woman to be the wife of a leader."

Horda rolled her eyes again. "Stop flattering me. It won't work."

"Stop rolling your eyes," Suka commanded more firmly. "It isn't becoming to the number one mate of a leader." She touched Horda's shoulder. "You know I'm not flattering you. You have a talent with people. That's important."

Horda ignored the compliment. "Mach and Thuro are too young to be leaders. They only have four hands plus two winters. Many older men are more qualified."

Suka shook her head. "Mach and Thuro are natural leaders. Zaaco and Elko both say the older men looked to them for guidance on the journey to save us. Anyway all the older members of the band volunteered knowing Mach and Thuro were the chiefs."

"Humph. I didn't volunteer," grumbled Horda. "I don't want to belong to this band."

"Well, you're not older. The Council didn't consult you." Suka patted her shoulder and grinned. "Sorry."

"You're not sorry," Horda muttered. "You're enjoying this."

"No, I'm not. I really am sorry because I know this is going to be a terrible job." Suka hugged Horda. "But you knew Mach had been chosen to lead before you mated with him."

Tears filled Horda's eyes. "I knew, but I thought we'd have more time. I hoped we'd have little ones for him to enjoy before he became responsible for a band of People." Once more she pressed her hands to her flat stomach.

"I understand. The band comes first even before the leader's family."

Horda's voice broke and she sobbed. "Mach doesn't have a family."

"That's a terrible thing to say." Suka looked back at the two children swinging from Mach's hands. "What are you? For that matter, what are Rain Drop and Storm Cloud?"

Horda dashed the tears from her face and glared at Suka.

"Well, you are a family. Aren't you? I thought Storm Cloud would stay with me, but he took one look at Mach and forgot I existed."

"The children didn't want to be separated. They are very close to each other. They helped each other survive for three turnings of the seasons."

"We would have taken both of them."

Horda giggled. "You'd have had to take Mach too. Sometimes I think they're permanently attached to him."

Suka nodded. "You've both been good for them. They aren't the ragged little waifs we found with Bear Claw's people."

"They've been good for us," sighed Horda. "We love them, but they're already growing up. They have a hand of winters. We long for our own little ones." Horda bit her lip and looked around to be sure she wouldn't be overheard before she whispered, "I tried to convince Mach to take another mate at this Gathering."

"I'm glad he didn't listen to you," Suka said. "That might have messed up the Council's plans for him."

"Do you mean his choosing a new mate would have kept him from being appointed chief?"

"It's too late," said Suka with a smile. "Anyway, the two of you will have little ones soon."

"Do you really think so?" Horda's eyes pleaded for reassurance. "Sometimes I just feel so guilty that Bear Claw killed our lit—"

"You're not responsible for Bear Claw's actions," said Suka firmly.

Horda rubbed her eyes. "I know that."

"Then be patient."

"I've been patient long enough."

Suka raised an eyebrow at the indignant expression on Horda's face. "Mother Life will give you children when she's ready and not before. Stop worrying."

"You sound like Unna and Nuroo."

"See, I know what I'm talking about." Suka lowered her voice and whispered, "Wilda doesn't appear to be pregnant either."

"No, she doesn't."

"Of course, I doubt she will be until she allows Thuro close enough to muss her hair."

"Suka, you're terrible." Horda clapped her hands over her mouth to muffle her giggles. "You shouldn't say such things."

"Why not? It's the truth and you know it." Suka shook her braids and preened in a perfect imitation of the flirtatious Wilda.

Abruptly sobering, Horda cried, "Suka, what am I going to do?"

"The best you can. That's all we ask." She hugged her again. "Our lives are changing. The council wants some of the younger men to have the authority to help the People meet those changes."

Zaaco's voice echoed in Horda's memory — *I didn't expect it to begin so soon, but I know changes are coming to our people. Our whole way of life must adjust, or we'll disappear like the smoke from the morning fires. Someday when the People need him the most, Mach will walk in my moccasins.* She swallowed the lump in her throat. "My father believes changes are coming."

"So do I."

She blinked. "I know you're right, but I just hate the thought of ..." Her voice trailed away.

"Hate the thought of what?" asked Mach joining them and hugging Horda.

"Congratulations, Mach," said Suka formally holding out her hand to touch his. "You'll be a fine leader."

He grinned. "I hope so, but I'm more than a little afraid I don't know enough for the job."

"It's a natural fear," said Suka.

"I hope so."

"Now, you sound like Elko."

"Elko?" Mach's mouth fell open. "You can't compare me to him. He has as many winters as my fa."

Suka smiled. "Not quite, though he does have many winters. But you must remember he was quite young when he was given his first band."

"He had over a hand more winters than Thuro and me."

"That's why there are two of you," said Suka primly. "He

was all alone. He nearly worried himself and me to death."

"He's a good leader," said Mach.

"I know that and you know that, but he doesn't always know it," said Suka quietly. "He still worries he doesn't know enough to be a chief."

Mach shook his head. "Sometimes I've felt he moved too slowly, but I learned the hard way how much he had to consider before making a decision."

"Sometimes he does move too slowly if you ask me," said Suka, "though I cannot fault his decisions once he makes them."

"Nor can I. What do you hate the thought of, Horda?" Mach returned his attention to his number one mate.

Horda stuttered, "We, ah, were, ah, just talking."

Suka said, "Horda and I were discussing the reasons she will be particularly valuable to you and Thuro as co-leaders of the new band."

Mach frowned at Horda. "You hate the thought of being the mate of a co-leader?"

"Not exactly," she hedged.

Suka took a deep breath and seemed to make a decision. "One reason you were made co-leaders is because she had experience with Meiran."

"Huh?" Mach blinked.

"Wilda is like the young Meiran," explained Suka.

"Oh," he said, "she is ... uhm ... unusual. Isn't she?"

"Very." Suka smiled at Horda. "Unless I'm mistaken, Mach was looking for you for his own reason."

"Oh, yes." He nodded. "I almost forgot. Zaaco wants to talk to you."

"I suspect I've already talked to her, but you'd better go. He might have something to add." Suka smiled encouragingly.

Hand in hand Mach and Horda walked through the shadows to find Zaaco.

Chapter 2

"COME, TAKE A SEAT beside my fire," Zaaco invited formally when Mach and Horda approached him. His mate Treema bustled around working on her dishes for the feast.

Zaaco smiled. "It's still hard for me to remember you no longer belong beside my fire, Little One." He embraced her.

"I know, Fa; sometimes I forget I am grown and gone." Her voice was even though she felt fear in her heart. When did her father become so frail? She remembered his body as hard and strong. Now his muscles felt soft. It seemed he had suddenly become an old man. How much longer would he walk the earth? How many more times would she see him? Talk to him? She closed her teeth on the inside of her lips and took a deep breath.

"It seems it was only yesterday I was tripping over all those warriors who were courting you." Zaaco looked at Mach. "I tell you, young man, there was quite a commotion at that Gathering."

"I know, sir."

"Meiran, bless her heart, was determined to increase her power through our daughter's choice of mate." Zaaco shook his head. "I didn't know how I was going to convince her." Horda watched the muscles in her father's jaw knot and knew he was remembering he hadn't had to convince her because she had gone to walk the Frozen Wilds before the Bid Ceremony that year.

"Eyah!" Zaaco exclaimed. "We would have found a way. She was a good woman in spite of some of her ideas."

"Yes, she was," agreed Mach and Horda.

"She was," declared Zaaco somberly.

Horda took a deep breath. "Fa, why did you do this to me? You know—"

Zaaco's raised hand silenced her. "I did not do anything to you."

"How can you say that?"

"Tut, tut, when did my daughter become so selfish?" he asked mildly.

"Selfish? Fa, that's unfair."

"Life is frequently unfair." Zaaco looked at the mountains reflecting the early afternoon sun. "Mother Life sometimes smiles on the worst people. She allows people who seem to have no real worth to continue on long after good people walk the Frozen Wilds. Father Death often takes away the best and the brightest of our young ones. We don't know why these things happen. They just do."

"Fa," Horda's eyes flashed her exasperation, "I know all of that."

Zaaco reached over to pat her hand. "I know you do,

Daughter, but you seem to have forgotten."

"I have not," she almost sputtered. "I just need to know why you insist on putting me with that woman. You know she hates me."

"Are you finished?" he asked quietly.

She took a deep breath, and Mach watched her gently touch each finger one time. "Yes, Fa. Please forgive my outburst. I just am trying to understand what is happening." She shook her head. "No, I understand what is happening. I just want to know why it is happening."

"Mach and Thuro have exhibited the qualities that make men great leaders from the time they were small boys organizing their friends for games."

Mach fidgeted uncomfortably. Horda sniffed. "I know that. You told me long ago."

Zaaco took a deep breath and waited. When the silence stretched and became uncomfortable, she looked at him. "I'm sorry," she said in a quiet little voice.

"Do you want to know why we made this decision? Or do you want to tell me why we should not have made it?"

"Please forgive me, Fa. I will listen."

"Mach is strongest at seeing what needs to be done and talking to the People then getting them to agree to help." Zaaco stopped and allowed a brief span of time to pass. When she didn't interrupt the silence, he smiled and continued. "While Thuro is strongest when it comes to making plans and seeing the little details necessary to complete the big picture Mach sees. Together they are the strongest leader of the People of the Frozen Earth."

Mach opened his mouth to protest, but Zaaco's sharp look closed it without a sound escaping. "You heard me say together. Together — they are strong because they listen to and complement each other. Apart they are weak in some aspects."

Horda sighed, and Zaaco smiled. "I am getting to the point, Daughter."

"I didn't say anything," she protested.

He shook his head. "As I was saying, Mach easily sees the end result while Thuro can plan the details. Mach sometimes speaks too quickly while Thuro refuses to speak if he can avoid it. The Council decided the best way to help each Mach and Thuro develop their weaknesses to match their strengths was to put them together."

"I pity the other People in the band," Mach muttered.

Zaaco's glare immediately silenced him. Horda frowned. "But Fa, why didn't you pair them as second leaders with one of the older leaders who is strong in their weakness?"

"That would have been a good idea, but in the areas they are strong, they are as strong as any of the second leaders."

"Oh." She frowned and chewed her lip.

"And, Daughter, they work well together. They are willing to talk problems out and neither takes unfair advantage of the other. So we decided it would be best to place them together."

"Thus placing Wilda and me together," she said softly.

"There is that," Zaaco said quietly. "Suka and I both mentioned how much you helped me keep your mother quiet and working well."

"No, I didn't," she said.

"Yes, you did, Daughter. From the time you could talk, you helped me help your mother. She did love power, but she hated the work she needed to do to earn it. You have never been afraid of work. You've always understood. I don't know what I would have done without you to help me help her."

"No, Fa, I didn't do any of that." She shook her head and backed away.

"Horda, I don't know what you are thinking. I have always told the Council you were the reason Meiran behaved in a more seemly fashion after I became the Chief of all the People."

Tears filled Horda's eyes, and she chewed on her lips. "No, Fa, that is not so."

Treema spoke softly to the crying young woman. "Horda, you always amazed me. You were so kind and gentle with Meiran that I don't think she realized what was happening most of the time. You never seemed to even think about it. You just showed her the way, and she followed you like you were the mother and she was the daughter."

"No," she cried. "I didn't mean to manipulate my mother. That is terrible."

"No, Horda," said Treema gently. "Manipulate is much too harsh a word. You did not manipulate her. You showed her the way she should be acting, and she chose that way to act."

"But I cannot do that with Wilda," she protested.

"Why not?" asked Zaaco.

"Because I didn't even know I was doing it," she said. "I didn't intend to do anything. If I go in planning to, it's not going to work. I'm sorry."

"I think you are underestimating yourself," said Mach.

"I don't think you know anything about this," declared Horda.

"No, I don't, but I know you. I don't think your behavior

is going to change at this late date," he said. "I suggest you give it a try. If it doesn't work out by next Gathering, we can be moved."

She blew the little tendrils of hair that had fallen into her eyes. "I don't want to," she protested.

"Sorry," said Zaaco. "The council has spoken. This appointment is for the greater good."

"So it really doesn't matter what I want. Does it?"

"No," said Treema. "It doesn't."

"Does it have anything to do with the fact Thuro and Mach are so excited?"

Zaaco smiled but did not reply.

"How about the fact so many of the older warriors and their mates were willing and ready to commit to this band?"

This time he nodded silently.

"Oh, Fa, I don't want to do this."

"I know you don't, Daughter, but the People of the Frozen Earth thank you for all your hard work."

"Fa, will you absolutely promise me we can join another band next Gathering if this does not work out?"

Zaaco did not say a word.

"Fa?" Horda's voice rose.

"Shh, it grows late. Gathering ends tomorrow."

"Promise."

"I will try if you need another band, but I cannot make any firm promises at this time."

"Just tell me you will do your best." Horda's light eyes bored into his.

"I will do my best if you need to join another band at next Gathering."

She held out her hand until he clasped it. "I don't like it, Fa, but I will try to help Wilda become the woman she should be."

"That's all we can ask of you, Horda." He pulled her into his arms and hugged her. "That's all we can ask."

"Why don't I feel more relieved?" she asked.

"Because it is past time to eat, and it will soon be time for the dancing and stories, but they cannot go on too long because the Ceremony of the Great Traveler will be very early tomorrow. I suggest you eat and get ready for the final festivities." He made gentle shooing motions and laughed quietly at Horda's indignant face.

Chapter 3

Mach stared at the sixty-one knots he had tied on the counting cord. When the sun rose above the prairie, two hands hands plus two hands plus one boys of the Frozen Earth would walk away from the Gathering grounds on their Great Travels. Clamping his jaws tightly, he swallowed the words of warning bubbling in his throat.

He forced his shoulders to relax. His words would do no good. If Mother Life smiled and Father Death was merciful, the boys would return to become men at the next Gathering. Realistically many would embrace Father Death and walk the Frozen Wilds with him — victims of accidents, cold, or wild animals.

Remembered pain, loneliness, and fear wrapped cold fingers around Mach's soul. He shook his head as if to clear it. So many ways for a young man alone to die. *Be careful. Watch out. Take care. Come back; we need you. Change is coming.*

Thuro placed a hand on Mach's shoulder. "We've never had so many Great Travelers before."

"No," said Mach, "I used a counting cord to number them."

Thuro counted the groups of knots on the cord. "So many leaving," he said softly. "So few will return."

"Yes." Mach fingered the knots and shook his head.

Thuro muttered, "It's a useless practice."

"Huh?" Even though he hated it, Mach had never questioned the value of the Great Travel.

"I know you hated your Great Travel as much as I did," persisted Thuro. "Surely you agree it's worthless."

"Well, I didn't exactly enjoy it," admitted Mach, "but I wouldn't say it was worthless. It is important." He shrugged resignedly.

"Why?"

"Why?" squawked Mach.

"Yes, why?"

"Ah, because it always has been."

"That's no reason." Thuro chuckled. "Those are empty words to silence whining little ones. We keep talking about change. Maybe this is one thing it's time to change."

Mach frowned. "I don't think so."

"Why not?"

"Because," said Mach, "the Great Travelers patrol the outer reaches of our territory. Without them we'd have to send scouts."

"Would that be so bad?"

Mach considered Thuro's question then he nodded. "Yes, it would be. Once a man takes a mate and has a family, he shouldn't be away for such long periods of time."

"Probably not." Thuro shrugged. "How much good do children do? I wouldn't have known what to do if I had found intruders. Would you?"

"I thought I would have, but probably not." Mach shook

his head ruefully. "What do you suggest?"

Thuro grinned. "Well, the outer bands are near the perimeter, and the tribe is growing so we could station more bands out there. It shouldn't be too difficult for the men and boys of those bands to patrol."

"Maybe not, but . . ." Mach paused.

"But what?" prompted Thuro.

"But the Great Travel forces boys to become men."

"What do you mean by that?"

"Don't you remember?" asked Mach.

"All I remember is being cold and hungry and lonely," replied Thuro, "and wanting to come home."

"Yeah, but when we started out, I thought I was all grown up. I was on my Great Travel, and I was a man. I thought the Great Travel was the end of the Rituals of Manhood," Mach said ruefully, "but really it was only the beginning. I still had much to learn."

Thuro laughed. "I'm pretty sure I was scared half to death by the time I left the Gathering Grounds, and it didn't get any better until I was back. I hated every bit of the time I was out there."

Mach frowned. "I hated it too. But I wasn't scared when we left. I was too stupid to realize I might meet Father Death out there. Oh, I know I had been told that all my life. I even knew boys who left and never returned, but in my heart and head, I didn't believe it could happen to me. I just got bored and really tired of my own cooking. I wanted someone to talk to, and I was homesick. Then I met the big cat.

"That's when I realized how serious the Great Travel was. I could have died out there, and I didn't like that at all. But that's also when I learned to look inside myself for strength.

It was really scary because I was afraid I didn't have it."

Thuro nodded his understanding, but he didn't interrupt.

Mach continued, "I thought I was a responsible person when we left. You know how we had gone through the Rituals and had practiced making decisions and doing things, but basically that was playing. If we made mistakes or things got too rough, we had our parents and others in the band to help us out. That's not bad, I mean, how are children going to learn if they don't have grown-ups to help them, but it's not the same. After the big cat attacked me, I knew I didn't have anybody to help me out there. I had to learn to depend on myself. I don't know if I would have ever learned that any other way."

Thuro nodded. "I remember," he murmured. "I grew up out there." For a long time he stared into the distance with a far away look in his eyes. Finally he spoke, "I guess the Great Travel does serve a purpose."

"Yes, it really does," agreed Mach. *But, Mother life, please take care of them and bring them back safely.*

Farewell: The ritual departure of the Great Travelers began well before sunrise on the last day of Gathering. Each mother rose early and prepared a special morning eat for her family. The eat consisted of whatever she thought her son liked the best. Almost all included fry bread, fresh meat, and porridge. Then there were berries, camas molasses candy, and other sweets. The mothers always prepared enough to pack leftovers for their sons to carry with them.

The parents were allowed to help the young men choose and pack their supplies. The mothers' preparations for this day began during the Moons of the Long Blizzards though the fathers and boys had obtained the hides and skins for leather and furs even earlier. Mothers prepared clothing and a small shelter to help their sons. During the Moons of Gathering Growing Things, they dried and preserved food and herbs.

The fathers helped with weapons. Though the men made most of their own points and blades, almost everyone traded with the most skilled flint knappers to provide their sons with the best points and knives possible. The parents prepared more than their sons could carry so the boys could choose the very best supplies for their journeys. The parents did everything they could to help their sons survive and struggled to keep their fears hidden deep in their hearts.

After the eat was finished, the families had a short span of time together before they moved to the assembly area. They told a few stories, gave a few warnings, but as Mach remembered, they mostly just sat and looked at each other. It did not matter that no fears were spoken. Fear sat behind each family member's shoulder like a dark shadow over the sun. Every one of them knew this might be the last time they would ever be together. The boy's childhood ended when he walked away from the Gathering grounds.

Father Death was well-known to the People of the Frozen Earth. If he did not claim the Great Traveler, he might claim one or both parents or brothers or sisters before the boy returned a man. Dark thoughts of Father Death swirled around the morning fires, but the People did not encourage his visits by talking about him.

Infrequently words told the boys how much they were loved; more often silent gestures and touches told them. Mothers, sometimes fathers, and occasionally the boys fought tears as they sat around that last cook fire. When the time of parting neared, the battles became more pitched, but no one acknowledged them. Tears were not allowed.

Finally the time had come. The families carried the Great Travelers' supplies to the High Place and the Circle of Light. The mother, father, and boy followed close behind sometimes speaking, more often not. The mother's hand was probably on her son's arm. The father most likely had slung an arm over the boy's shoulder. The boy would lean briefly on one and then the other. But still no tears might fall; no protests would be voiced.

Solemnly the boys arranged their supplies and checked them one last time before stepping into their assigned places. This was the only time any of the People of the Frozen Earth would turn their backs to the High Place. When the boys embarked on their Great Travels, they were the protectors of the land drawing their strength from Mother Life who manifests herself in the Sun anointing the High Place. They stood shoulder to shoulder around the High Place ready to go forth to protect their lands and People.

When the young men were in place, each family looked into their eyes and spoke words of comfort and encouragement before hugging them and sharing their breath. Then they nodded their blessing and moved without turning to their places in the Assembly area. After the families had spoken to their Great Travelers, other members of the People stepped forward to pay their respects and wish them well.

Mach and Horda waited with Rain Drop and Storm Cloud

to speak to the young men.

Rain Drop yawned and sighed, and Storm Cloud poked her. "Behave," he whispered.

"I am bein' have," muttered Rain Drop.

"Are not."

"I'm sleepy," protested the little girl rubbing her eyes.

"You must be quiet," whispered Mach to both children. "This is an important time for our people."

"I know," said Storm Cloud. "Thas' why I'm being very good."

"He was talk—" protested Rain Drop.

Horda leaned down and whispered to the two children. "You are both making too much noise."

"We're sorry." Rain Drop threw her arms around Horda's neck.

"We didn't mean to be bad," said Storm Cloud patting her hair.

"I know you didn't," said Horda standing up. "But I need you to be especially good this morning."

Mach nodded and winked at the children. "We will. Won't we, Little Ones?"

Both children opened their mouths to protest, but Mach shook his head. "Just say, 'Yes, Horda.'"

Frowning and obviously wanting to argue, Rain Drop and Storm Cloud obediently said, "Yes, Horda." Then their small group made its way around the Circle of Light speaking to each young man.

Mach had been involved in the Rituals of Manhood since he entered them two hands turnings of the seasons past. But watching him greet and speak with each of the boys, Horda wondered how he managed to remember and keep their names straight especially since he saw most of them only in the busy days of Gathering. Even as she wondered, she knew it was one of the traits that had marked him as a leader. He knew and cared about the People. He took a genuine interest in what they did.

It was a gift, she thought ruefully. A gift she almost wished the Mother hadn't given him, but then she had to admit it was what made Mach Mach. Perhaps she loved him in spite of the gift instead of because of it. She smiled to herself. If she were honest, she'd have to admit that wasn't so.

Finally the pink fingers of morning pushed above the far prairie driving away night's shadows, and the drums and flutes began to play. "The Song of the Great Traveler" was unlike any of the other songs. One of the ancient songs, it combined loss and mourning in a counterpoint with thanksgiving and hope for the future, a future that stood before the People in the bodies of the boys poised on the brink of manhood. Its lost haunting notes recalled memories of the cold, fear, hunger, and loneliness that walked the days of the long year of uncertainty that was the Great Travel.

The music whispered then soared as it reached a crescendo. The willow flutes trilled, and the cedar flutes sang their deeper notes. The large drums sounded the heartbeat of Mother Life, and the smaller drums echoed the marching feet of the Travelers. Then the Men of the Frozen Earth shook their gourd rattles and lifted their voices in joyous thanksgiving for the large number of strong boys embarking on the greatest adventure of their lives.

Even as Mach kept the beat and raised his voice in song, chill fingers of memories walked his back keeping time with the sad notes of mourning in the "Song of the Great Traveler."

Tears silently streaked down more than one mother's face. Fathers chewed the inside of their mouths and fought to look solemn. The smiles of many of the young men were nothing more than grimaces with gritted teeth. Then the sun pushed above the edge of the prairie bathing the Circle of Light and the High Place in its rays. As if one, the voices of the singers, the flutes, and the drums dropped to little more than a whisper.

Suddenly Zaaco, resplendent in the white wolf cloak, and Nuroo, equally imposing in black bear fur, stood silhouetted against the morning sky. Zaaco raised his arms. His voice rang across the assembly. "People of the Frozen Earth, we come to the end of this Gathering." Silence took over once more. The People stood in the early morning light — waiting, listening, anticipating.

After a short span of time, the light grew stronger, and the music began again — different — louder and more hopeful. Nuroo's strong voice sounded. "Oh, Mother Life, we come before you to ask your protection and guidance for these, our young men … aiiii mah nyah ahyy ahmoni." He began to sing, and the words of the songs ran together in a comforting rush of sound and warmth as the People raised their voices to chant the prayers.

While younger Nuroo sang, Horda watched her father. He stood straight and proud, but, he didn't look as strong as he once had been. Chewing her lips, she realized again Zaaco had become an old man. In the way of all things, he would go to the Frozen Wilds. Her heart twisted. How could he suddenly be so old? He was her fa.

But he would be gone — like so many others. His ma and fa — beloved old ones she knew from stories Zaaco had told her long ago. Xyla, Zaaco's first mate who had loved baby Horda and encouraged her as a little one so different from all the rest of the People of the Frozen Earth; Zephat, Xyla's son and Horda's favorite brother, killed by his Dance of the Sun. Their images – forever young and strong— smiled in her memory.

Then Selah, Zaaco's last mate, and her little warrior who never lived appeared in the mists of the Frozen Wilds shimmering in Horda's mind's eye. And finally Meiran, her proud, difficult mother, stood holding the tiny little one Bear Claw had stolen from Horda. Tears clogged her throat and threatened to spill down her face as she faced the realization her father would soon be gone as well.

She blinked rapidly to dry her tears as she thought of all the ones her father had loved. No, not just her father, she had loved many of them as well. Someday they would meet her, and she would walk with them into the Frozen Wilds. In her life time she had seen walking the Frozen Wilds first as a frightening thing she hoped never to have to do. Then she had seen it as a place to be free of pain. Sometimes she had thought she would welcome it, but now she knew she did not want to rush. There were many things she hoped to do, and she hoped her father would be there to help her. *Please, Mother Life, take care of him for me,* she prayed silently. *Don't let Father Death claim him. Please, tell those waiting to wait a little longer. Just let me keep him a few more turnings of the seasons.*

Zaaco's rich voice, the voice of her memory, cut across her thoughts. "Mother Life, we come today to commend these young men into your hands. We ask that you care for them and bring them safely back to us. Father Death, we ask that you be merciful and allow these young men to come through the trials you have prepared for them and to walk home to us, their families and loved ones." The People added their quiet entreaties to Zaaco's formal prayers. Then the words faded to silence, and Zaaco and Nuroo bowed to each of the four directions before saluting the sky and the earth.

Zaaco looked into his oldest daughter's eyes and almost smiled while she wondered if he could read her thoughts. He raised his hands and continued. "Mother Life, we beg you to protect these boys from their enemies as they protect us, the People of the Frozen Earth, from our enemies. Guide them; show them the way to walk the long, lonely paths and find their ways through the darkness that lurks beyond the light of the cook fires. Keep them safe we beg you. Lead them and bring them back here to us at the next Gathering. You know they are our hope of tomorrow."

The People echoed, "Our hope of tomorrow." Once more Zaaco and Nuroo made the ritual salutes to the four directions. Once more they paused and paid tribute to the sky and the earth. Then they stood in silence.

Zaaco raised his arms again and said, "Father Death, grant your mercy. Allow each of these boys to come home to us as men. Permit their vessels of time to fill slowly and protect them in your infinite wisdom."

Every adult man had survived the Great Travel, but every one of the People of the Frozen Earth had lost sons or brothers or uncles or friends on their Great Travel. Too frequently Father Death claimed too many of the young men before they came back to their families. Sometimes Father Death walked the earth as a bear or a big-toothed cat or some other wild animal, strong and ferocious or small and wily, somehow filling the boy's vessel of time too soon.

Other times the boys found strangers — usually traders but sometimes spies or warriors intent on harm. The Great Travelers had little experience and less time to decide whether the stranger's intent was fair or foul. Mistakes sometimes caused Father Death to walk with them.

These thoughts and more filled Mach's mind. Be careful, cried his heart, but no words escaped his lips. Excitement, sadness, fear, hope, all these emotions and more walked through his soul as he waited for the prayers and chants to end so the flutes and drums could send the boys on their ways.

Then Zaaco's voice rose again. "Be careful, young men. Walk gently. Watch out. We need you to come back to us." The old man lowered his arms and stood silhouetted against the morning sun.

Mach had never heard the informal words of caution before. He wondered if Zaaco felt the same sense of dread he did. What was happening? The instruments' volume rose again. The singers' voices rang across the assembly area. Zaaco raised his hands in one last salute and lowered them as he watched the Great Travelers. The drums played the insistent beat of a marching song. Then the Great Travelers lifted their packs and began their journeys slowly away from the Gathering Grounds.

First, the boys would walk two hands' turnings of the sun to the outer reaches of the territory of the People of the Frozen Earth. Once there they turned right and patrolled. They circled the lands watching for intruders. They were the first line of defense for the People of the Frozen Earth, who only relaxed their vigilance during Gathering because they felt safe with all the bands at the Gathering Grounds.

The Great Travelers were allowed to sit beside the cook fires of the outer bands briefly — no more than two turnings of the sun so long as they contributed to the eats. On rare occasions storms or blizzards might allow them to tarry longer, but no matter how bad the weather, they could not stay more than a hand's turnings of the sun. Basically they lived alone, feeding and fending for themselves in all kinds of weather and against all kinds of animals and danger.

The march had barely begun when an eagle appeared in the blue sky above the High Place. Majestically it soared in the clear air before it called once then flapped its wings and disappeared from sight. Watching a single feather drift down from on high, Mach grinned. "Good luck for these Great Travelers."

Storm Cloud whispered, "Why?"

Horda said, "Shh!"

Rain Drop sniffed. "Behave, Storm Cloud."

Horda's hands on each child's shoulder ended the discussion.

The songs and chants continued until the last of the Great Travelers disappeared into the morning mists. Then Zaaco spoke one last time. "Gathering is finished. May Mother Life look after us and protect us and bring us all back to this place after the next turning of the seasons. May Father Death smile on us and allow us to fill our vessels of time slowly. May our steps be steady and may we walk long upon the earth."

He and Nuroo raised their hands to each of the four directions. Then they lifted their arms and faces to the sun and stood quietly as the wind ruffled the fur of their capes, and the lone eagle soared across the clear blue sky once more. No one spoke, but the omen was clear. Mother Life was smiling on the People. She had sent her emissary. The People stared at the regal bird as it disappeared. Then Zaaco lowered his arms. The last Ceremony was done. The Gathering had officially ended, and most forgot the shadows they had seen.

Chapter 4

A FLURRY OF ACTIVITY BUZZED through the Gathering Grounds like a swarm of angry bees. Most bands were in a hurry to return to their own shelters. Some People left before it was full light; others tarried a little longer for one last visit with friends and family, but everyone would be gone by the time the morning shadows disappeared in the mid-day sun.

Hurrying to pack her belongings, Horda thought of the time between the end of Gathering and the first blizzard. The Gathering Grounds were the quiet home of the Inner Band until the next year. Most of the work had been done, and only little things remained as the summer breezes strengthened and grew colder with each passing day. The hot rays of the summer sun gentled first to warm caresses then to a cold source of light casting smudged blue and lavender shadows across the riotous golds, reds, and oranges of the aspens and oaks flaunting their autumn coats before they bid farewell to summer and went into the mourning of winter.

Memories of a Gathering in the days of her childhood flitted in the back of Horda's mind. Thunder Eagle, the trader from across the jagged mountains, had come to Gathering that year. His face bore slashes from a vicious fight with a young bear that had driven him into a raging river and had cost him his salt and his trade goods, and perhaps most important, his flute. Everything was gone, he'd said gingerly touching his eye swollen from the fever demons nibbling on his face.

Even his flute, a gift from his fa's fa, was lost. She could still feel the pain she had seen in his eyes and heard in his voice when he'd told Zaaco the flute had been made by a man who had walked the Frozen Wilds many turnings of the seasons. It was gone. He could never have it back.

She remembered Zaaco and Thunder Eagle sitting beside the cook fire and talking of endings and beginnings. Celebrations and memorials. Hope and despair. She hadn't meant to listen. No, that wasn't right. She had meant no harm, but she had meant to listen. She had longed to sit bedside her father and listen to the wisdom he gave to the young Thunder Eagle who had looked so sad.

Thunder Eagle usually brought wonderful trade goods from distant people, but her People mostly wanted his salt. Occasionally he had told stories, drawn pictures, played his flute, or sung around the assembly fires, but always before he had been there to trade, and he had never lost sight of his purpose. That assembly had been different. Wounded and almost empty-handed, Thunder Eagle suffered more pain in his heart than in the wounds on his face as he sat beside Zaaco's fire.

Closing her eyes, she could hear again her father's calm, comforting words reminding Thunder Eagle he had lost only things. Even his flute was but a thing. He still had his memories. He could paint pictures and tell stories, and all the things he had lost would be his once more. Memories give us essence, and essence gives us knowledge to hold even when the things or people were gone.

"You, son, can make another flute that will be your ancestors' and your own. It will walk forward through the years as his did until it too has been passed down to memories. But that descendent will use his knowledge and your essence to make a flute that is both his and his ancestors'."

Closing her eyes, she remembered Zaaco's rich voice and wondered how he had become so smart.

She saw the jagged angry wounds slashing across Thunder Eagle's handsome face and recalled her fear that this man would die. She had trained with Nuroo briefly, but she knew little more than gathering herbs and fetching and carrying. Nuroo knew her stitches were smaller and finer than his or Norlon's though she had never sewn up a person's face before. A quiet conversation between her father, Nuroo, and Thunder Eagle, and she had been asked to clean and stitch the trader's face.

She remembered her fear — what if she didn't know enough? But she also remembered the trust in Thunder Eagle's eyes and his words, "Will you help me? The wound makes it hard for me to see. Nuroo believes you can make the scar smaller than he can. I'd like that."

She could still feel how her shaking hands steadied at his quiet words. Cleaning the wounds and getting rid of the fever demons had saved the eye, and the last time she had seen Thunder Eagle the scars had faded to tiny hair lines bisecting his face. No longer angry they only added character to a face of dignity, pride, and humor. She smiled in memory.

The trader had no trade goods for that Gathering. His wounded face bore red and angry scars, but it seemed his heart and soul were also wounded. Though he stayed with the People of the Frozen Earth, he did not participate in any of the Gathering nor did he offer explanations for his lack of goods. He simply sat and watched.

After Gathering ended, Thunder Eagle had stayed with the Inner Band of the People regaining his strength and rebuilding his trade goods until the Moon of Melting Snows.

Slowly he regained his sense of self. As time passed, he told stories, painted, and knapped flint, chert, and obsidian, and then he made a new flute. The river prepared a beautiful piece of wood, scouring it and placing it where Thunder Eagle would find it. From it he carved a wonderful instrument whose music danced and soared even more beautifully than the one the bear and the river had taken away.

Thunder Eagle worked hard and finally laughed as that winter passed telling old and new stories to the People of the Frozen Earth. He painted pictures on the cave walls, on summer shelters, on clothing, and on little bits of leather that people cherished when he was gone. Even in his laughter, many of the People had heard his sadness. They saw him stand in the cave entrance and look across the snow remembering things they had never seen and places they had never been.

Zaaco had told Horda he believed Thunder Eagle would go when the snow did. Her father's words saddened her for she had grown close to this man whose face she had saved. His gentle ways touched the hole in her heart where her brother Zephat had once lived. She knew Thunder Eagle was not her brother nor did she try to make him so, but he had become her friend. “Oh, Fa, he smiles at Oshia. I thought he would choose her and become one of the People of the Frozen Earth.”

Zaaco had leveled a silent stare at his eldest daughter. “Do you really think that, Horda?”

She smiled sadly. “No, I see his restlessness, but still I hope he chooses to stay.”

“I, too, hope for my own selfish reasons. He is the best knapper in our band. His points are so much better than any I can make. I’ve almost depleted my trade goods getting as many as I can for when he is gone.” She remembered how Zaaco cut his eyes at her. “I almost asked him if he would trade a lifetime of points for my daughter.”

“Fa! That is not right!” She had given him his hoped-for answer.

A barely perceptible sigh of relief escaped Zaaco. “I said, ‘Almost, Daughter.’”

She had not been able to resist her own little jab. “That is not the way of the People,” she said primly. “Anyway, I am much too young to think about such things yet although you know Mach is my warrior.”

Horda had giggled at her father’s look of horror and had almost forgotten the pain she had felt at the thought of Thunder Eagle’s leaving.

That had been the one year she had taken no pleasure in the life coming back after the Moons of the Long Blizzards. She had watched Thunder Eagle paint a wild and vibrant picture on the wall of the winter shelter, but she had taken no enjoyment from the beauty because she had known when it was done, he would be gone, and he had been.

Horda paused and remembered that picture — the golds

and oranges and reds of all the trees with burning leaves interspersed with the evergreens of the pines, firs, and live oaks. The whole scene had been washed in the pale blue, pink, and lavender shadows that are only visible in early autumn, but he had also scattered the tiny beams that marked the return of spring. Meiran had seen it as the death of a season and his final ungrateful goodbye to the People who had taken him in and nursed him back to health and traded with him so he had goods to take him back beyond the jagged mountains, but even as a girl, Horda had realized the picture was not goodbye.

She stopped and remembered her father's words — words that had explained the feelings she could not understand. Zaaco said the burning leaves were a celebration of the turning of the seasons, but he believed in this painting, they were actually a celebration and a thank you for what the People of the Frozen Earth had done for Thunder Eagle. Then Zaaco had pointed to the tiny sunbeams and asked what they made her think of.

She still remembered his smile when she had replied they were the promise of spring coming back. "Yes, Daughter," he had said. "They are a promise." She could still feel her own smile when she realized those little sunbeams were Thunder Eagle's promise to return to them.

In her memory she saw Zaaco as she had seen him then — as big as the sky and the strongest man in her world. She swallowed hard against the hot lump of tears suddenly in her throat. Had her father grown smaller, or had her world grown larger? How much longer before her father's vessel of time was filled? How many more times would she get to talk with him? Touch him? Laugh with him? Share with him? She wiped the tears from her face and hurriedly packed the last of her belongings so she would have time to visit with her father just a little more.

She slipped across the Gathering Grounds to his cook fire, but she almost hid when Emol waddled past her also heading toward her father's fire. Taking a deep breath, she forced herself not to stare at the old man. Grease stained his stretched tunic and beads dripped from the broken sinew of the design. His little piggy eyes had receded even further into the fat of his face. If possible, he was bigger, dirtier, and more slovenly than he had been back at the Gathering where she first mated.

Looking him in the eyes, she said, "Greetings."

Emol waddled faster without acknowledging her. She wasn't sure whether to be angry or relieved as she waited politely for him to finish his business with her father.

"Greetings, Zaaco. Treema," she said when he was finally gone. "I see Emol is still his wonderful, agreeable self."

"Do not jest, Daughter," said Zaaco sternly. "The man grows ever lazier and more useless. I am ready to banish him."

Horda's eyes rounded. "Banish?"

"No, not really," said Zaaco, "because to hear him tell it, he works harder than any other leader of the People of the Frozen Earth."

"Can't someone teach him to work smarter instead of running around and around like a wolf cub chasing its tail?" asked Horda. Zaaco looked at her silently until she started to fidget. "Oops, my mistake," she said. "You already tried that."

"At least a hand of times," said Treema quietly. "He listens just long enough to tell us all the reasons we don't know what we are talking about and why our ideas won't work for him and his band."

"Do you point out that the ideas work for every other band in the tribe?" asked Horda.

Zaaco smiled in spite of himself. "No, Horda, we haven't thought of telling him anything like that."

Horda shook her head. "Of course, you have. It just seems so simple I can't believe he is still starving. Well, he's obviously not starving, Fa, he's the biggest man in the whole tribe."

"No, he's not starving, but some of his young ones and some of the older ones end up sick every winter until someone comes to their rescue with food and supplies." He shrugged. "I always say I am going to allow them to fend for themselves, but then I can't let the innocents starve because he is a hard-headed, hidebound, old bison bull."

"What did he want this time?" asked Horda.

"Nothing much," said Treema. "Just to join all of his people to the new band."

"Our band?" squeaked Horda.

"Umm, yes, as a matter of fact, it is your new band." Zaaco's eyes twinkled mischievously, but Horda was upset enough she did not notice.

"What did you tell him? Are you going to send us to his land? Please, Fa, it's bad enough you throw me to Wonderful Wilda. You know we don't know enough to do this, but—"

Zaaco placed a gentle hand on her arm. "Daughter, you should be honored. Emol believes this new group of People would cause everything to suddenly be wonderful in his band. There would magically be plenty of food and shelters and clothes and everything. Don't you know?"

"No!" Horda snorted in a most unladylike fashion. "I don't know. I don't know any such thing. I went through that once with the People of the Tall Grass. I won't do it. I refuse to be the slave for his lazy, worthless band. I tell you I won't, Fa. It's bad enough I'm supposed to teach Wilda to behave. I absolutely refuse."

"Well, Daughter, I know you are grown up and all that, but do you think you are showing appropriate respect to the Chief of the People of the Frozen Earth?" He bit his lips to keep from smiling when Treema grabbed a feather fan and energetically waved it in front of Horda.

Suddenly Horda heard her own words. Words of disrespect and anger. She felt the blood rush to her face. "Oh, Fa," she said. "I'm sorry. I did not mean to be disrespectful."

"Good," said Zaaco. "Then we will discuss this." He still sounded serious.

She took a deep breath and looked into his eyes. "No, Fa, we won't. I apologize for being disrespectful, but I must tell you I cannot do this thing. Please do not ask it of me — of us."

Treema smiled gently. "Zaaco, you are being mean."

"No, I'm not," he said quietly. "It's not my fault the girl leaps to conclusions."

"Perhaps not, but you were certainly pulling the hide tighter and tighter to help her bounce higher in her leaps."

"I was, wasn't I?" Zaaco grinned. "I haven't had a chance to tease her in a long time." He put his arms around Horda. "I never thought I'd have such a chance again."

"Fa." She sputtered stepping out of his embrace. "What did you really tell Emol?"

His warrior's stern face was marred by the gleam in his eyes. "That he was the leader of his band. He is in charge. It would not be seemly to have three leaders — especially not with two leaders so much younger than he."

"You didn't really tell him that. Did you?" She frowned suspiciously.

He nodded solemnly.

"Did he mention me?"

"Indirectly," Zaaco smiled. "He said he could handle the boys and girls and teach them to be good leaders in their time. I assume he is counting you as one of the girls."

Treema frowned. "I don't understand that man."

"Neither do I," said Zaaco. "Many times he has come to us whining because he needs help to feed and clothe his band. Now, suddenly he's telling us how well he can teach new leaders."

Horda giggled. "Perhaps he wants to serve as an example of what not to do."

Zaaco and Treema pretended to be shocked by her words. "Daughter, that is not a seemly thing to say."

Horda made a face at him. "But it's true."

Mach had joined them and stood silently listening to the exchange. Not quite understanding, he looked at all three of them before he said, "We are ready to leave when you are, Horda."

"Oh, dear, Fa, I came to talk to you. I wanted to tell you how much I love you and to tell you goo ..." She fought the tears burning her eyes.

Zaaco put his hand on her arm. "I love you, too, but do not say those words," he said softly. Touching his forehead to hers, he shared her breath before he hugged her with all his might. "We will see each other, Daughter. If not at the next Gathering, then farther on down the trail."

She sniffed and smiled a watery smile. "Yes, Fa."

Treema embraced her. "Good luck with all your helpers," she smiled mischievously.

"Yes, right," said Horda returning her hug.

Zaaco caught her in his arms once more. "I ask Mother Life to give my Little One a little one of her own."

"Oh, Fa." She could no longer deny her tears. "Thank you. Nuroo and Unna both say it will happen when it happens."

He nodded. "I know, but sometimes it is hard to wait on the Mother's own time."

"It is." She took a deep breath and squared her shoulders. Then she managed to smile. "You are a very special man. I am proud to have you as my fa."

"And you, Daughter, are a special woman. I'm glad to have you as my little one." Suddenly he chuckled. "Even if you are still easy to fool sometimes."

Laughing she hugged him one last time. "I'll see you when I see you."

"Later."

Waving one last farewell, she took Mach's hand and walked back to their camp area.

Chapter 5

SHEDDING WARM RAYS TO dispel the cool breezes, the sun climbed toward its zenith before Mach and Thuro and the members of the new band followed the Great Travelers down the winding path through the foothills away from the Gathering grounds.

"I don't see why we have to find a new place," whimpered Wilda.

"Because we're a new band," said Thuro for what seemed the fifth hand of times.

"Well, I don't see why we couldn't use one of the established winter camps."

Horda looked at Mach who turned his eyes toward the sky.

Thuro's smile was more a baring of his teeth at Wilda. "Because we're on our own. We have to find our own cave and establish our own winter camp."

"But it's almost winter," whined Wilda.

"That's why we brought all our possessions and our share of the winter food to Gathering."

"Humph!" Wilda shook her head and set the beads and

shells in her braids to jingling. “What if we don’t find a cave before the blizzards come?”

Thuro gritted his teeth. “We’re heading to a cave Mach found on his Great Travel.”

“Didn’t you find a cave on your Great Travel?” She peered up at him through her eyelashes.

Thuro touched the fingers of each hand twice before he answered Wilda. Horda almost shook her head in exasperation, but at the last moment she restrained her reaction.

“I found several caves on my Great Travel, but they were hardly large enough to shelter me.” Thuro spoke with exaggerated patience. “There’s no way we could enlarge one of them enough for a whole band before the blizzards come. Mach says this cave is naturally large enough, and it’s near the Big River. We’ll have plenty of fresh water and fish. Since none of the other bands hunt or gather the area, there will be plenty of food. It’ll be a good territory for our band.”

“How do you know this cave is suitable?” Wilda asked crossly. “Have you seen it?”

Mach coughed to cover the chuckles threatening to erupt from his mouth. Horda frowned at him. This wasn’t funny. Already Wilda stirred conflict.

“No, I have not seen it,” said Thuro firmly. “I know because I trust Mach’s judgment.”

“But you’re an equal leader with him,” pouted Wilda. “Shouldn’t you have an equal say where we build the camp?”

“By the Father’s dirty teeth, woman,” snapped Thuro finally losing patience. “I have a say. I don’t know any place better. I equally say we are going to this place.”

Tears filled Wilda's eyes, and her lower lip quivered. "I just want you to be respected for yourself," she whispered. "I don't want you to stand in Mach's shadow. It doesn't seem right for him to tell you and everyone else where we're building our winter camp and where our territory will be." Two fat tears rolled down her cheeks.

Seeing the thunderstorm on Horda's face, Mach caught her hand and shook his head. He slowed their steps until Wilda and Thuro were well ahead of them.

Horda's amber eyes shot sparks. "She just wants to cause trouble. Why didn't you help him?"

"Because it's none of my business. Nor is it yours." He stared at her. "Is it?"

"Well, Suka said I am to help him control her." Horda looked innocently at her mate.

Mach shook his head. "That's not exactly what she meant, do you think?"

"Not really," said Horda, "but you're the co-chief. She's trying to cause trouble. You should have said something."

"Listen to yourself," he said. "You agree it's none of our business in one breath and tell me to interfere in the next. Thuro will deal with her on this. She can't cause trouble unless he allows her to." Mach shook his head. "And I don't think that's going to happen."

Horda wasn't so sure. "Mach, what are we going to do?"

"The best we can," he said simply. "We'll support Thuro, but we won't interfere unless he asks for our help."

She shook her head and trudged on toward their new home. *Mother Life, what have I been put into the middle of now?*

Pine, sage, and juniper perfumed the cooling afternoon while the shadows stretched across their path. The sky behind the jagged teeth of the mountains blazed pink, orange, and purple where the sun disappeared for the fifth time since Mach and Thuro's band left the Gathering grounds.

"That's the Green River just ahead," said Mach. "The cave lies about a half day's trek up the river."

"Good," said Thuro. "Let's camp in those trees beside it. We can find our new home in the light tomorrow." Wilda sniffed but did not speak.

"That sounds like a good idea," said Horda straightening her back and flexing her shoulders. "My pack grows heavier the closer we get."

Mach chuckled. "That's because you have Rain Drop's pack too."

Horda wrinkled her nose at him. "You have your pack, Storm Cloud, his pack, *and* Rain Drop."

He smiled at the little boy and girl dozing on the top of his travois. "But *I'm* not complaining." She pretended to glare at him.

Thuro called, "Gather round."

Sensing their long journey neared its end, three hands of warriors, four hands plus two fingers of women, and five hands plus four fingers of children crowded around the leaders and their mates. Their excited buzz quickly dropped to silence.

"The cave is about a half day's trek farther up the river," said Mach. "Thuro suggested we camp in the trees just ahead. That way we'll reach our new home with plenty of light to inspect it and begin preparing for winter."

A general chorus of agreement met Mach's words, and the tired People pushed toward the grove of trees with renewed energy.

"Why did you let him do that?" hissed Wilda.

"Do what?" asked Thuro innocently.

"All the talking."

"What do you mean, woman?"

"It was your idea to camp in the trees, but he told the People. You should have told them. He's taking over the band. And you're letting him."

Thuro muttered an oath under his breath.

"Can't you understand?" whimpered Wilda. "I want you to truly be the leader of this band, Thuro."

"Didn't you hear Mach tell the People it was my idea to camp?"

"Yes, but it's not the same. The words should come from your mouth." She tossed her braids causing the shells and beads to jingle and clatter. "You have to stand up for yourself."

Thuro trudged away from her with a sigh.

Staying close on his heels, she muttered, "I just don't want anyone taking advantage of you. You're the bravest and smartest warrior in the whole band. We deserve a place in the Inner—"

Dropping the handles of his travois, Thuro whirled and glared at her. He leaned down until his fiery eyes were level with hers. "Will you never learn? Zaaco could have punished us for your presumptuous words before we mated. He won't be lenient if he hears of your prattling."

Tears filled her huge brown eyes and dripped down her

round cheeks. "Please, don't be angry with me. I'm only trying to help you."

Leaning tiredly against the travois, he rubbed his face. "I'm not angry with you. I'm just telling you I don't need protection from Mach."

"But you let him take advantage of you."

"No, I don't," Thuro said firmly. "Mach knows I don't like talking to large groups. He's not taking anything away from me that I want. Trust me."

Wilda pursed her full lower lip in a pout. "Horda takes things away from me that I want."

"What are you babbling about now?"

"The women all look to her when it's time to cook. None of them ever seek my opinion."

Thuro hooted. "You can't boil water without burning the cooking bag, Wilda. You have not yet helped prepare one of our eats. You always manage to be elsewhere when the women cook. Why would anyone in their right mind ask you anything about cooking? We would have already starved if it were up to you to feed us."

Though Wilda's brown eyes still glistened with her tears, they shot angry flint knives at her mate. Her voice quivered. "She's not such a good cook either."

"Maybe not," said Thuro agreeably, "but she is always there when it's time to cook, and none of us are starving."

"In the mornings when we get ready to march, they always ask her who should snare birds or fish and where to march and everything. No one asks my advice."

Thuro shook his head. "Have you snared a bird or caught a fish since your Rituals of Womanhood? Have you helped set up or break camp on this trek?"

She glared. "That is beside the point."

"Why?"

"I am the number one mate of the chief of the band. I should be consulted." The beads and shells in her braids jingled and rattled angrily.

"Perhaps if you helped prepare the morning eat and break camp instead of bathing and fixing your hair until the morning marches begin, the women would be more inclined to ask your opinions."

Wilda sniffed. "I have a position to uphold. It's my duty to set a good example."

"Horda's setting a good example preparing food and breaking camp." His soft words fanned the angry fires in the depths of his mate's eyes.

"That should not be the duty of the chief's mate."

"Then whose duty is it, may I ask?" Watching the People approach the trees, Thuro shook his head. "You have much to learn about being the number one mate of a chief, and," he looked at her meaningfully, "I hope you learn before you must be taught." Bowing his head, he picked up his travois and hurried to help the men set up the camp.

Speechless Wilda glowered at his back before making her way to the river to soak her tired feet. *Who is he to threaten me? He has much more to learn than I do. I know exactly what should be expected of the chief's number one mate.*

The sun's first pink rays glittered in the light frost glazing the trees and grass. The Moon of Gathering was almost gone, and the Moon of the Burning Leaves was coming in with its welcome cool breezes. The People hovered around the fire and reached out to embrace its welcome warmth. Preparing horns of hot yarrow tea, Horda said, "We eat lightly this morning, but we'll feast tonight in celebration of our new home."

Nods of agreement and sounds of laughter filled the crisp air while the women passed the tea and cakes of pemmican. The People quickly ate their food and rushed to break the camp, excited that their journey neared its end.

Only Horda remained beside the cook fire packing the bags and baskets when Wilda finally arrived. Horda didn't pause in her work. "There's pemmican on the tray and a horn of tea for you."

Wilda frowned at the deserted area. "We should have a hot eat to be strong and ready to work when we arrive at the winter cave."

Horda forced her voice to remain pleasant. "We wanted to finish the journey. We ate traveling food."

"Oh, I don't think that is a good idea," said Wilda firmly. "We need porridge with meat and fry bread to go with the tea. It's cool this morning. A good meal will help us."

"You're welcome to prepare whatever you want," said Horda evenly, "but the rest of us have eaten. We're ready to finish the trek to our new home." She returned the pemmican to the pack and stored the tray.

Silently fuming Wilda rescued the horn of tea before Horda could pour it on the fire.

Aiyana, a very pregnant young woman who had suffered the captivity with Horda and Suka, lumbered to the cook fire. "Premo asked Trefo and Garol to hunt with him this day, Horda. Will two antelope or deer be enough?"

Horda smiled at the younger woman. "That should be plenty since they're pretty big by now. Though tell them to feel free to bring more if they get a chance. We can make pemmican and dried meat since we've reached our new cave.

"Tonight we'll dig a fire pit and roast the meat. Lija and Zorya are looking for vegetables and greens. We've found a good supply of cattail tubers, pond lily bulbs, and onions along the way, but we can always use more. I hope they find watercress and cow parsnip."

"We need to know where the vegetables grow near the cave," said Aiyana. She frowned. "Do you want me to scout?"

"Not today." Horda shook her head. "But let's keep looking for berry bushes and vines as we walk. Maybe the birds haven't eaten all of them."

"I'll get my pack and help you." Aiyana waddled away as quickly as her pregnant stomach would allow.

Wilda glowered. "I still say we should feed the People a hot eat before this last day of the march. We'll be too busy to prepare a feast when we get to the cave."

Horda took a deep breath and forced herself to speak calmly and pleasantly. "I'm sorry you feel that way."

"You're sorry?" shrieked Wilda. "Is that all you can say?"

"What else can I say? The People have eaten and are starting to march. They expect a feast tonight. I don't plan to disappoint them." Horda shrugged.

"I should have been consulted before these plans were made," declared Wilda icily.

Horda blinked. "Consulted?"

"Yes, consulted."

Horda drew herself up to her full height and glared down on Wilda. "You have shown no interest in feeding the People. You never join us until everyone else has finished eating. Why would I think today would be any different?"

Wilda tossed her braids and glowered. "I should be consulted. I am the number one mate of the co-chief — in case you've forgotten."

"Oh, no, I haven't forgotten, but I thought perhaps you had. You help with none of the work."

Wilda grimaced. "I've been busy with other more important things."

"I find it hard to imagine anything more important than feeding and sheltering our People." Horda's voice dripped artificial sweetness as she helped Rain Drop adjust her pack. With a tiny sigh of relief, she then shouldered her own pack and walked away leaving Wilda silently gulping air like a fish left too long on the banks of the river.

Chapter 6

THE SUN GLARED FROM the top of the sky with a heat rivaling the middle of summer before Mach stopped and pointed to a large black hole half way up the side of a sheer cliff. "There's the cave." He gestured at the faint trail leading to the black hole. "There's a path, but we'll have to widen it."

Wilda's eyes followed where he pointed. Such a small opening disappointed her. She knew the cave wasn't suitable. She'd be the first inside so she could point out all its shortcomings. They'd simply have to move on. Thuro would find a proper home for them. She'd see to that. She rushed headlong up the trail past Mach and the others. Her actions were so uncharacteristic no one realized her intent until she clambered up the trail.

"Wilda, stop!" called Mach.

"Come back!" shouted Thuro. "You don't know what's inside the cave."

She continued on her course.

"It might not be safe. There could be large cats or bears using the cave for a den," yelled Mach. "We need to check it."

She snorted. *Do you think I am a total fool? You want to be the first one in the cave so you can tell everyone all the good things about it. Well, Mach, not this time. I'll get there first and tell them all the bad things.* She grinned to herself. *This time I'll force Thuro to take charge.*

She stood just inside the opening of the cave waiting for her eyes to adjust to the gloom. Phew! It smelled awful. Like something large and dangerous once lived in the cave though it had surely died — but not too long ago — the stench almost made her gag. Irregularly shaped lumps loomed in the semi-darkness seemingly monitoring her movements. She told herself bears and cats wouldn't be in their dens in the daytime — she didn't think.

"Wilda, come out of there this instant!" Mach's angry voice strengthened her resolve, and she inched farther into the foul-smelling shadows.

"Wilda, you don't know what's in there. You could be killed!" Thuro called. "Come out, right now!"

They're just trying to frighten me. She made her way farther into the cave. *By the Father's dirty teeth!* She almost stamped her foot. *Mach was right. In spite of the unpleasant smell, the cave would meet the band's needs without any major alterations for several turnings of the seasons.* Several small shafts of sunlight beamed through natural vents in the ceiling. It would require major cleaning, but she realized they'd have a hard time finding a more suitable winter camp.

A flurry of movement froze her in her tracks. Falling to the ground, she tried to burrow into the cave floor. A sudden whirring assaulted her ears, and a scream died in her throat. Her intrusion and the men's yelling had disturbed thousands of tiny bats and sent them streaming out of the cave. Though they flew near enough to jingle the shells in her braids, none actually touched her.

Panic stricken and shivering, she lay on the floor while genuine tears streamed down her cheeks into the dust. When the exodus finally ended, Thuro ran to his mate with Mach close on his heels. “Are you all right?” He pulled her to her feet.

Still shaking like a new leaf in a spring thunderstorm, Wilda couldn’t force an answer past the sobs tearing her throat.

Thuro caught her arms and shook her. “Answer me! Are you all right?”

She reluctantly raised her tear-filled eyes to him, but still she didn’t speak.

“Answer me, now!” Thuro gave her another shake. “Did any of them bite you?”

Finally she shook her head. Breathing a sigh of relief, Mach left Thuro and Wilda alone in the semidarkness of the cave. Thuro swept her into his arms and gently scolded her. “You could have been killed. Big cats and wolves and bears live in caves. Most of them sleep in the daytime. Don’t you remember anything? Are you out of your mind?”

Wilda sniffed and burrowed against her mate’s chest like a small, frightened animal.

“You’re lucky only bats came out of the cave. You’re even luckier you weren’t bitten. Don’t you know how dangerous bats are? They carry sickness and fevers. If you get them, you suffer agony, burning and begging for water. You can’t swallow, and it is awful. Then you finally die because once the bat bites you, there’s nothing anyone can do to help you.

Do you know how stupid you were to rush into the cave?"

Pausing at the cave opening, Mach listened to Thuro's tirade. Angry reprimands burned his throat, but he warned himself not to say a word. Thuro had to chastise his own mate. She'd already caused enough trouble. And Mach feared it was just beginning.

Disturbed by the commotion at the front of the cave, the bear cubs rooted against their mother's side. The she-bear stretched and glared at the noisy creatures invading her den. Neither she nor her little ones had ever seen such creatures up close. She squinted. She remembered seeing one of them walking upright in her territory a long time ago. He hadn't bothered her though, and she hadn't bothered him.

She sighed. Her cubs were restless. Born during one of the long blizzards, they were too young and too nosy to be cautious. She had to warn them. She barely made a sound, but they heard her and knew they had to be quiet and still while their ma listened and looked. The sounds were annoying. What was going on?

They weren't hungry — they had fed on fish and berries earlier in the day. Their bodies were round and well-padded with blubber for the long sleep. Their fur was thick and shiny. The feeding frenzy was over, and they were preparing for winter. A few more turnings of the sun, and the bears would settle down to hibernate through the long cold. What was happening?

Throwing back her head, the she-bear sniffed the air. The strangers didn't smell like any food she recognized, but they certainly were loud. She did not appreciate being wakened. She made her decision. With a fierce growl, she shook her twin cubs loose and stood up. Hardly pausing, she ran from her nest and jumped on Thuro knocking him to the ground and clawing him. His spears were crossed on his back behind his neck and their shafts slowed the bear when she tried to bite his head.

Wilda shrieked and scuttled through the dirt to cower in the crack between two boulders. Her noise and movement distracted the she-bear long enough for Thuro to scramble to his feet and pull the flint knife from his belt. Interested in Wilda's actions for only a few instants, the bear turned back to Thuro.

Almost casually, she reached out a paw tipped by claws longer than Wilda's fingers and batted Thuro's arm, knocking the knife away and slashing deep gouges from his wrist to his elbow. Unarmed, Thuro crouched into a fighter's stance, raised his fists, and waited. Blood dripped from the wounds on both his back and arm, but still he stood between his mate and the bear. *Please, Mother Life, spare us*. He looked desperately and hopelessly for some way to stop the bear from claiming him and Wilda for Father Death.

The low growls echoed through the chambers of Mach's memory. Deeper and more guttural, but Father Death still spoke and plunged Mach back to his Great Travel. Pulling a spear loose and dropping his pack in one motion, he roared angrily and charged back into the cave. The bear had flexed her legs ready to leap on Thuro. "Down, Thuro!" shouted Mach.

Thuro flattened himself on the ground as the bear jumped. Mach's spear used the bear's forward motion to rip into her chest and pierce her heart. With an agonized cry and blood gushing from her mouth, she fell on Thuro's prone body.

Pushing and shoving, Mach finally freed the bloody Thuro

from the dead bear's weight. "Mother Life! It's a she-bear," he muttered prodding her sagging teats. "Zeek, bring spears. Quickly."

Zeek raced into the cave with four spears. "She has cubs," Mach said taking two of the spears.

Zeek nodded. Cautiously they searched the dark cave until Zeek called, "Over here."

The two half-grown cubs stood up and growled at the men. Mach frowned. "I hate to kill her young. Somehow it doesn't seem right."

"It has to be done," replied Zeek watching one of the cubs prepare to charge them. At the last instant, Mach thrust a spear into its chest and twisted. The cub gave an almost human cry of pain and crumpled to the ground. Waving its front paws menacingly, the other cub stood on its hind legs and growled at Zeek. Zeek threw his first spear but missed when the cub suddenly dropped to all fours and charged him. Zeek recovered and side-stepped stabbing behind the cub's front leg with his short spear. The cub took two steps past Zeek and fell to the ground with a low moan. Zeek recovered his fallen spear and plunged it into the cub's heart silencing its cries.

Then Zeek helped Mach check the rest of the cave. They met beside Thuro who moaned softly. "That's all of them," said Zeek.

Mach nodded. "Let's get him out of here." He and Zeek carried the bloody Thuro into the sunlight so they could examine his wounds. No one paid any attention to Wilda, still in the cave.

"Kindle a small, hot fire then go to the river and bring me two hands of filled water bags. Someone, go gather two armloads of the goldenrod growing on the flat land back there. Hurry." Horda pulled her medicine bag, two horn cups, and a small grinding stone from her pack before racing to Thuro. She cried, "Is he ..."

"How badly are you hurt?" demanded Mach gently shaking him. "Thuro, tell me how badly you're hurt!"

Thuro managed a shaky smile at his friend. "I'm not sure." He squeezed the deep scratches on his right forearm in an attempt to control the bleeding.

"Stop that," commanded Horda gently pushing his hand away.

"But I'm bleed—" protested Thuro returning to his task.

"I can see that," snapped Horda. The young man's face had bleached white beneath his dark copper tan. Speaking more gently, she said, "Let it bleed. The flow cleanses the wound."

Reluctantly he removed his left hand from his right forearm and watched the blood blossoms grow and shed their petals. Nodding approvingly — the blood dripped instead of flowing — Horda walked around Thuro surveying the damage to his body. "Where do you hurt?"

"My back and my arm, I guess." Frowning he moved his shoulders. "It almost feels like my whole body is on fire. I know she tried to bite my head, but my spear and Wilda distracted her long enough for me to get away." He shook his head experimentally. "I don't think my head hurts."

Horda examined his head and neck. "You're lucky," she said. "Your hair's wet and slobbery, but the skin's not broken."

"Wilda saved me," he said.

"Yeah," muttered Horda digging in her medicine bag for dried leaves of buckthorn, mugwort, and alum root. *After she caused you to be there in the first place.* She was already grinding the plants into a powder with her bone pestle when Aiyana brought the goldenrod. "Thank you," Horda said. "I need you to fill those three water baskets half full and set them to heat. When the water begins to steam, add the goldenrod and let them boil."

As she spoke, she stripped several goldenrod stalks of leaves and blooms. Horda nodded her thanks when Zeek's mate, Dita, took over the task. Forcing a smile, she went back to Thuro. "Okay, it's time to stop the bleeding."

He nodded.

"This may hurt, but it has to be done." She took one water bag and poured its entire contents over his arm.

His face, which had taken on a definite green tinge while he watched his blood drip on the ground, turned first a mottled red then white. "May hurt?" He muttered. "Surely you're joking."

Horda grinned. "I didn't want to scare you."

Thuro spoke through gritted teeth. "You didn't scare me, Horda, you nearly killed me."

"No, I didn't," she denied. "The bear did that." *Along with your mate's carelessness.* She sprinkled the powdered leaves on his arm and bound it firmly with clean leather. "Now, your back." She took another water bag and repeated the process. The muscles in Thuro's jaws bulged and tears glistened in the corners of his eyes, but no sound escaped his lips.

She frowned, "Unless your arm keeps bleeding, I won't

stitch it, but I have to stitch your shoulder, Thuro, after I wash it with the goldenrod water."

He blanched. "You're going to wash it some more?"

She nodded. "Goldenrod helps keep away the fever demons." She patted his undamaged shoulder encouragingly and offered him willow bark and three lobelia leaves. "I want you to chew these and swallow the juice but not the pulp. It will help deaden the pain and fight fever."

With great effort Thuro unclenched his teeth and allowed her to place the medicine on his tongue. "You're not torn up as badly as you could have been." *Thank you, Mother Life.* She turned her eyes skyward. "Some of the scratches are deep, but none of the muscles appear to be particularly damaged. All we have to do is keep the fever demons from making an eat of you."

Thuro forced a smile and nodded.

Mach fingered the hairless, puckered scar on the top of his head, the result of his own encounter with a big-toothed cat on his Great Travel. He shuddered remembering how some healer woman in a distant band had finally burned the wound to stop the infection. He whispered, "Are you going to—"

Horda's snapping amber eyes silenced his question. "I'm going to stitch the wounds that need stitching then keep all of them clean and bandaged with the herbs. That should be enough."

At that moment, Wilda appeared blinking and crying in the cave opening. She shrieked, "Oh, help me. Please, I am ..." She started to wobble.

Thuro immediately tried to stand, but Mach and Horda restrained him. "Are you hurt?" asked Horda curtly selecting more of the leaves and putting them into a stone cup which she set on the ground.

"Hurt?" snapped Wilda forgetting she was about to fall. "Of course, I'm hurt. First those bird things knocked me to the ground then that bear attacked me. And everyone just left me in that dirty cave with those dead animals." She shivered and held out scraped hands then lifted her tunic to show skinned knees.

"Neither would have bothered you if you hadn't barged into the cave before the men checked its safety," said Horda choosing a tiny curved bone needle and a thin twisted strip of boiled deer gut from her medicine pack. "Wash your scratches and dust them with some of these herbs." She used her toe to push the stone cup toward Wilda.

Wilda forgot her pain and charged over to Thuro. "Are you going to let her talk to me like that?"

Thuro blinked at his mate like a confused owl. "Like what?" he finally managed to ask.

Wilda stamped her foot. "Like I'm some unimportant child."

"Children are important," Thuro said piously. "They're the hope of the future."

Wilda glared. "I'm hurt, and she's ignoring me."

Mach intervened. "Horda's ignoring you because she's busy taking care of your mate."

Wilda spun to face him. "I'm hurt too."

Mach shook his head. "You scraped yourself getting away. Thuro was almost killed."

"Thuro," whined Wilda.

Thuro fought to focus his eyes. "For the Mother's sake, Wilda, leave him alone," snapped Horda. "Stop making him try to concentrate. I've given him herbs to deaden his pain so I can sew up his back."

"Sew up his back?" Wilda squeaked. "What are you talking about?"

"I told you," said Mach patiently, "that bear almost killed him."

Wilda glared at Mach. "It should have been you." She spat in the dust before she walked away.

Horda looked at Mach and shook her head. *Mother Life! What are we going to do?*

"She really isn't hurt, is she?" Horda mouthed the words to her mate while she gently bathed Thuro's back with the cooled goldenrod water.

Mach shook his head. "I don't think so. She scraped her knees and hands. She said the bats didn't touch her."

Horda shivered though her hands steadily closed the gaping wounds in Thuro's back with tiny even stitches. "The bats wouldn't have to touch me to kill me. They could just scare me to death."

Thuro barely grunted when Horda applied the heated packing and wrapped his back with strips of clean leather. Then she inspected the bandage on his arm. "Your arm doesn't seem to need stitches. The blood hasn't soaked through the packing, but I want to wash the wounds."

Thuro grimaced when she unwrapped his arm. "More washing?"

"More washing." She poured the rest of the goldenrod water over his forearm.

A mighty yawn interrupted his smile. "It must be getting better. It doesn't hurt like it did the first time you did that."

"Good," said Horda. "I hope it's not too bad. I'm going

to be washing you twice a day for a hand of days."

Thuro snored softly before she finished packing his arm and bandaging it again.

Mach grinned down at her. "What about the bears?"

"What?"

"You said the bats could scare you to death without touching you. What about the bears?"

"I don't even want to think about them." She set a small rawhide shade over Thuro and left him sleeping peacefully.

Walking beside her, Mach suddenly sobered. "Do you know why Wilda suddenly ran ahead of everybody into the cave?"

"No." Horda bit her lip. "But she got mad this morning because we planned the feast and everything without consulting her."

Mach arched his brows. "Was she even awake?"

"Who knows?"

He shook his head. "I don't understand that woman. She doesn't do very much. Does she?"

"Besides fix her clothes and hair and fret and whine?" Horda smiled ruefully. "No, but perhaps she'll do better now that the trek is finished."

Mach grunted.

"It is finished, isn't it?"

"I haven't inspected the cave," he said. "But if those were the only bears in it, and if it's as big as I remember, and if we can convince the bats to roost elsewhere, it is."

She shivered again. "I don't like bats."

"Neither do I," he said with a laugh. "But it should be fairly easy to get them to move. We may have to run them out several hands of times."

"Run them out?"

"Yes, we'll keep a fire of mixed green and dry wood burning for a couple of days. Bats don't like the smoke and light."

"What will keep them from coming back?"

"We'll make a grass mat or a hide curtain for the shelter opening to keep them out until they give up and find another den." He grinned at her. "Maybe we can use the she-bear's skin. Unless you want it for a robe."

She shivered remembering Bear Claw's tattered bear skin robe. "No, thank you — not in this lifetime."

Seeing the pain in her eyes, he remembered too. "I'm sorry. I didn't think."

"It's all right. That's all over." She shook her head and squared her shoulders. "But I still don't want a bear skin robe."

"I don't either," he admitted.

"How long will it take to get rid of the bats?"

"I don't know, but it shouldn't take too long for us to make a cover, then they should find another roosting place pretty quickly."

"How long will it take us to clean the cave?"

"Probably longer than it takes to get rid of the bats," admitted Mach.

"I thought so." She laughed in spite of herself. "I have a big supply of soaproot if you men have strong arms for carrying and scrubbing."

"We'll help," announced Storm Cloud solemnly. Rain Drop nodded her agreement.

Horda shook her head. "I don't think so. You might catch some sickness from the cave."

Storm Cloud frowned. "We can scrub with soaproot. You taught us."

"Yes, we'll help get our new home ready," said Rain Drop.

Mach turned up his nose at the remembered smell of the bat guano. "Thanks, little ones, but your moccasins aren't quite big enough to help with this job. It's going to take more than soaproot to get rid of the smell."

The children frowned but did not argue.

"Make your smoking fire of cedar wood or juniper. It smells sweet and ought to help with the odor. Then we'll burn sage and some other herbs. It probably won't take much past spring to cleanse the cave," said Horda lightly.

"Spring?" Now Mach was doubtful.

"Probably."

"Are you serious?"

She laughed. "I hope not."

"Me, too," said Mach squeezing her hand.

Chapter 7

"HO, THE FEAST!" CALLED Garol flexing the muscles of his shoulders as he neared the end of his journey. He, Premo, and Trefo each pulled a heavily laden travois into the camp. "We found a large herd and decided to get meat while we could. We took a hand plus four deer. We can dry the extra for winter like Horda suggested." The young men stopped and looked around the chaotic camp.

"What's happened? What's wrong?" Premo's fear showed on his face. His small body seemed to shrink even smaller when he could not locate Aiyana immediately.

Garol and Trefo drew themselves up to their fullest heights and surveyed the camp. "What's happening here?" demanded Garol. "I thought we were having a feast to welcome us to our new shelter."

"Oh, Premo," Aiyana cried. Heedless of Garol and Trefo, she ran out of the crowd and threw herself into her mate's arms. Then the whole story tumbled out in no discernable order.

"Slow down," coaxed a visibly relieved Premo. "Tell me what happened. How many are hurt?"

"Only Thuro." Aiyana paused for breath. "Wilda screeched and howled, but she just skinned her knees and palms. She's not really hurt."

"Mach?"

"He was outside when the bear attacked Thuro. Mach killed it, but Thuro fought it. Then Mach and Zeek killed the cubs. They weren't very big, but Mach said they tried to attack just like their mother. Oh, and there were bats."

The young men shook their heads. Premo asked, "Why did Thuro go into the cave with the bats before he knew it was safe?"

"Because of Wilda."

Premo's mouth set in a grim line. "That woman doesn't have the sense of a deer fly," he muttered. Garol and Trefo nodded their agreement.

Joining the young men, Horda gave Mach a speaking look at Premo's words. *What are we going to do?*

Forcing a jovial tone into his voice, Mach said, "Praise to Mother Life. Thuro's wounds don't appear to be too serious, and your hunt was successful beyond our hopes. As was ours. The she-bear and her young ones were well-fed and ready for winter. We have much fresh meat and blubber ready to be preserved."

"Yes, the Mother smiles on us," said Premo formally.

"If our luck holds, we'll eat well in the dark days of the Moon of the Long Blizzards and into the Moon of the Early Green," added Horda. "The skins and furs of these animals will provide our People warmth during the coldest times."

"Yes, the Mother is most kind," agreed the young men.

"We must prepare for the feast." Horda clapped her hands and immediately was surrounded by the People. "The shadows lengthen as the sun moves toward the mountains, and we have much to do." She quickly assigned tasks, and the People scattered to do her bidding.

Wilda caught Horda's arm and spun her around. "How dare you!"

"How dare I what?" asked Horda.

"Continue like nothing has happened."

Horda's brow wrinkled. "Much has happened."

"But you're going to have a feast anyway," accused Wilda.

Horda fought to keep the sharpness from her voice. "We have a great deal to be thankful for, Wilda."

"Oh, yes," snarled Wilda. "*You* have a great deal to be thankful for."

"What do you mean by that?"

Wilda glared at Horda. "Because of my mate's unfortunate accident, your mate will lead in his place."

"And whose thoughtless actions caused Thuro's *accident*?"

Wilda jingled the beads and shells in her hair and sniffed. "Mach should have known it wasn't safe. He should have stayed to help Thuro."

"Neither of them would have been in the cave if it hadn't been for you," said Horda softly.

"That's right. Try to put the blame on me." Wilda twisted her fingers together. "I had no idea the cave might be unsafe."

"Both Mach and Thuro warned you."

A telltale blush crept up Wilda's bronze cheeks. "I, ah, didn't hear them." Horda's amber gaze bored into Wilda's soul.

Wilda glared at her. "I wanted to see the cave for myself. I wasn't listening."

"Perhaps you should have been." Horda turned to walk away.

"You can not blame me for Thuro's injuries. I do not want him to suffer. He is my mate. I do not benefit by his being hurt. You do."

Horda paused but decided not to reply.

"You ignore me. Everyone ignores me. It is not right," shouted Wilda. "You have taken my place as the women's leader."

"Your place?" Horda spun around and glared. "Pardon me. I thought your place was sleeping and primping while others worked."

Though Wilda's fullest height barely reached Horda's chin, she managed to stare down her nose at her. "As the number one mates of the leaders of the band, we have a position to uphold. You may spend all your time working if you want to, but I do not choose to spend my time that way. There are others to do the work. There is no reason for me to do it, but I should be consulted."

Disbelief rounded Horda's eyes. "Whatever gave you that idea?"

"I have rank. Power. Status. I am the mate of the chief. I do not have to do the work."

In spite of her anger, Horda laughed in Wilda's face. "My mother was the first mate of the chief of the entire tribe of the People of the Frozen Earth. Not a small band like ours — the entire tribe. She once thought like you do. My father quickly straightened her out. She did her share right up to the time she walked the Frozen Wilds."

Now Horda looked down her nose at the smaller Wilda. "The band is at our winter home so remember People who are able to work and don't, do not eat. If they continue not doing their part, they are banished. That is the way of the People of the Frozen Earth."

Wilda opened and closed her mouth several times before she found words. "Do you threaten me?" she finally screeched.

"Oh, no … oh, no," said Horda softly. "I'm only reminding you of the ways of our People." She turned and walked away. *Mother Life, what are we going to do with that woman?*

The camp soon became a beehive of activity. Some of the men skinned the deer carcasses and stretched the hides. Others assembled drying racks. The women who weren't preparing the feast sliced the extra meat into thin strips and pounded it with herbs. The children carried it to the drying racks.

Mach took four men with him to check the cave for other animals. When they were sure the cave was deserted, they began filling baskets with the bat guano. "Phew, this stuff really stinks," said Garol unnecessarily.

Mach only nodded preferring not to open his mouth in the cave.

"Anything that smells this bad ought to be good for something," observed Premo.

Everyone groaned except Mach. He left the cave and sought Horda beside the cook fire. "Do you remember when Zaaco found the bat cave during Gathering?"

Still upset by her encounter with Wilda, Horda didn't answer. Mach reached out to touch her arm but saw his dirty hands and stopped. "Horda," he called more loudly, "where are you?"

A little shake of her head brought her back to the present. "I'm sorry. Are you talking to me?"

"Yes, I am." Mach frowned tenderly. "Are you all right?"

"No!" She poured out the story.

Mach found himself smiling in spite of his anger. "Do you mean she's trying to blame me for Thuro's injuries?"

"It isn't funny," said Horda.

"Yes, it is," said Mach gently. "She behaves like a small child. All we have to do is help her grow up."

Horda shook her head. "What do we do? Wave a magic stick and say three times 'You're a grownup.' Do you think it's going to be that easy?" Exasperation sharpened her voice.

"No, I don't think it's going to be easy at all." He smiled at his mate. "What would you do if she really were a child?"

"I'd make her sit and think about what happens when everyone doesn't do their share."

"Well?"

"Well, what?"

"Maybe that's what she's doing after your pointed … ah … hint."

"Humph."

"We can always hope," said Mach trying to hug Horda without touching her with his hands.

"What will we do if she doesn't start to work?" asked Horda wrinkling her nose and stepping out of his clumsy embrace. "What if we have to banish her?"

"We will banish her if we have to." Mach frowned. "But first we'll remind her and see if she gets the message. If not, we'll warn her formally." He chewed the inside of his cheeks and shook his head. "I hope we don't have to do that." He looked around the camp. “Where is she?”

“I think she’s sitting with Thuro. She said he needed her and flounced off when we started to work.”

“It’s time for me to check on Thuro,” said Mach starting away.

“Not without scrubbing your hands in the hottest water you can stand.” Horda went to a nearby pack for a large piece of soaproot. “I don’t know if you should touch his wounds even then.” She shivered. “Did you find me just to discuss Wilda?”

“No, I forgot what I came for though I don’t know how.” Mach looked at his dirty hands and wrinkled his nose at their pungent smell. “Do you remember the bat cave Zaaco found during Gathering several turnings of the seasons ago?”

Horda nodded.

“What did they do with that guano?”

She thought for a moment before she replied. “I think they put it where the fruits and vegetables grew.” She nodded. “Yes, I’m sure that’s what they did with it. Nuroo said it would make them grow better.”

“That’s what I thought, but I couldn’t remember for sure.”

“Why?”

“Well, we have enough bat guano for most of the tribe. Do you want us to put it somewhere special?”

“I don’t know where the plants grow in the spring.” Horda frowned. “I guess you could make a pile — away from the camp, please — and we’ll use it when we see where we need it.”

“You don’t want it just outside the cave?” Mach smiled at her.

Horda scowled though her eyes were twinkling. "Not hardly."

"I can't imagine why not," he teased waving his hands under her nose.

"Stop that. We have work to do." She put the soaproot into his hand without touching him. "Do not put that stuff near the river."

He leaned down and touched his lips to hers. She shared his breath. "Everything will be all right," he whispered against her mouth.

Would it? She certainly hoped so.

Mach found a droopy-eyed Thuro propped up on his good arm listening to Wilda. "Greetings, Thuro — and Wilda."

"Greetings, Mach," mumbled Thuro around a yawn. Wilda turned and pointedly looked away without responding.

"Let me look at you." Mach peered at the bandage on Thuro's arm before going behind him to look at his back. Though he'd scrubbed his hands, the odor of the bat guano still clung to them, and he did not touch Thuro. He nodded approvingly. "No blood shows on either bandage. That's a good sign."

"Humph," sniffed Wilda.

"How do you feel?" asked Mach ignoring her.

"Like a small herd of bison ran over me," admitted Thuro.

"Well, good. If it was only a small herd, you should be all right soon."

Wilda snorted like an angry bear. Thuro stifled another

yawn and blinked at his mate's back.

"Why don't you sleep?" Watching Thuro struggle to keep his eyes open, Mach laughed in spite of his concern. "Horda gave you enough lobelia to put you out."

"I was asleep," mumbled Thuro with another mighty yawn. "Wilda woke me."

Taking a deep breath, Mach walked around to face Wilda. "Do you have a problem?"

Her eyes shot daggers at him before she spoke. "My mate and I have a problem," she said haughtily turning her back to Mach once more.

Thuro reached out. "Wilda, don't —"

She glared at him. "I'm not afraid of the mighty Mach though you seem to be." She faced Mach. "This is all your fault. You planned for my mate to be hurt so you could take over the band like your mate took over the women."

"I what?" yelped Mach.

"You planned this." A tear quivered prettily on her sooty lashes.

"I planned this?" asked Mach. "What are you talking about, woman? Thuro wouldn't have been in that cave if not for your foolhardy action."

"You were in the cave with us. When you decided it wasn't safe, you deserted us — hoping we'd both be killed."

Mach clenched his huge fists. Hitting a woman went against everything he had ever been taught, but for just a brief span of time he allowed himself to consider the satisfaction of smashing this woman's troublesome mouth. He forced his fists to relax. He spoke softly. "You know that is not the truth."

"Are you accusing me of lying?" screeched Wilda.

"Yes," said Mach firmly.

"Yes," echoed Thuro. Wilda spun around to scowl at him.

Mach forced the anger from his voice. "I left you and Thuro alone in the cave because it was his place to scold you for your foolish actions. I didn't expect the bear to share the cave with all the bats."

She dissolved into tears. "I didn't know. You should have warned me."

"We did warn you," said Thuro thickly.

Mach said, "We both called you back, but you didn't pause. After the bats were all out, we had no choice but to enter the cave to get you. Only Mother Life's grace kept Thuro and you both from being killed by *your* foolish actions."

"You'd be glad if we had been killed," accused Wilda.

Mach stared at her a long time before he finally replied. "No, Wilda, Thuro and I are co-chiefs. More important, we're friends. We need each other very much. I would have been very sorry if he'd been killed by your stupidity." He turned and walked away without another word. *If Thuro had been killed, I would have been obligated to offer you a place beside my cook fire, and that would have been a fate worse than death.*

"The very idea," she muttered rubbing the angry tears from her face. "He didn't deny he'd be glad if I died. Why didn't you challenge him?"

Thuro looked at her for what seemed a very long time. Finally he said, "You need to help with the work for the evening eat."

"No, I'll sit with you. You may need me."

"All I need is a chance to sleep."

She tossed her braids jingling the shells and beads. "Then

go to sleep. My place is right here watching over you."

"No, Wilda, it isn't," he said sharply. "You know the way of the People. The able-bodied must work if they are to eat."

"But I am the first mate of the ch— "

Slurring his words, Thuro said, "As mate of the co-chief, you must do your share of the work and stop shirking your responsibilities. Go help the others."

Fresh tears gathered in her eyes. Her full lower lip quivered. "You're angry with me. You blame me too."

Though pain pounded through his injuries like a bison stampede, Thuro held out his good arm to his mate. "No, Wilda, I just want you to be a good leader of the women." His eyes drifted shut.

"But, I can tell them what to do," she insisted.

Thuro forced his eyes open. He fought to make them focus on her face. "That's not the way of the People of the Frozen Earth."

"I knew you were angry."

His exasperation penetrated the fog in his brain. "I have told you I am not angry. Will you please do what needs to be done and let me sleep?"

"You said I was lying."

"You were," he said sadly. *What is wrong with her? Did the fright damage her mind?*

"I wasn't," she declared. "Your injury is Mach's fault." He winced when she burrowed against his neck jostling his injured arm. "He should have stayed with us since he knew the cave was dangerous."

"No, he shouldn't have. He was right to leave us alone. You shouldn't have run ahead. You were wrong."

"You do blame me." Sobbing hysterically, she lowered her head so he couldn't see the anger in her eyes.

"I blame myself." Tipping her face up with his uninjured hand, he gritted his teeth against the pain until he could continue. "I should have been more careful. I should have made sure you understood the danger."

She sniffed. "Don't make me leave you. I want to take care of you."

"I don't need any care. I just want to sleep for awhile." He closed his eyes. *Please, Mother Life, make her go away.* "Won't you please go help the others?"

She frowned. "I have a position to uphold. I shouldn't have to work."

"Didn't you even listen in the Rituals of Childhood?"

She rolled her eyes. "Of course, I listened. What are you talking about?"

"Able-bodied People who do not work, do not eat," he quoted. "If they still do not work, they are banished."

She pushed herself to a sitting position against his chest causing him to groan. Then she ran her fingers down his jaw. "Oh, you sound just like Horda," she teased.

He pushed her away. "Because she's right."

"No, she's not." Wilda glared. "As the number one mate of the chief, I'm special. I shouldn't have to work."

"As the number one mate of the chief, you have to work harder than any other woman in the band. Everyone looks to you for an example. Look at Horda."

"You look at Horda if you want to. I don't want to be like her. She's nothing but a big, old bison cow." She scowled. "I still don't see why everyone thinks she's so wonderful. Just because Bear Claw kidnapped her. She deserved it, I'm sure."

"Wilda, you know nothing about that terrible time." Thuro's mouth set in a straight line and his eyes flashed.

"Oh, yes I do! I know you didn't care enough to stay with me where you belonged. You left me standing alone during the Mating Ceremony while you ran off after Horda. It was embarrassing. I hated it."

"The kidnapped women were raped, beaten, and tortured," he said softly. "They suffered things you cannot even imagine."

"And you won't tell me. I still say she did something to make Bear Claw take her. I suspect there are many things we don't know about the high and mighty Horda."

Horda's bruised and battered face flashed in Thuro's memory before he looked away. "I know the women suffered horribly. Bear Claw killed one of his own women and nearly beat Horda to death." His mouth snapped shut.

"Why did he suddenly decide to beat the precious Horda?"

"He didn't suddenly decide to beat her." Thuro hedged. "I understand he and his people beat all the women from the day they captured them."

"Well, that doesn't make any sense. Why capture women to enlarge their tribe if they were going to beat them to death?"

"How would I know? I didn't understand the workings of Bear Claw's twisted savage mind, Wilda."

She sniffed. "I still say more happened than we know about. Someone said there was a Band Council before you came back."

Thuro looked away.

"Well, was there?"

"Was there what?"

Wilda glared. "Was there a Band Council?"

"Yeah," he mumbled and closed his eyes hoping she'd think he was asleep and wouldn't question him anymore.

"Why?"

He cursed the fuzzy mind that had made him confirm his mate's words. " Wilda. I was not a member of the Band Council."

"But why did they call a Band Council?"

"The members of the Band Council do not discuss their business with the People unless the People have a need to know about it." He quoted the teachings of the Rituals of Childhood.

"But *you* know," she accused. "I'm sure it had something to do with Horda and Mach." She watched Thuro closely hoping to learn if she had guessed correctly.

Thuro's warrior face gave her no clues. "No one told me why the Council was called." He hid behind true words.

Suddenly she changed her tactics. "The People should look up to me and consult me, but I shouldn't have to do any of the real work."

He shook his head, but his expression didn't change. "Maybe someday when you've earned their respect and the band is much larger than it is now, you won't have to work as hard, but you'll always have to do your share. That's the way of the People of the Frozen Earth."

"Then we should change it."

"Wilda, we can't change it."

"Why not?" she whined. "I've never thought it was fair for the important People to work like everyone else."

Especially since you see yourself as important. Thuro struggled against the herbs to keep from slurring his words. "It's going to take all of us working together to get this place ready for the winter." He rubbed his face and straightened his shoulders. "If you don't do your share, I will formally reprimand you."

Her eyes shot sparks. "You wouldn't dare!"

"And if that doesn't work ..." He leaned back and closed his eyes. "You will be banished."

Once more she managed tears. "You don't love me."

"I love you, but your actions are unacceptable. You must do your duty just as I must do mine." Though he still fought to stay awake, his eyes rolled back and his eyelids drooped shut.

She shook him.

He opened one eye and stared at her. "I won't let you destroy this new band with your childish behavior. Go help prepare the feast."

She glared at him, but she slowly made her way through the afternoon shadows to the cook fire.

The good smells of bear stew, venison roast, wild onions, and sage drifted over the camp while the sun slipped into the jagged teeth of the mountains. When the stony-faced Wilda joined the women preparing the feast, anxiety flared through Horda. *What will she do now?* Taking a deep breath, Horda ignored Wilda and continued grinding cattail and yampah roots into flour for frybread.

Wilda wandered around the cook fire. She gave a desultory

stir to one of the cooking bags and knocked one side off the supports. "Be careful," cautioned Horda when Wilda reached for the falling bag.

Wilda caught it. "Ouch!" She dropped the bag and stuck her burned fingers into her mouth. The rich stew sizzled and smoked as it spilled into the cook fire.

Grabbing rawhide mitts, Horda managed to pull the bag from the fire before it completely emptied. Without a word, she replaced it on the rack above the fire then returned to grinding flour.

"I'm hurt," whined Wilda.

Horda pretended not to hear her.

She stuck her hand under Horda's nose. "My fingers are burned. I need the healer woman to treat them."

"They aren't even blistered," said Horda icily. "Next time, use the mitts so you don't waste the stew."

"That's all you have to say?" shouted Wilda. "Some healer woman you are. You ignore People who are hurt and need your care."

"I ignore People who have nothing better to do than complain. I'm busy. The flour must be ground so we can make the bread. Then the food will be ready."

Wilda seemed to debate continuing the argument she would probably lose. "I came to help."

Horda swallowed her surprise. "Okay. You can grind the flour while I start frying the bread."

Horda stood up hiding her smile at the dismay playing across Wilda's face. *She hadn't expected to be given a job so quickly.* Horda mixed crumbled sage and rosemary with a little of the salty cow parsnip before she blended it into the flour. She rubbed a piece of the fresh bear fat on the flat frying rock. While she waited for it to heat, she added enough water to the mixture to make a thick paste.

Wilda still stood looking at the cattail and yampah roots. "You'd better get busy. It won't take long to fry this batch," said Horda.

Wilda sat down and began to grind.

❂

The clear white light of the autumn moon smiled on the summer shelters of the camp. "It won't be too long before we can move inside the cave," promised Mach carrying first Rain Drop and then Storm Cloud into the shelter.

"I'm ready," said Horda straightening their fur bed. "This shelter isn't really big enough for all four of us."

Mach stripped off his moccasins and breechclout and dove into the freshly straightened bed quickly churning it to disarray. "We'll have to make a bigger one before next summer."

"We?" teased Horda slipping off her moccasins.

"I'll get you the bison skins."

One golden eyebrow arched. "In the winter?"

"I'm a mighty hunter. I'll — Humph!" The air whooshed out of his lungs as she lay down and neatly elbowed him in the stomach. "Ouch!"

"Oh, did I hurt you?" Her voice sounded innocent.

He rubbed his midsection. "Don't worry about it. I'm sure it was an accident. You wouldn't hit me. I'm the co-leader — Oof!" She wiggled against him and none too gently kneed his side.

"Yes, I would. I don't want you getting conceited like

Wilda."

"You don't have to worry about that." He smiled. "You keep me humble." He pulled her into his arms and tickled her.

She giggled and fought against him until his mouth found hers, and they shared breath. She melted into his familiar embrace. "I love you," she whispered.

"I love you." He fumbled with the lacings of her tunic until she helped him. Sitting up he lifted the tunic over her head. Naked she snuggled into the sleeping furs beside her mate and shared his warmth. Their hands and mouths worked their magic. Together they walked above the clouds and danced the ageless dance of lovers. Together they floated back to earth and Mach slept.

Horda lay awake a long time staring at stars twinkling through the smoke hole at the top of the shelter. *Please Mother Life, let this be the time we make a little one.*

Chapter 8

SHIVERING IN THE COOL air, Horda carried a load of green wood and watched the apricot, pink, and lavender sunbeams chase the grey out of the morning sky. Fine trees surrounded the small clearing adding their crisp, tangy scent to the smoke from the meat-drying fires. She added her wood to the fires. Soon we will have more than enough meat for the winter. She rubbed her hands in the meager warmth before she headed back to her cook fire.

In the early light a few bats flew toward the cave. Horda grimaced. *Now, if those last pesky bats will give up and the men get the path widened, we'll move into the cave and be ready for the long cold. Two hands' turning of the sun have passed. Thuro's nearly well, and the fever demons haven't found him so they probably won't. Even Wilda's trying to do her share. Not that she's much good at anything yet, but she's trying, and she isn't griping.* Horda reached up to embrace the morning sky. All was well in her world.

"Horda! Where are you?" Wilda's shrill cries brought Horda running to the cook fire.

Oops! I thought too soon. "I was tending the smoking fires.

What's the matter?"

"It's Aiyana. Premo couldn't find you so he called me."

"What's wrong?" Horda yanked on a fire mitt before she picked up a bag of hot water.

Wilda looked blank then she finally replied, "They need you."

Her medicine pack in one hand and the water bag in the other, Horda headed for Premo's shelter with Wilda close on her heels.

"Is something wrong? Is Aiyana bleeding?"

"I don't know."

Horda frowned.

"He couldn't find you, and I panicked, I guess," Wilda admitted. "I don't know much about birthing."

Horda smiled. "You'll learn soon enough. Most of the time it's just catching the little one and cleaning up after."

The two young women skidded to a stop outside the shelter.

"Premo," called Horda softly.

He pushed back the door covering and pulled Horda inside. Wilda followed close behind.

"Greetings, Premo. It's a beautiful day to become a father," said Horda.

"Do something," he commanded.

Aiyana moaned when a contraction knotted the mound of her stomach.

Horda put down her medicine pack and hung the hot water bag on the shelter support. She lifted the furs covering Aiyana's lower body and smiled. Only the faintest tinge of pink colored the wet furs. "Tell me what's happened," she said taking a piece of soaproot from her pack and turning to wash her hands.

Premo blushed furiously. "We woke this morning in a puddle. Aiyana said her water broke." His Adam's apple bobbed. "I got up to get clean furs, and the pains hit her. What's the matter? Is she dy . . ." His last words faded to silence.

Horda fought to keep from smiling at the distraught young man. "She's having the baby." She dried her hands on a piece of clean leather from her pack.

"That's all?" Relief relaxed Premo's tense features.

Another pain caught Aiyana and she moaned. The color blanched from Premo's face, and it tightened once more. Wilda turned a definite shade of green.

Horda walked over to the laboring woman. "Premo, go fill two large water bags and put them on to heat. Then clean yourself up and have some hot tea. Wilda and I will help Aiyana."

He protested faintly. "But shouldn't I h ..."

Horda did smile. "You've done your part. This is Aiyana's job."

Another blush painted Premo's face, but he collected two water bags and clean clothing before he left the shelter.

"Now, Aiyana, let's see if everything is going as well as it appears to be. Then we'll clean you up."

"It hurts."

"I know it does," consoled Horda. "Just think about the little one you're going to have in your arms soon." A pain of loss stabbed Horda in the pit of the stomach, but she kept her smile in place and her voice smooth.

Wilda turned a darker shade of green when Horda pushed the tunic above the mound of Aiyana's stomach and began to examine her. “There’s no real bleeding, and you’re opening up nicely.”

Aiyana’s stomach knotted, and she groaned and began straining.

“No, no, Aiyana. Don’t. It’s too soon to push. Breathe, like this.” Horda sucked in her cheeks and panted. “Ride the pain.”

The harsh sound of Aiyana’s breathing filled the small shelter.

“That was a good one. It won’t be long now.” Horda washed the young woman’s lower body with warm water. “Can you stand up?”

“Maybe.” Taking Horda’s hand, Aiyana started to climb to her feet, but another pain caught her, and she sat back gasping. “Maybe not.”

Horda laughed. “Breathe like I showed you.”

Aiyana rode the pain until it ebbed away.

“Hurry,” Horda urged her up. “Wilda, come hold her. Don’t let her fall if another pain comes. I have to prepare the birth bed.”

White-faced and obviously frightened, Wilda put her arms around Aiyana and lent her support. Horda quickly stripped away the fouled furs then fashioned a kind of seatless chair from others.

“Argh!” A mighty contraction twisted Aiyana in Wilda’s arms.

“Breathe,” commanded Horda. “Breathe, don’t fight it. Work with it.”

Aiyana struggled for control and lost. A scream tore her throat. “I’m coming apart,” she screeched.

Wilda’s dark eyes grew enormous in her white face. She

shook like a leaf in a spring storm, but she held on to the straining girl until Horda reached them. Together they set Aiyana on the bed of furs and positioned her lower body.

Examining Aiyana, Horda grinned. "I thought so," she said triumphantly. "The baby's coming. I can see the top of its head."

"It's killing me," cried Aiyana.

"No, it's not," said Horda matter-of-factly. "Wilda, hold her shoulders and help her push with the next contraction."

Wilda bit her lips and swallowed convulsively but took the place Horda indicated. Massaging the mound of Aiyana's stomach, Horda said, "Your baby is ready to be born. Now, you must help it. Do you hear me?"

Aiyana nodded.

"With the next pain, I want you to push hard as you can. Do you understand?"

Aiyana nodded again and waited for the next contraction to begin.

"Push, Aiyana," commanded Horda kneading the mound of her stomach. "I can see its head. Keep pushing." Horda placed her hands under the little one's head and guided its shoulders free while the contraction lasted.

"I can't do this," said Aiyana.

"Yes, you can," soothed Horda. "You're almost done. One more big push, and you'll have a little one."

The next pain hit Aiyana, and she moaned. "Don't waste your breath moaning, Aiyana," scolded Horda. "Now's the time to push."

The power of Aiyana's pushing turned her face red and caused a blood vessel in her forehead to pulse like a small dusky rose-colored snake. But between her push and Horda's gentle pull the little one slid free until it was only connected to its mother by the thick, pulsing, purple umbilical cord. "It's a boy!" Horda cleared the little one's mouth and nose and wrapped it in a soft rabbit fur blanket. "Here, Wilda, hold him while I cut the cord."

"A boy?" asked Aiyana faintly.

"A boy. A fine strong boy." Horda laughed when the little one yowled indignantly at being passed to Wilda's trembling hands. Horda tied sinew in two tight knots around the umbilical cord then slashed it with a fine obsidian knife.

"I want to see him," demanded Aiyana.

Wilda carried the squalling infant to his mother.

"He's beau —" Another pain twisted her stomach terrifying her. "Am I d —"

Horrified Wilda took a step back and clutched the squalling infant to her chest.

"Don't worry," said Horda. "It's just the afterbirth." She massaged Aiyana's flattening stomach to help her expel all of it. She wrapped it in a fine fawn skin and put it aside. She would bury it under a juniper tree when she finished her other tasks. Then she washed Aiyana's body and wrapped her in clean furs.

After that she prepared a shallow bowl of warm water. "There. Wilda, give me the little one and go tell Premo his child is born. As soon as I get him cleaned, his mate will introduce them."

Wilda thrust the infant into Horda's arms and fled.

"That's all?" asked Aiyana blinking.

"That's all." Horda fought images of her own dead child while she unwrapped the baby and washed his tiny body. "Where's your baby pack?"

"Over there." Aiyana gestured to a gaily decorated pack hanging from one of the shelter supports. "It wasn't nearly as bad as I expected."

"What?"

"The birth. I thought it would take longer and hurt more."

"Sometimes it does."

"My mother always made me think she labored for days trying to give birth to me."

"It is possible," said Horda. "Sometimes it takes a long time for a baby to be born."

"She was disappointed that after all the pain I was a girl." A tear quivered on Aiyana's eyelash. "She's never forgiven me."

Horda blinked. Aiyana had gone through the Rituals of Mating when she had but three hands of winters. Much too young in Horda's mind. She'd wondered why this girl had rushed so to become an adult. Now she knew. "I wish I could take the pain away," she said simply.

"Oh, it's stupid to let old memories hurt me now." Aiyana sniffed against the tears filling her eyes. "But I've always wanted her to be proud of me."

Horda took down the pack and searched for the supplies she needed. She chose her words carefully. "She should have been proud of the way you survived our captivity."

"She wasn't. She reminded me that if I'd listened to her when she said I was too young for the Rituals of Mating, I wouldn't have been captured."

"Oh." Horda tried to find other words of comfort. "She'll be proud of a grandson."

"Maybe." Aiyana wiped her eyes and watched the little

one wave his arms and legs while Horda padded his behind in combed flax and soft moss before wrapping him snugly in strips of soft leather and putting him in a thin rabbit skin sacque. Happiness glowed in Aiyana's features as she admired the tiny scrap that was her son.

Horda ignored the pain in her heart and smiled down into the little one's lopsided red face. "You're a beauty. That you are. You're much too pretty to be an old warrior." The baby stopped fretting. He seemed to be trying to focus on her face. "You'll break all the maidens' hearts in a few turnings of the seasons."

Aiyana watched them. "Do you really think he's beautiful?" she asked in a small voice.

"Yes." Horda placed the little bundle against his mother's breast. He began to snuffle and root trying to nurse. "He's strong and smart too." She smiled sadly watching the baby's movements. *Mother Life, haven't my arms been empty long enough?* "You'd better let him eat before he chews his way through your covering."

Aiyana rearranged the furs and offered him her nipple. The baby snuffled once and latched on with a noisy slurp. She giggled.

"He's a greedy one," said Horda.

"Like his father."

"Maybe they don't outgrow it." The two young women shared a smile.

"Horda." A blush tinted Aiyana's cheeks at the sound of Premo's voice outside the shelter. "Wilda said my mate waited to introduce our child."

Horda lifted the cover over the shelter opening. "Please enter, Premo. Your family awaits." She stepped outside to stretch her cramped muscles. Looking at the midday sun, she realized the birth really had taken only a short span of time. On her way to her cook fire, she smiled in delight. Wilda had been a help, and Aiyana had delivered easily and quickly. Life was good.

Then she heard Wilda's hysterical sobs. "It was awful. I couldn't bear such a thing. I'd die. I thought she was going to be torn in two."

"Shh, shh, calm down." Thuro rubbed his mate's back as if she were a distraught child.

"I've never seen anything so terrible. You can't imagine. I couldn't do that. I don't want to do that. Please, please. Promise me ..."

Surprised Horda watched Wilda sob and babble.

"It's okay. Don't worry. It's all right." Thuro looked helplessly at Horda.

She shrugged and mouthed. "It was an easy birth."

He still rubbed Wilda's back. "Horda said it was an easy birth."

Wilda screeched and turned on Horda. "How can you tell such lies? Aiyana suffered terribly. I thought she was going to die."

"There is pain involved in giving birth," said Horda trying to reassure her. "It's the way things are."

"I don't want to suffer like that — ever," cried Wilda piteously. "Please, promise me I won't have to."

"I can't promise you that, Wilda," said Horda. "There are herbs that ease the pain some, but nothing takes it away completely."

"You didn't give Aiyana herbs," accused Wilda.

"She didn't need them."

"Didn't need them? She moaned and screamed. She suffered agony."

Horda shook her head. "No, she didn't. You need to talk to her. She was surprised it was already over. She expected more pain."

"More pain? She's out of her mind. I know what I saw, and I don't ever want to go through it," cried Wilda. "It hurt too much. I couldn't stand it. Please, Thuro, promise you won't make me go through that."

I have no place in this conversation. Where is everyone else? Horda edged away from them and continued on her way.

CHAPTER 9

A SHORT TIME LATER LOUD laughter drew Horda to the flat area where the path to the cave began. Looking at the crowd of men, she asked, "What's going on?"

"Horda, how's Aiyana?" Mach chuckled.

"She and her little one are fine." Horda frowned. "What's happening?"

"Storm Cloud and Zeek's little boy Bran wanted to help us widen the path up to the cave, but they got their feet tangled and rolled down the path instead."

"I don't see anything funny about that."

"Well, they ended up in the bat guano and now the only parts of them that aren't black are the whites of their eyes and their tongues." He pointed to Bran and Storm Cloud standing in the circle of laughing people and enjoying being the center of attention.

"Mach," gasped Horda. "That's bat guano. They could catch all kinds of sickness from it."

"Oh, Horda. Don't be such a spoilsport. They're having a

wonderful time. Here comes Zhrul's boy Domo."

"Stop, Domo!" she commanded.

Urscia came running down the path. "Why are you yelling at my son?"

Horda took a deep breath and immediately regretted it. "Because I don't want him to get into the bat guano, Urscia. I'm afraid this may cause some sickness, and he was heading into it." She chewed her lips to keep from telling Urscia what she was really thinking. "I'm sorry. I didn't see you. I would never have reprimanded him if I had."

Urscia caught her little boy's hand and pulled him to her. Rushing up the path, she muttered, "It's not her place to scream at m —"

Zhrul's glare silenced her as he fell into step beside her. His voice rumbled low in his chest. "Perhaps you should remember, as People of the Frozen Earth, we work together."

"I will take care of my own —" Zhrul caught her arm, and the rest of her words were lost.

Horda stalked to the center of the circle and caught Storm Cloud's and Bran's hands. She scowled over her shoulder as she hurried the protesting children away. "I hope a good time is all they have."

Her steps didn't slow until both boys were seated in a shallow pool at the edge of the river. "Sit still, Storm Cloud. You're next." She scrubbed Bran, a sturdy little boy beginning the fourth winter of his life, with fine sand from the pool's bottom.

"Why?" Storm Cloud's lower lip pushed out in a pout. "We were having fun."

"No bafh," giggled the younger Bran trying to slip out of

Horda's grasp. "Have fun."

"It's not fun to play in animal droppings."

"Animal droppings?" The whites of Storm Cloud's eyes grew larger in his black face. "Guano?"

"Yes, guano."

"Guano," echoed Bran.

"Yes, guano," said Horda.

"Oh-kay." Bran stuck the first three fingers of his right hand in his mouth and began to suck vigorously.

"Wait. Your nails ..." Horda pulled on his hand. He sucked harder.

"Why's he doing that?" asked Storm Cloud. "The guano tastes terrible."

"How do you know?" Horda finally got Bran's hand out of his mouth and scrubbed it.

"I got a mouth full the first time I fell in."

"The first time?" Horda rolled her eyes. *Mother Life. Please take care of these children.* "How many times did you fall in?" She rinsed the little boy.

"Only once."

Reeme, Bran's mother, huffed up to them with several large pieces of soaproot. "Oh, Bran, what have you done?"

Horda explained what had happened and traded the little boy for one of the pieces of soaproot. Reeme began to wash her son again while Horda scrubbed Storm Cloud vigorously.

"Good, I'm glad you only fell in once," said Horda.

"After that we jumped."

Horda and Reeme squeaked together. "You jumped?" Both boys nodded. "Why did Mach let you jump into that pile of bat guano?"

"Everyone laughed. It was fun." Storm Cloud shrugged. "It was soft and squishy and kind of warm."

"Jumped lots," said Bran around a mouthful of fingers.

"Please, Bran." His mother pulled his fingers out of his mouth, but it had become a game. He gleefully stuffed all ten fingers back into his mouth.

"Take your hands out of your mouth," commanded Horda without thinking.

Reeme's sigh reminded Horda of the earlier confrontation with Urscia. She took a deep breath. "I'm sorry, Reeme."

Still scrubbing, Reeme looked at her. "Why?"

"I should not be reprimanding your child. It is not my place. Since I work with the children so much, sometimes I forget. Please, forgive me."

"I don't have much luck making him do what I want him to," admitted Reeme. "He likes to play with me, and I enjoy it. Sometimes I feel like a failure. Other times I just enjoy him. He minds just about everybody except me. Most of the time it doesn't bother me because I know he has to behave to keep him safe, and I know you people who love him will make him mind and do what's right."

Horda considered Reeme's words. She wasn't sure she approved of the woman's attitude, but it was better than Urscia's. "When we finish here, we're going to the cook fire," she said. "I'm going to wash them again in hot water with soaproot, and then I'm going to rinse them with goldenrod water. After that, they're going to drink a tea of mugwort."

"Ah, Horda," protested Storm Cloud. "We don't need three baths and some smelly old tea."

"No more bafs. Don't need no 'melly old tea," chimed Bran.

Horda glared at them. "I hope you're right, but you are going to have to do what I say today."

"Yes, more baths and mugwort tea," said Reeme firmly.

Horda divided the next few days between caring for Aiyana and worrying about Storm Cloud and Bran. Traditionally new mothers of the Frozen Earth remained in seclusion, where they were pampered and cared for during the first hand of days of their babies' lives.

The new band had set up one of the hunting shelters away from the main camp and designated it their birthing shelter. The location was beautiful, but it was a long walk from the main camp to the birthing shelter to care for the mother and baby.

The sun had barely risen the fourth morning when Horda arrived to find the young mother peeking out. "Greetings, Aiyana. Premo thought you were still asleep."

She jumped. "I'm tired of sleeping."

"Good, I hope you still feel that way by the next moon." Horda smiled. "Let's go inside. I brought you porridge and tea."

Aiyana frowned, but she moved away from the opening. "What I really want is to go down to the river and take an all-over bath."

"Well, you can't for two more days." Horda set the tea and porridge on the ground cloth beside the sleeping furs.

"I'm going crazy in here."

"No, you're not," said Horda. "You just think you are because you're young and healthy and don't need all the time to recover."

"Then let me out."

"No. Tomorrow is the last full day. Use this time to get to know your son."

Aiyana grinned down at the infant strapped to her chest. "I know my son. He's happy so long as he's full and warm and dry."

Horda touched his downy cheek. The baby immediately began to make smacking noises and suckle the air. "I can almost see him growing."

"I know. He eats and eats and eats."

Horda chewed the inside of her cheek, but she kept her smile in place. *Oh, please, Mother Life.* "Have you and Premo chosen his name?"

"On the first day, we're going to call him —"

"Shh! You can't tell anyone his name before you tell Mother Life and Father Death at the Naming Ceremony."

"You asked me."

"I was only trying to make conversation. I didn't ask what name you chose. I asked if you had chosen a name."

"I forgot. I'm sorry."

"No harm was done, but you must be careful."

Aiyana's sense of humor returned. "Not too careful since you're the only other person I see."

"No, not too careful." Horda shook her head. "Since you're so restless, why don't you sew or something."

"I don't have any leather or furs in here."

"I'll bring you some. What do you want?"

"Is it allowed?"

"If it keeps you inside and quiet, it's allowed."

Aiyana giggled. "Well, I'd like to make a baby bunting. I

made one a long time ago right after we mated, but it's kind of lop-sided. I can do better now."

"What do you need?"

"Just rabbit furs or a fawn skin from my small furs in the storage cache. I have my needles and sinew in here."

"Do you have your knives?"

Aiyana nodded.

"Finish your morning eat while I find the skins. It may take a little while."

"Yes, Ma. I'll be a good girl 'til you get back."

Aiyana didn't see the pain that flashed in Horda's amber eyes. *Aiyana didn't think. She didn't mean to hurt me. She was only teasing.*

Horda hurried back through the dappled morning shadows to the other shelters and almost tripped over Bran. "Ho! Bran, come here and let me look at you."

"No." The sturdy little boy ran away.

Laughing, she chased him. "You can run, but you can't get away from me." She scooped him into her arms. "I just want to check you."

"Me oh-kay." He struggled to get down.

"I want to see for myself." Fear pounded through her as her sensitive fingers discovered a small, hot kernel underneath Bran's jaw bone on the right side of his neck. *Maybe it isn't anything.* But there was another under his left arm. She blinked. *Oh, please, just let me be imagining things.* When she found a third and fourth in the creases of skin where his legs joined his torso, she could no longer deny the child carried fever demons in his body.

She clutched him to her chest and hurried to the cook fire.

"Me down," cried Bran drumming his feet against her stomach.

"Not yet, I want to make you some tea."

"No." He drummed harder.

"Ouch."

"Ouch?"

"Yes, ouch. You're hurting me."

"Not." Bran giggled and kicked some more.

"Yes, you are. You need to stop — now."

"Me down."

"No." She cradled him in her arms.

"Down. Big boy. Not baby."

She buried her chin in his neck without replying.

"Ouch." He cried and twisted away almost causing her to drop him. "Hurt."

"I'm sorry. I didn't mean to hurt you." Setting him down beside the cook fire, she washed her hands and began rummaging in her medicine pack.

"Oh-kay." He giggled and climbed to his feet.

"Sit still while I make you tea."

"No."

"We'll have a ceremony," she coaxed.

"Cer'mony?" He eyed her.

"Like at Gathering."

His brow furrowed. "No."

"We'll play like you're the chief."

"Like Mach?" His eyes gleamed at the thought of his hero.

"Yes, like Mach."

"Oh-kay."

"Okay, you wait right there while I fix your tea, Chief."

"Oh-kay."

Horda pulverized a small amount of mugwort and willow bark and set it in a waterbasket to brew into strong tea. "Now, Chief, what are we going to do today?" She placed some camas molasses and mint leaves into a small drinking horn.

"Hunt," he said solemnly.

"Oh, what are you going to hunt?" Reaching into her medicine pack, she pinched less than her little fingernail's worth of pinion pitch and rolled it into a ball.

"Bis'n."

"Umm, bison are a good choice. The meat's good and the hides make wonderful winter robes and covers for summer shelters."

"Yes."

She handed him the tiny ball of pitch. "Chief, I want you to eat that. Chew it up and swallow it."

Bran frowned at it and scrunched up his face. "No."

"It's strong medicine for the Chief's hunt," coaxed Horda.

He still eyed it doubtfully when Mach walked up.

"Hey, Bran, is Horda looking you over again?"

"Chief," said Bran pointing to himself.

"Huh?"

"He's the chief, and he's going to hunt bison after he drinks his tea," explained Horda straining the medicine into the drinking horn with molasses and mint.

"Why don't you leave him alone?" asked Mach. "Face it, he's not going to get sick."

"Not eat," Bran handed the pellet back to Horda.

"Please, eat this for me, Chief."

"No."

Mach saw the sheen of tears in Horda's eyes and realized something was very wrong. He kneeled so his face was level with Bran's. "Are you going to hunt bison with me, Chief?"

Bran cocked his head like a bright-eyed bird and looked at his Mach. "Yes."

"Good." Mach held out his hand for the pellet. "Then you need to eat this."

Reluctantly the little boy allowed Mach to put the medicine plants in his mouth. He frowned. "Tastes bad," he said through his scrunched-up lips.

Mach grinned. "Then chew it fast and swallow it. Horda has some tea to wash it down."

Horda showed him the horn of medicine. He opened his mouth to show it was empty. "Gone."

She held the horn while he drank a big mouth full. "Ugh!" He spewed. "Nassy."

"It's strong medicine to help you find the bison," said Mach. "If you don't drink all of it, we may not find them."

Bran wrinkled his nose but obediently drank every drop. He shook his head. "A'ful."

Mach laughed. "Strong medicine usually tastes awful."

Horda held out the horn of sweet mint water. "This tastes good. It'll wash the other out of your mouth."

Bran looked at her. "Still be chief?"

"Yes."

"Hunt bis'n with Mach?"

Mach nodded. Bran drank the water. He smiled. "Tastes good," he announced.

"I'm glad, Chief." Mach helped the little boy to his feet.

"You go find your spears. Then we'll go on our hunt."

"Really?"

"Yes, really."

"Come now."

"I need to talk to Horda first."

"Me wait."

Horda grinned. "If you wait, it'll make you later getting started on your hunt."

Bran's eyebrows drew down to his nose. "Oh-kay." He left in search of his toy spears.

As soon as the child was gone, Mach turned to Horda. "What's wrong?"

Tears filled her eyes. She took a deep breath. "He has hard, hot kernels in his body. The fever demons are inside him waiting to break free."

He shook his head. "Are you sure you aren't just imagining things?"

"I tried to tell myself I was, but I found four." Her voice caught on the lump of tears in her throat. "I didn't imagine that many."

"Will the medicine stop them?"

She rubbed her ears to stop Nuroo's voice from reciting the fearsome list of diseases one could get from droppings. The voice droned on. She clasped her trembling hands. *I can't drown them out. They're written on my heart. Please, Mother Life, let Bran get well.* "I hope so," she whispered.

Mach crossed two spears on his back and went in search of Bran. "Are you ready, Little Chief?"

Bran ran back with his spears in his hand. "Ready."

"No, you aren't," said Mach shaking his head.

Bran frowned. "Am."

"No."

The little boy caught Mach's hand and pulled. "'et's go."

Mach knelt down. "Look at my spears, Little Chief."

Bran looked and frowned. He tried to put his spears on his back, but he didn't have the harness. Mach laughed. "Let me help you."

"Hurry."

"Yes, sir." He took a long piece of braided leather and fashioned a criss-crossing harness on the little boy's back. Then he slipped the two small spears under the sides of the cross. "Now," he said patting the boy's shoulder and standing. "We're ready."

Bran tried to look behind himself. He turned around in a complete circle trying to see his spears. Finally in desperation, he stamped his foot. "No!"

"Why not?"

Bran's face looked like an angry thundercloud. "We can't go, Mach." He turned around one more time before he said, "No spears."

Mach grinned. "Watch me." He raised his hand over his head and reached back and caught the shaft of a spear. With an easy motion he lifted the spear and had it positioned in his hand to throw. "Can you do that?"

Bran reached up and caught one of his spears by the point and pulled it out of the harness.

"No, Bran, you'll cut yourself." Mach reached for the small spear. He found the "point" was actually a tiny, flat river rock in the approximate shape of a point. "Oh," he said. "Your point isn't sharp, but you still shouldn't learn to grab weapons like that. It won't be long before your spears will have real points."

Holding the small spear by the rock, Bran glared at Mach. "My spea's have real points."

"Then don't touch them." Mach replaced his spear in the sling over his shoulder without touching the point. "Watch me."

Bran carefully placed his chubby fingers below the point of the spear and began trying to poke its shaft into the harness on his back. As his frustration mounted, his efforts became more frantic. He almost dislodged the second spear, but he could not replace the first spear. Tears were not far below the surface.

"Okay, this is not working," said Mach. "Let me think."

"No, not workin'." The little boy was suddenly drenched with perspiration. He thrust the spear into Mach's hand. "You fix it."

Mach strode to his arms cache. Bran's eyes lighted up, and he reached for one of the smaller spears. "No," barked Mach. At the quivering of Bran's lips, Mach said, "Oh, please stop that. I didn't mean to scare you. Look." He picked up the spear and gently drew the point across the pad of his thumb. Droplets of blood beaded along the tiny cut.

Bran frowned. "Sharp?"

"Very sharp."

The boy traded spears with the chief and dragged his thumb down the side of his toy spear's point. He examined his thumb, mashing and looking at it. "Not sharp," he finally said.

"Not yet." Mach took the toy from Bran then showed him how to place his fingers around the shaft of the real spear. He touched the point on one side and the feathers on the other. Mach opened the little boy's hand and balanced the spear on his palm.

Bran's eyes lighted. "A real spear?"

Mach nodded. "Come outside and we'll practice throwing."

Apparently tired, Bran handed Mach's spear back. "Hunt, Mach."

"Don't you want to learn how?"

The little boy placed his small chubby fist on his hip and looked at Mach as if he were the child instead. Then he picked up his own spears. "Know how. 'Et's hunt." He started away from the camp.

Mach followed quietly. "Eh, Chief," he whispered.

"Shhh!" Bran kept walking.

Mach looked around wondering if he sometimes expected hunters to follow him blindly. He certainly hoped not. "Eh, Bran." He tried again to get information.

Bran turned around shaking his head and pointing to his chest. "Chief."

Stopping and sitting on the ground, Mach waited for the little boy to come back to him. "What's the matta?" Bran asked.

Mach pushed out his bottom lip. "I don't know where we are going," he complained.

"To hunt buffalo," said Bran pointing toward the plains.

"Oh," said Mach sagely. "That explains everything." He squinted, "Do you see the buffalo?"

Shielding his eyes with his hand, the little boy peered

across the plains. "Yes, I see them." He pointed to the right. "There."

Rising to his feet, Mach sighted down Bran's arm. "Ah, yes. I see them now."

Bran blinked and looked again, "Weally?"

"Well, really, pretend," said Mach.

"Yes, weally, pretend. Fix these." Bran gave his spears to Mach who replaced them in the little harness. "Now, carry me." commanded Bran. After rearranging the spears on his back, Mach lifted Bran to his shoulders and marched down the path. It wasn't long before Bran pulled on Mach's ears. "There the bis'ns."

Mach dutifully slowed and looked in the direction Bran pointed. "That's a big herd," he whispered. "How many do you think, Chief?"

"A finger's hands," said Bran with authority.

"Humm, that many?"

"'es!" Bran drummed his heels on Mach's shoulders. "Don't let them run away, Mach." He pulled Mach's left ear one more time.

Mach pretended to sneak up on the beasts. "Oops, they are getting nervous," he whispered. "Be very quiet." He lifted Bran off his neck and together they lay on their stomachs behind a small rise of land,

"Good job, Mach," whispered Bran. "I'll show you when to run. Oh-kay?"

"Okay."

The man and boy lay in the warm grass for a short span of time. Mach listened to the lazy insects singing, whistling, and screeching their autumn songs. "Noisy, isn't it?"

Bran didn't look at him but continued to survey the land

in front of them. A sudden silence enveloped them. Mach listened with every fiber of his being. Something or someone was in the area. He slowly and silently raised his head and looked around, but he didn't see anything.

"Don't scare them."

It took Mach a little while to remember Bran was talking about the pretend herd of bison. "I won't, Chief." He lay in the grass waiting for the sounds of the insects to return and feeling a slight chill of fear in the warm sun.

Suddenly Bran yelled, "C'mon! Now." Then the little boy leaped to his feet and ran across the prairie. Mach followed though his approach was more cautious as he tried to tell himself he and Bran had frightened the insects to silence.

Bran paused and threw his spear. "Got him!" He ran to retrieve his spear. "Now you." He looked at Mach.

Mach knelt beside him and asked, "Didn't you scare the rest of the bison away with all that noise?"

The little boy's eyes twinkled. "Nope." He stared across the plain so convincingly Mach almost rubbed his eyes so he could see the bison Bran had spotted. Then Bran leaned over and whispered in Mach's ear. "They can't hear us."

A cloud covered the morning sun casting a chilly shadow over Mach. "Why not?"

Bran's look clearly said he thought Mach had left his brains for Horda to use tanning hides. "'Cause they can't." He leaped to his feet and raced across the prairie again pretending to spear a bison. Mach was close behind him.

Chapter 10

THE PRETEND HUNTING TRIP was over, and Bran was still ready to play, but Mach was almost as tired as if they had killed and butchered real bison. The sudden silence of the insects continued to bother him. It wasn't natural. He stood on the path and stared at an area just beyond the river. Once more the insects' cacophony sounded, and cloud shadows danced across the dried grasses waving in the warm autumn breezes.

Then silence screamed from one area, and one shadow danced a different song — not quite in sync with the others. That shadow appeared to be in the grasses not on them. Blinking, Mach shook his head and rubbed his eyes with the backs of his hands. He almost convinced himself it was his imagination.

Then an errant sunbeam flashed. Had he not been staring so intently, he never would have seen it. Suddenly, adrenalin pulsed through his blood stream tensing every muscle. Some small crystal lying in the grass? Or some small crystal sewed on the beading of a breast plate? Mach's patience and caution asserted themselves. He watched the shadow without appearing to until it moved once more. “Thuro.” He called his friend from his work beside the river.

A short time later, Thuro stood beside Mach on the path. “Do you see what I see?” Mach barely breathed the words.

“I don’t know. What do you see?” Thuro also stared without being obvious. The shadow moved a little more. “Ahh, are we watching whatever is in the grass?” His words were hardly more than the autumn breeze.

The slightest inclination of Mach’s chin acknowledged Thuro’s words.

“It could be a bear or a big cat.” Thuro cupped one hand over the other and used hunter’s signs while he stared a little more openly.

Mach shook his head.

“Why not?” Thuro’s hand asked.

“Watch the way it moves,” Mach signed. Thuro’s suddenly tense shoulders told Mach all he needed to know.

“Friend or foe?” Thuro whispered.

Mach only shrugged. They knew this was not one of the People of the Frozen Earth. They did not sneak into each other’s territory, but that did not make the intruder an enemy. Cautious, smart, but not necessarily an enemy.

With barely more than flicks of their wrists and juttings of their chins, Mach and Thuro agreed to keep the shadow in sight and to tell the rest of the men about him. Gestures and a few whispered words had everyone on the move. Effortlessly, with no seeming haste the men exited by ones and twos and faded into the grass. They had surrounded the intruder before Mach and Thuro marched boldly down the path behind the camp out of sight.

Then the young leaders glided into the grass where their

movements unconsciously mirrored those of the shadow they had watched. The grass brushed Mach's leggings and sighed as he passed. It bowed down but did not break as his feet slipped across the prairie toward the figure. Mach watched Thuro move around and behind the shadow.

Suddenly the shadow became a man. He stood up and leaned on a trader's pack before Mach reached him. "Greetings, my little brother." The man showed his empty hands. "I, Thunder Eagle, come to you in peace bringing fine trade goods." Memories of Bear Claw and the People of the Tall Grass chilled Mach's spine. As they had, this man spoke the language of the People with a slightly different accent. Mach surveyed the area for others.

Thunder Eagle? Thunder Eagle – the trader. Mach looked closely. He could not recognize the trader in this man.

He did not remember hearing that Thunder Eagle was an accomplished hunter, but he might have been. This man certainly must be an excellent hunter. It was only by the Mother's blessing he and Thuro had seen him. Mach hesitated still trying to determine whether the man was alone or not before admitting his presence. The apparently unarmed trader smiled and waited to be acknowledged.

Finally feeling like a small boy caught in some mischief, Mach stood and showed his own empty hands before he said formally, "Greetings from Mach. I am a leader of this band of the People of the Frozen Earth. I trust you have had a pleasant journey."

He watched Thunder Eagle watching him. This man looked familiar. One old scar ran down the man's right cheek from the corner of his eye half-way to his mouth, and another began a finger's width beneath the first and continued across his chin. Unlike Bear Claw's scars which had been treated to make them wide and dark, these were no wider than a hair and had faded to faint lines of lighter skin. Instead of detracting from the dignity and serenity of the trader's face, the scars somehow enhanced it marking him as a man with stories to tell and experiences to share.

Thunder Eagle's smooth dark skin held the warm, golden undertones of the sun, and his thick, straight hair hung around his shoulders like a shawl. Instead of the raven's wing black strands that his unlined face made one expect, his hair was threaded with the grey of the elders. Almost as black as obsidian, his eyes glittered not with the cruel ice Bear Claw's had held, but with the warmth of laughter waiting to be shared. Mach did not realize it, but he looked into eyes that mirrored the contentment he would feel when he neared the end of his journey.

Thunder Eagle waited while the young man observed him. Recognition danced in the back of Mach's mind as he searched for words because he had not prepared himself to be caught. The laughter in Thunder Eagle's eyes almost caused him to speak sharply, but he took a deep breath and forced himself to be quiet.

"I am unarmed. My weapons are in my pack," said Thunder Eagle. "Tell the others it is safe. I am alone."

"Others?" Mach fought to keep his voice level.

"Yes, others. Only a very stupid man would meet the unknown alone if he didn't have to." The older man now smiled. "Mahlo assured me long ago that his son would not be a stupid man."

"How do you know my father?" Mach asked before he could stop himself. Silently he cursed. Now, the intruder knew who he was. Then he cursed himself for a little boy. The intruder had already known who he was.

"My, my, but you are suspicious. Aren't you?"

Mach glowered, but did not speak.

Thunder Eagle gestured to the men still hidden in the grass. "I am a trader and storyteller. I hoped you would remember me, but I'm not surprised you don't. I bring salt and other wondrous things from distant places beyond the high mountains. I have walked in the mountains above the clouds, Mach."

Mach looked closely at the man. Recognition dawned, and a smile spread across his face. Then he nodded. "Your hair was darker, and your face was thinner."

Laughter rang across the plains. "What a tactful way to say I am older and fatter than when you were a boy!"

"I didn't mean …" Mortification painted the younger man's face dark scarlet.

"Why not? It is true."

"But …"

Thunder Eagle held out his hand to Mach. "Son, I was lucky to recognize you. The last time we met, you had fewer than three hands winters. You paid little attention to me, and I paid less to you."

"I paid attention," Mach said quietly. "You told the People about walking above the clouds. Later I listened to you talking with some of the younger men, and you told them more. My father said it was a story you told young boys who didn't know any better. I didn't quite believe him." He shook his head. "Actually, it was the first time I doubted anything my father told me. I don't believe him. My mate and I will walk above the clouds and look down on the earth someday."

Mach signaled to the men to join them before he touched the trader's hand. "I apologize for being inconsiderate."

"Inconsiderate?" Thunder Eagle's rich laughter echoed across the plains once more. He shook his head. "I was the one who was inconsiderate. I saw you as a child. I had no knowledge of your interest in my travels, nor did I realize you would soon be a leader with goods to trade." His dark eyes sparkled in his solemn face. "I should have made your acquaintance and saved us all this trouble. I'm tired and hungry. Are you going to invite me to sit beside your cook fire or not?"

Reaching into his parfleche, the trader held up two cleaned hares. "I have food to share." He smiled. "Your mate may have the skins if she'd like." Then mischief danced in his dark eyes as he held up a small packet of fine leather. "I also have salt to add to the food's savor."

"Zeek, come here," Mach called.

The oldest warrior in the band rose and joined them. After the slightest pause, Zeek touched Thunder Eagle's hand. "Storyteller, I wondered what had happened to you. Where have you been?"

"I've been over the high mountains all the way to the restless waters." His smile faded. "I grow old. My feet are not as sure as they once were. I wanted to settle down, but I still have a taste for the salt. I took a mate. I thought I would live with a band beside those restless waters."

"Congratulations," said Zeek scanning the trees. "Does she travel with you?"

"No," said Thunder Eagle quietly. "There are no congratulations. An early spring flood brought mud down on our village. I was hunting. My mate and my son walk the beyond."

Zeek held the younger man's hand in both his own. "There are no words."

"No, there are not, but I thank you for your support." For a brief span of time Thunder Eagle looked across the mountains to a world Mach and the others could only imagine. Then he shook himself almost as if he were awaking from a bad dream. "It is done," he said. "I am back. I am fine…I am fine. I was afraid I wouldn't reach your People before the blizzards set in in earnest."

"We are glad you made it," said Zeek. "Do you have your flute?"

"Am I breathing?" asked Thunder Eagle.

Zeek laughed. "How about your pigments?"

"Of course."

"And new stories to tell?"

"I told you I lived beside the big restless water with my mate and my son since last I visited the People of the Frozen Earth." The trader smiled sadly. "I have visited the cook fires of many bands. I shared feasts and ceremonies. Yes, I have many stories from different peoples to share."

"It will be good to have you tarry with us for a while," said Zeek.

Thunder Eagle looked at Mach. "I have not been invited to stay with your People, Zeek."

Mach felt the hated blush as he tried to think of words that wouldn't insult the older man.

"Are you satisfied, Mach? Do you believe I am who I say I am? May I approach the shelter?"

Zeek laughed softly at Mach's discomfort. "Put the boy

out of his misery, Thunder Eagle."

The trader turned to the young leader. "I was told you had the makings of a fine chief. I wondered if it was so or if it was simply your father's pride speaking."

"I apologize. I did not mean to insult y—"

"On the contrary," interrupted Thunder Eagle, "you did not insult me. You complimented me."

Mach frowned, and Thunder Eagle's rich laughter sounded once more. "You saw me as enough of a threat to remain cautious. That is a compliment to a fat old man."

Mach was mortified. He knew he sometimes spoke before he thought, but he was certain he had not called this trader either fat or old, though it seemed every time he opened his mouth his words were twisted. "I did not say you were —"

Now Zeek put his hand on the young man's arm. "Be silent," he said kindly. "Thunder Eagle uses words like he uses his flute and his paints. You will not be able to best him. He likes to tease. He knows you did not insult him."

"Are you sure?" asked Thunder Eagle with a smile that made the thin scars on his cheek crinkle.

"Yes," said Zeek. "I seem to remember similar conversations between you and other leaders. You would think a man who travels as much as you do would be more hospitable to his hosts."

"Ah, but when one brings salt, he is forgiven much."

"Yes, that is true. Where do you get that stuff?"

Thunder Eagle's smile did not alter, but Mach sensed a change in his eyes. "Oh, I find it many places. Sometimes I trade for it beside the big restless waters that are filled with it, and some I find in the ground where I suspect big restless waters used to be. It is not near here. It's all farther on down the trail."

Mach listened to the answer that wasn't an answer and wondered as the trader turned to him and spoke formally. "Please forgive my jest. I do not mean harm. I am usually alone on the trail, and I sometimes play word games in my head to pass the time. Then I forget my manners."

"I am afraid I forgot my manners," said Mach. "I did not recognize you. Please accept my apology."

"You spoke the truth, Mach. There is no reason to apologize."

"Okay, children," said Zeek with a grin. "I thought this man said he was hungry."

"Before we go, I would say one more thing," said Thunder Eagle solemnly. "I am pleased to see the things I have heard of you are true. You do have the makings of a fine leader who keeps his people's welfare foremost in his mind."

The compliment was so unexpected Mach stood staring. Now both Zeek and Thunder Eagle laughed as Zeek signaled the others to go back to the shelter. "You must tell this story often, Thunder Eagle, for none of the People of the Frozen Earth will ever believe Mach was, even for a short span of time, speechless."

Premol hurried to the camp to tell the women Thunder Eagle, the trader, was a friend who would be passing time beside their cook fires. Horda was with Aiyana and did not hear the message.

The men walked into the camp just as the sun sank behind the jagged mountains casting shadows across the land. The children raced out to meet the men — surrounding them, shouting questions, and running back and forth. Suddenly four children were hanging from Mach's hands and two more were pulling on his legs. Thunder Eagle did not speak, but his face screamed his dismay.

Mach stood still and clapped his hands. "Children, your manners!" Immediately the noise level diminished, and the children stood quietly. Mach smiled. "May I present Thunder Eagle. He is a trader from beyond the jagged mountains. He brings salt and other fine things, but more important, he brings us stories of places we have never been."

Rain Drop looked up at Thunder Eagle. "That's wonderful," she said. Then she creased her brow. "Tell me, Thunder Eagle, what is salt?"

Leaning down, Thunder Eagle spoke directly to the little girl. "Do you know what cow parsnip is?"

"Oh, yes," she sighed, "Horda puts it on the meat. It makes it taste good."

"Horda?" Thunder Eagle traced the scars on the side of his face. "Is she the daughter of Zaaco and Meiran?"

Rain Drop frowned and shrugged. Storm Cloud said, "She is Mach's mate."

Mach said, "Yes, Horda is the daughter of Zaaco and Meiran. Why?"

Thunder Eagle sensed the challenge in the younger man's question and chose his answer carefully. "Many turnings of the seasons ago the Big River took me and tossed me among the rocks and carried away all of my possessions and trade goods." He touched his right cheek. "I despaired. I was alone, and I had nothing left. Even the clothes on my back were waterlogged and torn. The rocks had beaten me black and blue and slashed my face like angry enemies. I was ready to give up.

"One of Zaaco's elder sons found me and took me to the Inner Band. Nuroo treated my injuries, but he knew his young student, Horda, would be able to fix my face with the least disfiguration. She did."

"My mate is the healer woman of our band."

"I felt certain she would be. She had the touch even as a small child."

Mach's spirit warred within him. He was proud that this man recognized his mate's talent as a healer woman, but he did not like him to speak about her touch. He remembered the beautiful picture of the Moon of the Burning Leaves on the wall of the Inner Band's winter shelter. This man truly had many talents.

Chapter 11

EVENING SHADOWS CAST THEIR lavender smudges across the camp when Horda returned from the birthing shelter. Rain Drop and Storm Cloud ran to her each trying to tell about their visitor and thus keeping her from understanding either of them.

She stopped at the assembly fire and spoke to Mach without seeing the guest. "Do you know what they are trying to tell me?"

He gestured to the man seated near him. "Yes, Thunder Eagle has come to trade."

She took a deep breath and lowered her eyes. "Welcome to our camp, Thunder Eagle. I trust you had a pleasant and uneventful journey."

Standing, Thunder Eagle inclined his head to her. "Yes, my journey was pleasant. I trust you have had happy days since last we met."

Memories of the kidnapping swirled through her mind, but she pushed them away. "Mostly happy days. Thank you. And you?" Just as Thunder Eagle had watched the pain swirling in her eyes, she watched pain and loss swirl in the depths of his dark eyes. She vowed to herself that they would talk together sometime before he left their camp.

Thunder Eagle forced a smile. "I have had many happy days, but there have been sad days too." He shrugged. "That is life." He reached up and touched his cheek. "Your mate tells me you are a full-fledged healer woman."

She smiled. "I am."

"As you can see, your stitches have disappeared into the fabric of my life."

She stepped closer and examined his face. Nodding she said, "I did well, didn't I? I was frightened when Nuroo told me to stitch your wound."

Thunder Eagle's rich laughter echoed through the camp. "You were frightened? I had pretty much despaired and decided I had nothing to live for, but when he told a child to sew me up, I realized I wasn't ready to go to the Frozen Wilds just yet. I didn't want to seem ungrateful, but I wanted to tell Nuroo not to let you touch me."

She laughed. "Your eyes warned me you were not happy about me sewing you up."

"You cleaned the wound with goldenrod water and some other stuff that really burned."

"Uh-huh, and then I took an obsidian knife and trimmed the ragged edges before I stitched it."

"It worked. I thank you for doing a good job."

She smiled at her friend again. "I thank you for trusting me when you really had no reason to."

"Nuroo trusted you."

"Well, that trust helped make me the healer woman I am today. Thank you."

Thunder Eagle's smile told her she had earned his trust

as well.

Mach said, "Thunder Eagle has agreed to tell stories tonight after the evening eat."

"Then perhaps I should get busy."

Thunder Eagle opened his pack and handed her the two hares he had shown Mach earlier. He also gave her a packet of salt.

Nodding her thanks, Horda hurried to her cook fire where she had an antelope haunch baking for the Naming Ceremony the next day. Now she wondered if she should use it and hope to find something else for the ceremonial feast .

Mach followed her. "Do you need me to do something?"

"Skin the hares," she said handing them to him. She grabbed a fire mitt to check a thick stew of fresh antelope meat, pumpkin pieces, greens, and wild onions thickened with acorn flour. She sniffed and tasted.

Mach had finished skinning the hares, so she washed them and rubbed them inside with the salt and cow parsnip. Then she spitted them and set them to roast over the cook fire. With the hares and the last of the wild berries, they would have plenty for the evening eat, and she wouldn't have to use the food she had prepared for the Naming Ceremony.

❂

Thunder Eagle played his flute and told stories of faraway places and long-ago people. The assembly fire burned low. The cedar wood popped and sparks danced in the sky following the smoke on its way to the Great Beyond. Thunder

Eagle stood and looked at all the People of the Band.

He said, "I have one more story to share with you tonight. It is a very special story about a little girl. She was a strange little girl. She did not look like her people. Her hair was light and curled, and her eyes were the color of agate stones instead of the color of obsidian. But you know what? She was a beautiful little girl — inside and out. Many of the people didn't understand her, and they made fun of her because she was taller and lighter and different than the rest of their people.

"But the part they didn't understand was her strength. She was so much stronger than the regular people, but she wasn't selfish. She always shared her strength. Mother Life had chosen her. Mother Life had given her this strength to share.

"Just as Mother Life taught the first People to use the plants and animals for food and medicine, she taught this little girl to use plants and animals for food and medicine.

"Not everyone realizes Mother Life still teaches the People so they can teach each other. No one realized how different this little girl was until the medicine man started to teach her.

"Early on, he realized there wasn't much he could teach her because she already knew so much more than he did. Now, don't get me wrong. This little girl' didn't know she knew. So she went through the training like a normal person learning to be a healer woman, but all she was doing was remembering what she already knew. She worked gathering the plants and bark and leaves and seeds and all the rest. She practiced drying and preserving everything. Then she practiced caring for people — dosing and bandaging and wrapping and soaking and stitching. The medicine man said he had never seen anyone as talented as she, but she didn't believe him.

"She went through all the training and studying and practicing even though the Mother herself had taught her what to do. But this wasn't a bad thing. It was a good thing because it reinforced all the things she knew, and it made her the best, most skillful healer woman since Mother Life walked the earth."

When he finished this last story, Thunder Eagle saluted Horda with his eyes and retired to his hunting shelter set up a little way away from the main camp.

"I'm sorry Aiyana couldn't listen to the stories tonight," said Horda covering Storm Cloud and Rain Drop with their sleeping furs.

Mach shrugged. "I guess Thunder Eagle will stay with us a while."

"I don't know whether he will or not," said Horda. "He's always been restless."

"I don't remember seeing him except at Gathering a couple of times."

"He's been to Gathering a few times, and he stayed with the Inner Band when he was injured." She yawned.

Mach looked at her. "He told a story about you."

Her mouth fell open. "What are you talking about?"

"Yes, he did. I realized it was about you before he had hardly begun."

"No, no. Thunder Eagle tells stories of long ago and

far away. You're being silly. He wouldn't tell a story about me."

"You weren't listening."

"Yes, I was. You're imagining things."

"Horda, he told me this afternoon you fixed his face when you were just a little girl. And you have told me before about the picture he painted from the Moon of the Burning Leaves. I've always known you have a bond with him." He hugged her. "I just realized today that he has a bond with you."

She shook her head. "What are you talking about?"

"The last story he told about the little girl who was studying to be a healer woman." He stared at her. "That little girl was you."

"You are imagining things."

"Want me to ask him?"

"No!"

He drew her close and shared her breath. "It makes me feel good to know someone else realizes how special you are."

"I'm not," she sputtered. "You must not go around saying things like that."

"Oh, yeah," he laughed, "I'm going out tomorrow and tell the whole band the trader was talking about my mate when he was talking about the little girl that Mother Life taught. Sure I am. And, oh, yes, I'm going to be sure Thunder Eagle is at the next Gathering so he can tell everyone just how special and wonderful my mate is. Sure."

"Mach, he was not talking about me."

"Are you sure?"

"Yes, I'm absolutely sure. Aren't you?" Mach only raised his eyebrows and grinned. She said, "You're only teasing me.

You know he wasn't talking about me, but you're enjoying this."

Mach covered up in the sleeping furs, closed his eyes, and pretended to snore.

Horda finally pulled the furs off his shoulders and poked him. "Answer me."

Opening one eye, he said, "Yes, I am teasing you. Yes, I am enjoying this. But no, I'm not at all sure he wasn't talking about you. And no, I am not going to ask him or tell anyone else I think he is talking about you."

"Good." She covered herself with the sleeping furs and closed her eyes. "I hope you don't mess up the Naming Ceremony," she murmured.

"Horda!" he yelped. "That was cruel."

"No more so than you have been. Sleep well. You can practice the ceremony at the morning eat."

❂

At sunrise on the sixth day after the birth of a child, the mother and father introduced the little one by name to Mother Life and Father Death before presenting him or her to the band at the Naming Ceremony. Naming Ceremonies provided happy times of feasting, chanting, praying, singing, and dancing. Not only did they welcome new life into the bands, they also provided one of the few formal celebrations held any place other than Gathering.

Four participants played active roles in the Naming Ceremony: the leader of the band, the mother, the father, and the baby. Everyone else from the oldest to the youngest member of the band played supporting roles.

The stars winked out leaving the area in cool darkness, but Mach's smile lighted his face when he joined Horda beside the cook fire the morning of the Naming Ceremony. "How's the little one?" he asked.

"Fine. He looks like he's grown half a hand taller already, and his eyes follow his ma when she talks to him."

"Do you think Aiyana will let me hold him after the ceremony?" Mach grinned sheepishly. "It's important for the leader of the band to get to know every member."

Pain laced the laughter in Horda's heart. *Mother Life, he does love babies very much.* "I imagine Aiyana will let you hold him," said Horda handing him a horn of hot rose hip tea. "Do you want to go through the ceremony this morning?"

"I don't think so." He shrugged. "Zaaco went over the words with me before we left the Gathering grounds. I just hope I don't forget anything important."

"I don't think you'll forget anything. You woke me up about four hands of times saying them in your sleep."

"I didn't either." Mach frowned. "Did I?"

Horda smiled. "Actually it was only four times."

"I'm sorry," he said. "I guess I'm a little worried."

"Really? I never would have guessed."

"I want everything to be perfect for the first child of our band." His smile died. "I just hope Wilda doesn't make a fuss."

"What's Wilda doing now? Between helping Aiyana and dosing Storm Cloud and Bran, I haven't had time to worry about her. Is she still upset about how terrible giving birth is?"

"I guess. She does her work, but her eyes always look like she's been crying."

"What makes you think she might cause trouble?"

"Because Thuro wants no part in the Naming Ceremony."

"He really should have a part."

"I told him that, but he says he doesn't want one."

"He's the co-chief."

"Thank you, Horda; we are both well aware of his position in the band."

Horda glared at him.

Mach frowned back. "He told me the People know he's the co-chief and his getting up and saying words he doesn't want to say won't make any difference."

"But —"

"Horda, I've argued with him all I'm going to. His mind is made up."

"It doesn't seem right."

"I told him that, and he told me to leave him alone."

"But what will Wilda do?"

"I don't know."

"I'll talk to him," said Horda.

"I wouldn't."

"Why not?"

"Mainly because you have enough to do helping Aiyana. The sun is about to rise."

Horda looked over her shoulder where the eastern sky had faded to grey. "Oh, I must hurry."

"By the way, Horda, where are Storm Cloud and Rain Drop?"

"Reeme knew I was going to be busy so she's feeding them their morning eat." She leaned down and shared breath with him. "If Thunder Eagle comes by, there is plenty of porridge and tea. Don't touch the cooking bag. It's for the Feast. Don't —"

"Yes, Ma," he said.

"I'm gone. I'll see you at the ceremony."

Shaking his head, Mach smiled at her retreating back and drank his tea.

"Greetings, Mach," called Thunder Eagle. "I trust you had a pleasant sleep."

"Greetings, Thunder Eagle. I trust you had a pleasant sleep." Mach gestured to the cook fire. "Please sit. Join me in the morning eat. I have porridge and tea. It is warm and filling."

"Thank you." Thunder Eagle sipped the tea Mach dipped for him. "My sleep was pleasant if a little short. I am afraid I talked too long last night."

"I don't think so," said Mach serving him porridge. "We enjoyed your stories and your music."

"You are kind, and I thank you. I enjoy sharing my stories and my music."

Taking a deep breath, Mach decided to see if Thunder Eagle would help him. "My sleep was a little restless."

"Restless?"

"Yes, I am about to lead my first Naming Ceremony."

Thunder Eagle nodded. "It is a great responsibility to be the leader of a band."

"I'm actually the co-leader."

"I have never found that dividing the responsibilities caused them to be less."

"No, I haven't exactly found that to be so either," said Mach. "I'm kind of dancing around asking you to help us."

"If I can."

"Well, you see, we have two drums and two flutes, but our flutes are the little flutes that usually play the counterpoint. We need a strong flute to lead the songs, and I was wondering if you would bring your flute to the Naming Ceremony and play the Naming Songs for us?"

Thunder Eagle laughed. "Of course, I'd be honored. I was afraid you were angry with me."

"Angry? Why would I be angry?"

"I know you knew."

Mach nodded. "Yes, I knew. I was honored that you realized how special she is."

"Did she recognize herself?"

"She denies it, but I believe she knows. I had to promise her I wouldn't ask you about it."

"You didn't."

"No, I didn't, but you aren't going to tell people it is a story about her. Are you?"

Thunder Eagle shook his head. "No, I'm not, but by telling this story now as she grows older, the story will grow, and she will be talked about around assembly fires long after we are gone."

Mach smiled. "She is special."

"I heard about the captivity."

Mach looked a warning at him.

"No, Mach, I'm not going to tell that story. Not to the People of the Frozen Earth at least. But it's an important story."

"Why?"

"Because it is a story of love and commitment and of good triumphing over evil. Don't you think it is a story that should be remembered?"

"No. It is a story of breaking rules and thinking you can get by with it and getting caught. It's a story of death and destruction. No, it is not a story that should be remembered."

Thunder Eagle smiled indulgently at the younger man. "I beg to differ with you. I believe you have missed the entire point of the whole thing."

Mach glared. "Are you going to hold us up to ridicule?"

"No, son, I'm not. I told you I believe you have missed the point of this story, but I give you my word I will not tell this story to any of the People of the Frozen Earth for at least two hands turnings of the seasons." Thunder Eagle offered Mach his hand. Then he said, "Doesn't this ceremony begin at sunrise?"

"By the father's dirty teeth!" Mach leaped to his feet and the two men hurried toward the High Place.

Chapter 12

"AIYANA, ARE YOU READY?" Horda called as she neared the birthing shelter.

"Almost. Won't you come in?" Aiyana was feeding the baby when Horda entered. Her clean hair hung straight and shining past her waist. Her doeskin tunic dyed a soft shade of blue using juniper berries and decorated with small chips of agate, blue-dyed porcupine quills, and the white down feathers from several baby eaglets waited for her to don it.

"Greetings, Aiyana. You look beautiful." Horda fought the longing in her heart.

"Greetings, Horda. Thank you. It feels wonderful to be clean all over."

"It seemed a little chilly to me."

"It was plain cold, but it was worth it." Aiyana's dark eyes gleamed. "I'll be glad when we move into the cave and build a bath pit. I can hardly wait for a hot bath with dried flower petals."

"It'll be a while yet. A few bats keep coming back."

"Ugh! I hate those things." Aiyana frowned. "How are Bran and Storm Cloud?"

"Storm Cloud seems to be fine, but Bran has hot kernels in his body, and he seemed hot to the touch yesterday. I haven't seen him this morning."

Aiyana shook her head. "I hope the fever demons don't really feast on him."

"Me too." *Oh, Mother Life, me too.* "We need to hurry. The sun is almost up. Do you want me to take care of the baby while you finish dressing?"

"Please, just let me burp him first." Aiyana placed the baby on her shoulder and rubbed his back. He rewarded her with a loud burp. She laughed. "My, that was a good one. You are just getting so big. I don't know what ma's going to do with you." The infant kicked his feet and waved his hands before Aiyana handed him to Horda.

Horda tucked him under her arm and went to the baby pack. "He's really growing."

"I know." Aiyana dropped her cloak and slipped the beautiful tunic over her head. Then she braided her long black hair and twisted it up with strings of shells and beads. "All he does is eat and sleep – and grow."

"That's what tiny babies are supposed to do." Horda laughed against the pain in her heart. *My baby didn't have a chance to grow or eat or sleep. Please, Mother Life. Haven't I waited long enough?* She quickly dressed the infant in a blue tunic and leggings decorated much like his mother's.

"He's not that tiny," said Aiyana watching Horda smooth the wrinkles out of the little leggings.

"No, he's really not," agreed Horda handing him back to his mother. "Did you hear the flute last night?"

Yes, I heard the flute and some of the stories, but I couldn't hear all of them. I'll be glad to be back with the People."

“Oh, I know. I don’t think I could exist alone,”

“Me either. Premo says I would talk to a tree if I didn’t have some one to talk to. I probably would.”

Horda laughed. “Are you ready now? It’s almost sunrise.”

“I think so.” Aiyana looked around the birthing shelter and then at herself. “Do I need to clean?”

Horda shook her head. “We’ll do it later. No one will be using it for a while. It’s time for me to go.” Horda gave them a quick hug and stepped outside where she met Premo. “Your mate’s ready.” She smiled and slipped away to join the assembled people.

At Mach’s nod, the soft cadence of the small drums signaled the beginning of the Naming Ceremony. The willow and antelope bone flutes whispered the dancing melody. Then the deeper notes of Thunder Eagle’s flute urged the procession up the hill. When the parents and the baby took their places at the head of the procession, the instruments sounded triumphantly across the early morning air. Premo and Aiyana led the members of the band up the trail to the high sacred place Mach and Thuro had marked and purified.

Mach and Thuro stood together, but Mach greeted the new family and escorted them to their places. The others stood in a semicircle around them and waited for the return of the sun.

When the sun’s first ray touched the baby’s dark head,

Mach began the chants that welcomed the new life into the band. "The Naming Ceremony reminds the People of the Frozen Earth that Mother Life came down to give us the earth and all its good things. She brought us animals for clothing, tools, and food. Then she taught us the plants to use for food and medicine."

"Thank you, Mother Life, for your bounty and goodness," the People replied.

"Mother Life protects us and keeps us safe, but Father Death walks with us from the day of our birth. He waits to take us to the Frozen Wilds where we will live forever."

"Yes, Father Death waits for us."

"Babies are the greatest gift the Mother gives us." Horda watched proudly as Mach reached out to touch the little one's straight black hair. "They are the future of the tribe, but they are also a personal gift from Mother Life to all of us to make our lives better and happier."

"Thank you, Mother Life." The People joined together in a song of thanksgiving.

"Who brings this child to the Mother?"

Premo held the squirming infant up to the sun. "Mother Life, I thank you for this fine little one. I promise to educate him in the ways of the People of the Frozen Earth. To teach him our values and beliefs. To show him that I revere you and treasure our ways. I will protect him with my life."

When Premo's words were finished, he handed the baby back to his mother. Aiyana glowed as she held the little one up and made the same solemn pledges. Watching Mach beam down at the mother and father twisted Horda's heart. There was a pause. Mach cleared his throat and cut his eyes to Aiyana's hands. Premo jumped and a blush colored his face when he placed his hands over Aiyana's on the baby.

The sun rose above the horizon and together the parents held the child up to its gentle rays. In a clear strong voice, Aiyana said, "Mother Life, our first-born son Zakon." They turned to the west where the dying sun would set and raised the baby high. Again she spoke clearly, "Father Death, our first-born son Zakon." Then they turned to the waiting People, and once more Aiyana announced, "Our first-born son Zakon."

The drums sounded a soft heartbeat in the background; Thunder Eagle's flute sang the melody and the other small flutes' notes soared and dipped in counterpoint while Mach led more chants and performed the dances of thanksgiving for the new life. The People spoke the words of welcome; offered gifts of clothing, furs, hides, tools, and food — gifts of love — to baby Zakon and his parents; and danced the dances of welcome.

Finally Mach took baby Zakon and held him high over his head. "Mother Life and Father Death, we thank you for Zakon, the first new member of our new band. We ask that you in your mercy smooth the paths of his life. Please, endow him with your wisdom to share with the People of the Frozen Earth.

"We beg you, fill his horn of time slowly that he may watch his children's children's children play around cook fires not yet kindled and may they grow to adulthood before he walks the Frozen Wilds and becomes a memory like the smoke of cook fires long grown cold. If it be your will, grant Zakon all these things."

"Please, Mother Life and Father Death," whispered the People.

Mach turned with Zakon to salute the four directions and said, "May the Winds of Life blow blessings through all Zakon's days."

When that was finished, Thuro stepped forward and placed his hands with Mach's on the baby. They looked into the baby's eyes and spoke in unison, "May we, Thuro and Mach, as your leaders, guide you in the ways of the People and help you grow to the man Mother Life has planned for you to be." The ceremony was finished. Mach handed Baby Zakon to Premo who with Aiyana led the People down the path to the waiting feast.

Horda blinked rapidly to keep the tears pushing against the back of her eyes from falling. A sob almost choked her, but she turned it into a cough. She forced a broad smile as she joined the procession. *Please, Mother Life, grant us our own little ones.*

The crisp scents of burning cedar and sage mixed with the odors of roasting meat and vegetables to perfume the almost-warm morning air. People wandered from cook fire to cook fire and ate and visited until the sun was high in the sky. When the feasting was finished, the men and boys threw bones, played games, and ran races. The women sat in the sun watching the children and gossiping.

Wilda suddenly jumped up and ran away. "What's wrong with her?" asked Aiyana.

"I don't know," said Horda. "I thought she looked pale."

Lena, Zeek's number one mate, chuckled in her

throat. "Looks like she waited too late to decide not to be pregnant."

"What?" Horda's eyes rounded.

"I've been watching her these last few days. She's either laughing or crying." Lena nodded sagely. "I thought the sickness would come."

"Do you mean ..."

"Yep, I mean that one's breeding."

"Are you sure?"

The older woman giggled again. "Horda, you are our trained healer woman. You're very good at what you do, but I've spent many turnings of the seasons watching breeding women. Trust me, she is breeding."

Oh, Mother Life. How can I deal with her now? "She's going to have a fit."

"Probably."

Wilda came back to the circle of women looking more than slightly green. "I'm sorry. I guess I ate too much."

"Sure," said Lena with a knowing grin.

Bran wandered up to Horda. She noted his glazed eyes and flushed cheeks before he climbed into her lap. A cold finger walked down her back. "He's burning up."

"Ah, it's nothing. He's just hot. He's been running and playing," said his mother Reeme.

The little boy snuggled against Horda. "Cold," he whimpered. His teeth began to chatter.

Horda wrapped her arms around him trying to stop the chill. "No, the fever demons are eating you. We have to get some willow tea down you."

"No, hurt." Bran shivered and snuggled against her.

She gently touched his neck and found the kernel bigger,

harder, and hotter. She handed him to his mother and pulled dried willow bark from the medicine pack that was never far from her hand. "Help me get his fever down."

Reeme stared at her. "What do you want me to do?"

Horda said, "Bathe him in water from one of the water bags."

"Bathe him?" echoed Reeme. "He's already shivering. It'll freeze him."

"No, it won't." Horda took a deep breath and prayed for patience. "We must get his fever down. Bathing is the quickest way."

Lena stood and took the little boy from his mother. "I'll get him ready while you get two full water bags."

Dipping a horn into the water bag simmering over the banked cook fire, Horda gave her a grateful look. "I'll be there to help you soon." She crumbled the willow bark into the hot water and stirred it. She frowned at the horn in her hand then stuck its point into the embers at the edge of the cook fire and took up her medicine pack once more.

Quickly she found a packet of wyethia roots and another of juniper twigs. She ground a small portion of each into a coarse powder. Next she poured the strong willow tea into another horn leaving as much of the bark behind as possible. Then she mixed the powder into the tea and added a small sprig of mint and a large dollop of camas molasses.

Horda stirred the mixture fighting memories of another boy consumed by the fever demons. *Please, Mother Life, help me save this one.*

Squaring her shoulders, she took her medicine pack and the horn of tonic to treat the tiny Bran. Her heart almost stopped when she heard Reeme scream. Bran's eyes had rolled back in his head so only the whites showed, and his body jerked in a fever convulsion. *No, Mother Life.* Screams of denial clawed Horda's throat, and she bit her cheek until she tasted blood, but she managed to keep her anguish locked behind her teeth. It wouldn't help.

Horda gathered the tiny burning body in her arms and held him gently but firmly so he wouldn't damage himself thrashing in the convulsion. "I need a stick padded with soft leather," she called.

Lena brought her one and together they slipped it between the little one's teeth to keep him from swallowing his tongue. Finally after an eternity that really lasted only a short time, Bran spat out the padded stick and relaxed against her. Then he began to whimper. She soothed him with wordless sounds of comfort.

He looked up at her accusingly and muttered, "Hurts, Ho'da. Hurts."

"I know, little one, I know." She held him in her arms and offered him the horn of tonic.

He took a sip and spat it out. "Nassy."

"I know, but it will help the hurt."

"No." Closing his mouth, he shook his head and leaned against her.

Lena brought a water bag and a finely tanned rabbit skin and sat on the ground beside Horda. Horda held out the horn of tonic. "Reeme, please put more molasses in this."

Reeme hurried to do so without speaking.

Horda dipped the skin in the water bag. Then she washed Bran's hot little face and head. He shivered once more. "Don't, Ho'da!"

"I have to," She continued to sponge him with the cool

water.

"No." He struggled weakly.

"Yes, Bran, this will help you feel better." Reeme returned with the horn of tonic. Horda dropped the skin in the water bag and took the horn. She smiled her thanks. "Now, Bran, your ma put molasses in this so it will taste better. You must drink it for me."

"No." Bran's little mouth puckered, and his fever-glazed eyes begged her not to make him drink.

She put the horn to his lips. "Open your mouth."

He turned his head. "No."

"Yes." She pressed the horn to his lips once more.

Reluctantly he took a small sip. She slipped her hand over his mouth so he couldn't spit it out. He glared at her but didn't protest. "Good," crooned Horda when he swallowed.

"Nuff?" he asked hopefully.

"No, Little Chief, drink some more."

He frowned but took several small sips. "Nuff," he declared.

"Very good, but not enough." She smiled at him. "Drink a little more for me."

"Nope, Ho'da. Nuff."

"Please?"

He shivered violently. "No."

She handed the horn back to Reeme and resumed sponging him. His body stiffened, and his eyes rolled back in his head as another convulsion seized him. Lena grabbed the horn of tonic as Reeme threw up her hands and shrieked. Horda held the child firmly against her bosom until the convulsion ended, and he fell limply to her lap.

Mach skidded to a stop beside Lena. "What's happening?"

"The fever demons are consuming Bran," she said.

Mach knelt in front of Horda. "How can I help you?"

Tears gathered in her eyes, but her voice was firm. "We've got to cool him down before the fever demons steal his life force. I've sponged him, but it's not enough."

Mach took him from her arms and strode away.

"Where are you going?"

"To the river," he said. "Come on."

She jumped up and followed him. He waded into the shallow water.

"Don't go too deep," she called. "The water doesn't need to be cold."

"Okay." When the water was a little above his knees, he sat down and cradled Bran so the shallow water covered him from his neck down. Horda waded out beside them and splashed the cool water on Bran's head.

Lena called from the shore, "Do you think you can get some more of the tonic down him?"

"We can try." Horda started to rise.

"Stay there," said Lena wading out to join them. When she saw Bran's closed eyes, she said, "He can't drink this. He's asleep."

Horda shook her head sadly. "No, he's not. He's unconscious."

"Oh," said Lena.

Horda frowned. "There's a hollow reed in my medicine pack. Will you get it for me, Lena?"

Lena splashed away.

"Mach, can you support Bran's head a little more so I

can open his mouth?" He nodded and turned the child so he could hold his head in one hand. "Good," said Horda squeezing Bran's cheeks so his mouth opened. Lena returned with the reed. "This is the hardest part," said Horda.

Lena frowned. "What do I do?"

"Catch some of the tonic in the reed and dribble just a little bit into his mouth. Then I'll rub his throat so he swallows. It takes a long time to get the tonic down him this way, but we can't hurry or we might choke him." Horda put her fingers on Bran's throat. "Are you ready?"

Lena's eyes showed her fear, but she nodded. "Okay," said Horda. Lena dripped a few drops of the tonic in Bran's mouth. Horda smiled. "You can give him more than that."

Lena drizzled more of the liquid into the open mouth. "Enough," said Horda massaging the little throat. Bran swallowed. Horda smiled. "Again." They repeated the process until the horn was empty.

Horda put her hand on Bran's forehead. "I think he feels cooler."

Lena touched his head and nodded.

Mach said, "His body feels cooler, and he's not shaking anymore. Should we get out?"

Horda shook her head. "Not yet. Let's give the tonic time to do some good." She resumed bathing his head and face. "I wish he'd come back."

"He will," said Mach.

Horda and Lena both looked at him. "I hope so," whispered Horda fighting the memory of another small boy who never came back.

Mach spoke quietly. "Horda, he can't possibly be like Brash. You've been dosing him and treating him all along.

You know the fever demons consumed Brash because no one treated him until it was too late."

"Was that the reason?"

"You know it was," he said.

She looked into her mate's eyes for a long time before she spoke again. "Please hold Bran so I can examine the kernels in his body."

He cradled the child against his chest. Horda's skillful fingers located and inspected each of the hard, hot kernels that ranged in size from Bran's thumb to Mach's thumb. She looked at Lena and Mach who had both watched her closely. Then she closed her eyes and sighed. "I wish Nuroo was here," she said in a tiny voice, "or Norlon or Unna." Then she smiled. "I'm not particular. I just wish someone else with healer training was here."

Lena put her hand on Horda's arm and smiled into her eyes. "Trust yourself, Horda. You are a well-trained healer woman. You will save him."

"I hope so. Oh, Mother Life, I hope so." She fingered the kernels one more time before she reached a decision. "I'm going to lance them and pack them."

Mach looked startled, but Lena nodded. She said, "I'll bathe his face and head while you get ready."

Horda stood and waded out of the river without speaking again.

She found her medicine pack where she had left it beside the crying Reeme. Zeek looked up at her with a fear-ravaged face. "Horda, what's happening?"

She took a deep breath before she answered this man who had done so much for her and Mach. "Bran is very ill. The fever demons are consuming him. He had two convulsions because we couldn't get his fever down fast enough to stop them. We've bathed him and fed him tonic, but he's unconscious right now. We hope it is temporary, but we don't know for sure. I'm sorry."

Reeme sobbed quietly. Zeek said, "Reeme thought he departed."

Horda bit her lips and shook her head. "No, he hasn't departed, but he is very ill."

"Unconscious, you say?" asked Zeek.

She nodded.

"That's bad. Isn't it?"

Oh, Mother Life, give me the words to answer him. "It might be, but I think — I hope — it is temporary. Mach put him in the river. The water has cooled him, and Lena and I managed to get the rest of the tonic down him. I think he will come back soon."

"What if he has another convulsion?"

"I'm going to keep a close watch on him. I'll try not to let the fever demons get that much hold again." She picked up her medicine pack.

"What are you going to do now?" asked Zeek.

"I'm going to lance the kernels and pack them with prairie flax seeds and figwort leaves. The packing will help draw the poison out of his body."

The color drained from Zeek's face, and he closed his eyes. Reeme sobbed loudly once more.

Horda took a deep breath. "I believe the packings and the tonic will drive the fever demons away."

Zeek stared into her eyes as if he were trying to see her soul. "Will my son be all right?"

She longed to look away so she could tell him what he

wanted to hear, but she couldn't. She owed her life to this man. She owed him the truth even though it would hurt. "I hope so, Zeek. I'll do everything in my power to make him all right. The rest is up to Mother Life — and Father Death."

Zeek swayed beneath the weight of her words, but he quickly steadied himself and squared his shoulders. "What can I do to help my son?"

She smiled. "I need wood to build up the fire, and someone needs to get all the big water baskets Unna made and fill them. It'll be too cold to put Bran in the river tonight if we need to bathe him, but he'll fit in those big baskets."

Zeek nodded and hurried away. Reeme followed Horda to the cook fire and sat watching her. First Horda pushed the flat rock she used for fry bread into the cook fire and stirred the embers into flames. She filled two small cooking bags with water and set them on the supports over the fire to boil before she went into her shelter and returned with her large medicine pack and a small grinding stone.

Next she took out an obsidian knife and a large bone needle and dropped them into one of the cooking bags. Zeek and three others returned with their arms full of dry wood and stacked it beside the fire.

"Thank you," she said. "Zeek, please, build up the fire until it is very hot." He nodded and set about his task while she took several strips of boiled leather bandages, a ball of lodge pole pine sap, and a hand of packets of roots, twigs, leaves, and bark from the medicine packs and lined them up. By the time she finished, the men had gone to help with the water baskets.

"Reeme, will you help me?" Horda asked.

Reeme looked startled, but she wiped the tears from her face and climbed to her feet. "How?"

Horda smiled. "I need you to pour the hot water for me to wash my hands." Reeme took a small water basket and dipped water from the bag beside the fire. Horda scrubbed her hands with soaproot then held them out while Reeme rinsed them. "Thank you."

Reeme nodded and sat down again. Horda set the ball of pine sap to melt on the stone then pulverized wyethia roots, juniper twigs, willow bark, and mint which she placed in the smallest cooking bag of boiling water. She moved the bag to a rack at the edge of the flames so the tonic could steep. "This will be better than the tonic we made so quickly this afternoon."

Reeme nodded but did not reply. Horda stirred the pitch with a wooden paddle before she pulverized two handfuls of prairie flax seeds and two hands count of figwort leaves. She stirred the pitch once more and pushed it to the edge of the stone, then she took wooden tongs and lifted the knife and needle from the boiling water and lay them on the coolest side of the stone. Zeek and Thuro followed by four other sets of men came back from the river with full water baskets and set them outside the shelter.

Taking a deep breath, Horda turned to Zeek. "Please, ask Mach to bring Bran." She paused and bit her lips. "I'm ready." *Mother Life, help me save him.* "Reeme, would you bring some sleeping furs? We don't want him to get chilled."

Once more Reeme struggled to her feet and walked away.

Thuro came back and offered Horda a fawn skin. "I thought you might need to dry the child."

Tears filled her eyes. “I didn’t even think about that, Thuro. Thank you.”

“Horda, don’t cry.”

“I’m not crying. Well, not exactly. I’m frightened.”

He clumsily patted her shoulder. “Bran will be all right. I’m sure of it. You’re doing everything Nuroo would do. He’s going to be okay.”

Her heart screamed. *You don’t know anything about it, Thuro. You wouldn’t realize if I was forgetting something.* Guiltily she clamped her teeth together to stop the words she knew she must not say. *He’s only trying to help me. To show he believes in me. Please, Mother Life, let me believe in myself.*

“I hope so, Thuro. I surely hope so.” She couldn’t stop the tears now trickling down her face. “Pray, Thuro — please, pray like you’ve never prayed before.”

“I will.” He turned and walked away.

She took a deep breath and blinked rapidly trying to dry her eyes without touching her face. *Mother Life, I’m scared. Help me save Bran. Please, Father Death, don’t take him away. He’s so little. He has his whole life before him.*

Chapter 13

REEME RETURNED WITH AN armload of furs and fashioned a bed beside the fire for Bran. Horda nodded her approval. "That's good. We want him to be comfortable." Reeme smiled her thanks and returned to her seat.

Mach and Lena followed Zeek who carried Bran. They joined Horda and Reeme beside the fire. "Thuro brought a fawn skin to dry him," said Horda.

Lena took the skin and patted away the water droplets speckling the little boy's skin like so many teardrops. "He's much cooler, but he hasn't come back."

"I'm glad he's cooler." Horda gave the pitch another stir before facing Zeek. "I'm also glad he's not back yet because this is going to hurt."

Zeek laid the boy on the bed of furs. Horda looked down at him then up at his father. "Do you want to help me and Lena, Zeek, or would you rather Mach did?"

"Help you do what?"

"Hold him. He mustn't move when I lance the kernels. The pain may bring him back."

Zeek's face blanched white, but his voice was steady. "I'll

help you."

Horda nodded. "Reeme, help Zeek and Lena wash their hands, please."

Horda stirred the warm pitch into the prairie flax seeds and figwort leaves then turned the mixture back onto the stone to cool while Zeek and Lena washed.

"We're ready," he said in a gruff voice. "What do you want us to do?"

She picked up the bone needle before she answered. "One of you needs to hold his head and the other his body while I open the kernel on the right side of his neck."

Wordlessly they took their places. With another silent prayer, Horda knelt beside the tiny boy. She located the kernel with the fingers of her left hand and lifted it as close to the surface of his skin as she could. Taking a deep breath, she plunged the needle into the lump and gave it a twist.

Reeme shrieked. Zeek paled, but he did not waver. Bran whimpered and wiggled but did not waken. Bloody pus gushed from the cut. *Thank you, Mother Life. This needed to be done.*

After wiping the needle clean, Horda dropped it back in the bag of boiling water. "Are you all right?" she asked Lena and Zeek.

Tears shined on Lena's face, but she nodded. Zeek closed his eyes and swallowed hard.

"Zeek, are you all right?" Horda asked a little more insistently.

He took a deep breath but did not open his eyes. After swallowing once more, he said, "Give me time, Horda. I will be."

Despite Mach's stricken look, she asked, "Do you want

Mach to take your place?"

Zeek managed to open his eyes, and Horda was glad to see most of the color had returned to his face. "No," he said hoarsely. "I'll do this for my son."

Horda nodded. "There are three more."

"I know," he said. "Let's get on with it."

She smiled. "The next one is under his left arm. You don't need to hold his head. This time I need you to hold him steady while you raise his arm and hold it over his head. Lena, you'll still hold his legs."

They nodded and got in position while she picked up the small obsidian blade. She located the kernel — much larger than the first, gritted her teeth, and plunged the blade into it then gave a half twist. Once more bloody pus squirted from the cut.

Watching, Reeme shrieked and began to sob and gag. Bran moaned and tried to pull away, but Zeek held him steady though tears filled his eyes. Moving to the fire, Horda gave Mach a speaking look, and he tried to comfort Reeme.

Horda dropped the blade in the bag and used the tongs to lift the needle from the hot water.

"The next one is at the top of his right leg. It's about the same size as the one under his jaw so I'll use the needle. Zeek, hold his upper body. Lena, hold his legs." She waited while they adjusted their positions. "Are you ready?"

They nodded. She finished quickly. "The one on his left leg is the last. It's the biggest." She took the obsidian blade and made the cut.

"H-ee-rt," croaked Bran blinking up at his father in accusation.

"Yes, Son, I'm sure it does, but Horda has to do this so

the fever demons won't eat you."

"No." Bran's lower lip quivered.

Horda smiled down at him. "The worst is over, Bran. Now, I'm going to clean the wounds. Then we're going to pack them so they will get well."

"No." He struggled to sit up. She nodded and Zeek set him on his lap.

"We don't want him to get any more upset than he has to," she said washing away the bloody seepage from the cuts. Then she stirred the sap mixture with her wooden paddle. "Bran, I need to try to get the rest of the poison out of your neck."

"No." Bran burrowed against his father.

"Now, Little Chief," she coaxed, "Don't you want to hunt bison with Mach again?"

Bran turned to look at her. "When?"

"As soon as you're better."

He pursed his lips but let her probe his neck. A little more of the corruption drained before he cried, "Nuff!"

Zeek took a deep breath. "Do you want me to hold him down for you?"

Horda shook her head. "There doesn't seem to be any more that wants to come out now. Anyway, the packing will draw the poison." She took a small portion of the sap mixture on the wooden paddle and tested its heat with her finger. She took another wooden paddle and cut the mixture so it would cool some. After testing it again, she turned to the child.

He eyed her warily.

She smiled. "I want you to lie down while I bandage you so you'll get all better and can hunt bison with Mach.

Okay?"

Bran frowned but said, "Oh-kay." Zeek laid him on the bed of furs and held his hand.

Horda packed the warm sap mixture on the wound and wrapped it with a boiled deerskin bandage. Bran struggled to rise, but Zeek stopped him with a shake of his head. "Not yet, Son. There are three more."

"More?" asked Bran.

"More."

"Oh-kay."

Horda packed and bandaged the rest of the wounds then helped him to sit up on his father's lap. "Now, Bran, I want you to drink some tonic."

"No, nassy."

Horda laughed. "No, it's not nasty. There's mint in it, and I'll add lots of camas molasses to it. It won't taste bad." She dipped a horn of the cooled tonic and made a show of adding the molasses. "Enough?"

"No."

She added more and stirred. "Enough?"

"No."

"I'll put in one more bit," she said. "That will have to be enough because it's all the horn will hold." She showed him the full horn.

He eyed it thoughtfully. "Oh-kay."

"Your fa will hold it while you drink it. Okay?"

"Oh-kay."

She handed the horn to Zeek and felt the little boy's forehead. *Mother Life, no.* Zeek's eyes met hers, and she knew he realized Bran's fever was climbing once more.

Reeme said, "Oh, he's so much better. He'll be fine

tomorrow. Thank you, Horda."

Tears formed in Horda's throat. She could not make herself face Reeme. "Do we need to bathe him?" Zeek asked.

"Not yet. Try to get the tonic down him first, but don't let him get too hot."

"I won't." Zeek helped the little boy drink.

Bran protested after the first few sips, but Zeek and Mach coaxed until he drank most of it. Then Zeek said, "He's getting hotter."

Reeme shrieked. "What do you mean?"

Horda said, "The fever demons aren't gone yet, Reeme. We have to bathe him again."

"No," she screamed and began to keen.

Frightened by his mother's cries, Bran howled. Horda went to her. "You must stop this. The more upset he becomes the faster the fever demons return. Stop! This instant!"

"I can't," shrieked Reeme. "He's my baby. He's going to be just like Br—"

"Then leave this cook fire," ordered Horda. "Now."

"I will not leave my baby."

Zeek said, "If you can't do as Horda asks, then you must leave."

"But —"

"He mustn't be upset," said Horda. "We have to keep him calm so he can use his energy to fight the fever demons."

Go," said Zeek. "See to the other children. I'll take care of Bran."

Reluctantly Reeme walked away. Zeek lowered Bran into one of the large water baskets.

"Cold," protested the little boy. "Out."

"Ah, the cold is good," said Mach. "It will drive away the

fever demons so we can hunt bison sooner."

Bran's lower lip quivered, and he glared at Mach. "Twooly?"

"Truly," said Mach sponging Bran's face and head. Horda busied herself picking up her medicine packets and straightening the area. Before she finished, Mach looked at her. "This water feels warm."

"Put him in another basket then."

By the time the water in the last basket became too warm, Bran's skin had cooled enough that Mach and Zeek lay him on the sleeping furs and covered him lightly with the soft fawn skin. Zeek sat beside his son and held his hand while the little boy drifted in a feverish sleep.

Mach joined Horda on the far side of the fire. "Is he better?" he whispered.

Horda shook her head. "Not as long as the fever demons come back."

"What are we going to do?"

"Fight them," she said fiercely.

"How?"

"The same way we have been."

Mach looked sick. "You mean …."

She glared at him. "Yes, I mean we'll keep lancing and packing and soaking him until the fever demons consume him or go away."

He looked at the tiny child sleeping fitfully on the other side of the fire and shook his head. "He's so little to already have three winters."

"I know." Horda bit her lips and fought the tears that gathered in her eyes. "He was born in the Moon of the Early Green after the winter of your Great Travel." Abruptly, she turned away.

He caught her arm. "I know this is my fault. I didn't think . . ."

She shrugged. "You weren't the only man there."

"I should have known better."

"So should they."

He pulled her into a fierce embrace. She allowed herself to melt against his comforting warmth for a moment before pushing away. "I need to fix some broth for him. Someone must have some fresh meat."

"The hunting was good yesterday," said Mach. "Thuro took a deer. He'll give you all the meat you need."

Her eyes widened. "You didn't eat tonight."

"Neither did you."

"Are you hungry?"

He shook his head. "Not really. I ate a lot at the Naming Feast."

Horda looked dazed. "That was today."

"I know." Mach smiled wryly. "It just seems like a moon ago."

"At least."

He gave her a little push. "Go on and get the meat. Bran won't need you for a while."

Horda heard Wilda whining before she reached the shelter. "I don't understand why you gave her my best fawn skin."

She couldn't understand Thuro's murmured reply, but she heard Wilda's response. "It just doesn't seem fair after the way they cut you out of all the important things about being a leader."

Thuro's voice rose. "I will not tell you again I have not been cut out of anything important about being a leader."

"You certainly had a small enough part in the Naming Ceremony today." Horda heard Wilda sniff. "I'd say that is being cut out of something important."

Thuro nearly shouted, "I told you I didn't want a larger part in the Naming Ceremony. That's the only reason I didn't have one."

Wilda sobbed. "Well, you should have."

Horda prudently decided to seek meat for Bran's broth from Premo and Aiyana. Approaching their shelter she called, "Aiyana, may I enter?"

A smiling Aiyana lifted the door covering. "Greetings, Horda. Does this visit mean Bran is better?"

Horda shrugged. "I don't know. I hope so, but his fever still rises."

"Oh, I'm sorry. Come sit with us."

"Greetings, Premo," Horda said politely.

"Greetings, Horda. Come sit and see our son."

She smiled. "I'd like to visit, but actually I need your help."

"Help?" asked Aiyana.

"Yes, I need some fresh meat to make a broth for Bran, but I don't have any."

"Because you cooked it all for Zakon's Naming Feast," said Aiyana with a broad smile. "It was a wonderful day for us. I'm just sorry Bran became so ill." As she spoke, she took a pack of fresh meat from her cache and held it out to Horda. "Will this be enough?"

"Oh, no, I mean, yes. It is more than plenty. I don't need nearly that much for one small boy," protested Horda.

"Take it," said Premo quietly. "Maybe Zeek and Mach will eat some of the meat and broth."

"Thank you," murmured Horda taking the pack. "I must get back."

"I'll hunt tomorrow and bring you more fresh meat," said Premo.

"Thank you, Premo. I'm sure I'll need it."

"If I can help you again, Horda, let me know," said Aiyana placing a hand on Horda's back.

Horda turned and smiled at her friends. "I will. Thank both of you very much." She returned to her cook fire and prepared a rich meat broth while Bran slept. When he awoke, they dosed him with tonic-laced broth. Then they washed him again before his fever rose too high.

"Hurts," mumbled Bran when Horda tried to give him the tonic again.

"I know, but you have to take it," pleaded Horda.

Though his fever-glazed eyes still accused her, he drank the tonic without further complaint and soon he slept again.

Then his fever started to spike. "No, no, no, no," mumbled Bran though he did not resist when his father lowered him into the water basket once more.

Horda coaxed him to drink some of the broth while Mach and Zeek bathed him. After no more than a hand of swallows, he turned his head away and whispered, "Nuff."

Fear's icy fingers twisted Horda's stomach as she watched the feisty little boy turn lethargic, but once more he cooled and fell asleep.

"He's worse. Isn't he?" said Zeek.

"I'm afraid so," admitted Horda. "But I don't know anything else to do."

Mach's eyes flashed. "He's going to be all right. It will just take time."

"Lots of time," said Horda.

"Well, then we'll give it lots of time," said Zeek.

Horda smiled. She knew she couldn't nurse the little boy all alone. There were any number of women willing to help her, but of all the members of the band, these two warriors were the little boy's favorites. Just having them close would help keep him content and maybe help him survive.

The next morning Horda and Mach were cleaning Bran's wounds and repacking them when Thuro came to the cook fire.

"How is he?" asked Thuro.

"About the same," whispered Mach.

"I'm sorry," said Thuro looking embarrassed.

"It's going to take time," said Horda, "but he's going to be fine." She smiled down at the quiet little boy. "Aren't you, Bran?"

"Hunt?" croaked Bran hopefully.

"Yes, Little Chief, we're going on that bison hunt as soon as you're better," assured Mach patting his arm.

Bran smiled wanly and closed his eyes.

Thuro's face was darker than the morning shadows as he kicked the dirt beside Horda's cook fire, but he didn't say anything else. The third time Horda almost fell over him, she asked, "Thuro, is something the matter?"

He flushed a dark red. "I hate to bother you, but Wilda's sick. She just keeps vomiting and vomiting. I don't know anything to help her, but I hoped you would."

Horda nodded. "Give me time to finish here and I'll get some herbs for her." She almost stepped on his foot once more. "Thuro, sit over there until we finish." Thuro didn't seem to hear her. She touched his arm and patiently repeated her suggestion.

"I, ah, I'm sorry," he said. "I guess I'm worried. She seems awfully sick."

Thoughts of her own unending morning sickness swirled through Horda's memory. "She is awfully sick, but I don't think it's serious nor will it last too long."

"What do you mean?"

Horda smiled. "I wasn't going to mention it to you because I don't have time to examine her now, but Lena thinks she's breeding."

"Breeding?" Thuro's face blanched white. "She can't be. She made me promise she'd never have to have a little one."

Mach grinned at Thuro. "Looks like your promise came a little late, old friend."

"Breeding?" whispered Thuro. "Mother Life! I can't tell her that."

"I'd just as soon you didn't," said Horda. "She may just have some kind of upset stomach, but either way, I'm sure it's not serious."

"Not serious? Horda, there's no telling what she'll do if she's breeding."

"Well, yes, Thuro, there is," said Mach.

"What?" asked Thuro.

"It's pretty easy to tell exactly what she will do if she's breeding." Mach smiled at his friend. "She'll have a little one."

"Oh, I don't know, Mach." Thuro's fear was a tangible thing painting dark shadows on his face and bowing him down. "You haven't heard her. I don't know what she will do. She's terrified. She's absolutely certain nothing is worse than giving birth."

Horda muttered one of the oaths she learned from Bear Claw's people. Thuro and Mach looked at her in shock. A blush tinted her cheeks. "I'm sorry. It just slipped out. It's so totally unfair. Some women would give anything to be pregnant, and here we're worrying about what she's going to say. Giving birth is not something to be afraid of. Women do it all the time. That's the only way anybody ever gets here." Horda's voice caught on a sob, and her pain showed in her face.

Mach touched her hand. She closed her eyes and gave a small shake of her head. She knew if she looked at him she would really begin to cry, and she didn't have time She had to care for Bran before she could get the herbs for Wilda. She took a deep breath and said, "Thuro, sit over there out of our way until we're finished here. Then I'll get you some herbs to help with her nausea. Later, I'll have some of the other women talk to her. I'm sure she'll be okay."

None of the three spoke again though tear tracks still

marked Horda's cheeks when she handed the packet of mint, ginger, and alum root to Thuro and told him how to use it.

Thunder Eagle had stayed quietly in the background since the Feast, but he joined Mach and Horda at their cook fire after Thuro left.

"Greetings, Mach — Horda."

"Greetings, Thunder Eagle. Please accept our apologies. We have been negligent hosts."

Thunder Eagle smiled. "Nonsense. You have been busy with much more important things than an old trader who is used to feeding himself."

"You are kind, Thunder Eagle," said Horda. "I had hoped for time to talk with you, but it doesn't seem like that's going to happen this visit."

"No, it isn't," said Thunder Eagle. "I must be on my way."

"So soon?" asked Mach.

"Yes, I have promised to visit several more bands before the long blizzards come."

"Where will you spend the Moons of the Long Blizzards?" asked Horda.

"I'm not sure. I may stay with the Inner Band this year, but I may also go south where there are no really long blizzards so I can cut across to the restless waters. I'm really not sure what my plans are. A lot depends on how my salt holds out." He offered Mach a large sack of salt.

Shaking his head and refusing to take it, Mach stepped back. "We have nothing to trade for this much salt."

Horda's eyes rounded. This sack held at least a hand's handfuls of salt. The packets he usually traded had half a hand full. "That is too much," she said.

Thunder Eagle smiled at her. "You paid for this and more when you were just a little girl. I don't know if you realize it, but you saved my life then. This is but a small payment on my debt to you."

Mach smiled because Thunder Eagle did not mention the story although he was sure Horda realized what he was telling her. His smile died when Thunder Eagle took his hand and said, "This is the stuff of another tale, Mach. I will be back to see how it ends, and then I will be telling it around the assembly fires of the People."

"You gave me your word," said Mach.

"Not about this story," said Thunder Eagle. "It is a wonderful story of the beautiful young woman fighting Father Death and winning. You aren't going to tell me I can't tell this story. Are you?"

"You will have to ask her. It's her story," said Mach.

"You aren't going to deny me, are you, beautiful Horda?" said Thunder Eagle with a smile.

Horda was too tired to be listening to what she had considered nothing more than joking men's talk. She shook her head and asked "What? What did you say? I'm sorry, but I wasn't listening."

Thunder Eagle laughed. "Then just say yes, my pretty one."

Mach's warning look had Thunder Eagle saying, "I was only joking, Horda. You are much too tired to think about this now. We'll discuss it when I come back this way." With a salute, he was gone as quickly and quietly as he had come.

Chapter 14

Bone-weary, Horda, Mach, and Zeek still cared for Bran. Three fingers less than three hands turnings of the sun of unremitting lancing, packing, dosing, bathing, and feeding passed with Bran's fever always climbing back. During that time he became a pale, silent shadow of the sturdy, talkative little boy he had been.

The band had moved into the cave and waited for the winter snows to begin in earnest when one night in the cold darkness after the moon set, Horda touched Bran's face and found him sweating. *Thank you, Mother Life,* she breathed. Then she called, "Mach! Zeek!"

Mach who dozed beside the fire sat bolt upright, searching for a weapon. A look of terror on his face, Zeek stumbled out of the sleeping area. "What's wrong, Horda?"

She smiled though tears glistened in her eyes. "Bran is sweating."

Mach banked the fire. Zeek picked up a water bag and emptied it over the flames.

Eyes wide, Horda asked, "What are you two doing?"

"The fever demons. It can't be good for him to be too hot.

We'll put out the f—"

Horda shook her head. "No, you don't understand."

Stupefied, the two men looked at her.

She smiled through the tears streaming down her cheeks. "The fever demons have given up. He's going to be all right."

"What?" croaked Zeek.

"People don't sweat while the fever demons feast on them. It's only when the demons give up their hold that the person is able to sweat and cool himself." She wiped the tears from her eyes. "Don't you understand? Bran's going to be all right."

"All right?" echoed Zeek.

"Are you sure?" Mach touched the little boy's damp cheek.

"Yes."

"We won?" Tears streamed down the old warrior's face as he traced the fragile veins lining the back of his tiny son's hand. "We won!" said Horda laughing and crying together.

"We won!" shouted Mach grabbing Horda and Zeek in a mighty hug. Then he built up the cook fire in the cave until the shadows were driven away, "Did you hear that? Everybody wake up! We won. Bran's going to be all right."

The entire band soon gathered around the sleeping child offering congratulations and thanks. Through all the commotion, Bran slept peacefully.

❂

Dark clouds piled high over the jagged teeth of the mountains and raced to cover the morning sun while casting irregular shadows across the land. The wind whistled across the flat land.

"Storm's coming," said Mach to his hunting party. "Let's go back."

Zeek cast a weather eye toward the roiling clouds rushing across the sky and followed Mach toward the cave. Premo, Trefo, and Orol were close on their heels.

Premo glared at the darkening sky. "It doesn't feel like it's going to snow," he muttered.

"No," said Zeek, "but it's going to storm." The distant grumble of thunder underlined his words.

"Thunder and lightning in this season?" Orol raised his eyebrows and hurried his steps. A finger of lightning tore a hole in the clouds allowing the rumble of thunder to pour through. The wind roared down on the men pushing them toward their destination.

The journey became a nightmare when the thick clouds blotted out the sun and cast the morning world in twilight shades of grey. Flash after flash of sheet lightning followed while thunder rumbled and grumbled making its protests audible even above the shrieking wind. But the worst was yet to come.

The deadly streaks of lightning reached down from the sky to touch the earth around the frightened men. The thunder crashes followed immediately. The short hairs on the back of Mach's neck stood up. He looked at the flat lands around them and then at Zeek. Except for a stunted tree or two, the men stood taller than anything else. "We have to find shelter."

Zeek shook his head and shouted, "Too late. Lie flat." Zeek spread-eagled his body on the ground as if to sink into the crust of the earth.

Before Mach could react, thunder crashed, and lightning flashed brighter than before outlining the prairie grasses and bushes in sharp shadows. Then the light died away. he shouted, "Lie down!" before following Zeek's example. He knew the last bolt of lightning struck nearby, but he dared not raise his head to see about his men. More lightning bolts battered the earth all around him. The crashes of the thunder melted into a continuous roar.

Mach waited for the rain that should accompany such a vicious storm, but none came. The tempest moved away leaving bitter cold but neither rain nor snow in its wake. The lightning faded away, leaving the world painted twilight shades of grey once more. The roar of the thunder died. But when he cautiously raised his head to look back at his men, one last bolt of lightning found a twisted tree a short distance behind them and exploded it in a shower of sparks.

Please, Mother Life, not a fire. Mach dug his face into the earth. The rotten egg odor almost choked him as he waited for the scent of smoke to tell him to warn his men to run. No smoke came, but a hint of charred flesh, like meat left too long on the fire, wafted on the now-gentle breeze.

The storm moved away. The sky lightened, and the midday sun played peek-a-boo with the tattered clouds drifting across the crystal blue sky. Mach raised his head and looked at Zeek.

Zeek nodded and climbed to his feet. "You can get up now," Mach called standing and dusting himself off. He turned and watched two other men stand. "No!" The word tore from his throat like a curse. He raced up the trail to where Orol sprawled unmoving.

Even before Mach reached Orol, the smell of his burned

hair and flesh assaulted Mach's nostrils causing him to gag. Orol's hands had become no more than burned claws clutching singed spear shafts. His leather clothing smoked and smoldered in places. Mach knew then what the first bolt of lightning had struck.

Mach squared his shoulders as the sad procession bearing Orol's remains neared the cave. Memories of the young man played through his mind. Orol with closed eyes and bowed head when Elko had told him Marmal, his first chosen, had not survived the long captivity by Bear Claw. Orol's quiet grief through the next winter. The sad, resolute way he chose a mate when Gathering time came again. Then the way the melancholy, stoic warrior had changed by this past Gathering. Orol's delighted happiness with his pretty, little Ryssa — pregnant Ryssa. *Father Death, you took him. You give me the words to say to Ryssa.*

Thuro met the procession beginning its slow climb to the cave. "Ho, it was quite a storm of lights and noise, wasn't it?" He looked at the clear, cold sky. "No rain or snow though. That's too bad."

"Yes," said Mach.

"What's wrong?" Thuro realized the travois did not carry fresh meat. "No."

Mach nodded.

Thuro asked, "What happened?"

"The storm caught us in the flat open. Zeek told us to get down. Orol was not quick enough or flat enough." So few words to tell about the end of a life. *Why, Father Death?*

Mach swallowed the rage burning the back of his throat like bile. Curses and questions without answers fought to escape his mouth. He couldn't let them out. He clamped his teeth so the muscles in his jaw knotted, but he couldn't stop the questions chasing each other around his brain. *Why didn't you take him while he was suffering so? Why did you let him find happiness? So you could snatch it away? Why? Why? Why?*

The sun still stood high in the afternoon sky when they reached the opening of the cave. Storm Cloud and Rain Drop greeted Mach catching his hands and swinging. "There was a storm," said Rain Drop. "The lightning flashed and flashed and the thunder roared. I wanted to go outside to watch, but Horda wouldn't let me. Storm Cloud was scared."

"Was not."

"Was too." The little girl grinned at Mach. "He stuck his fingers in his ears and closed his eyes."

"Did not."

"Did too."

Mach nodded and released his hands from the children's grasps. "Go to Horda," he said.

"But I want to tell you —" protested Rain Drop

"Go to Horda," Mach ordered.

The children frowned at him but did as he commanded. Mach turned to the others. "Wait here." He squared his shoulders and walked with Thuro to Orol and Ryssa's area of the cave.

Ryssa stopped her work and watched their approach. When they reached her, Mach saw tears trickling down her face. *Father Death! She already knows.* "Ryssa, I am sorry —"

She clapped her hands over her ears. "Please, don't tell me," she begged. "Please, don't." The anguish in her eyes pierced Mach's heart.

Stepping forward, he caught her hands and pulled them from her ears. "I wish I didn't have to," he murmured.

"Then don't," she snapped. "Let me pretend for a little while longer."

"I'm sorry, Ryssa. Pretending will not change what is," Mach said. "Father Death reached down from the sky and took Orol to walk the Frozen Wilds with him."

"No!" She pulled her hands from Mach's grasp and ripped two great, bloody hanks of hair from her head. Startled, Mach and Thuro tried to restrain her, but she fought like an angered she-cat, scratching and spitting at them and keening her grief to the skies.

Glaring at Mach and Thuro, Horda skidded to a halt before Ryssa. "Ryssa! Stop!" she commanded and caught the younger woman's flailing hands in her own. "You must stop this now. Think of your little one."

The sudden silence in the cave sounded deafening. Premo and Trefo followed by Zeek bore Orol's charred body to his cook fire. Ryssa's fight deserted her, and she threw herself sobbing across the remains of her beloved mate.

Horda looked at Mach. "What happened?"

Mach shook his head. "I thought the storm was a blizzard, and I wanted to get back to the cave. We were traveling the hunting trail across the flat when it caught us. There was no shelter. Zeek told us to lie down. Orol wasn't fast enough or flat enough or something. A lightning bolt struck him." He closed his mouth against the curses still bubbling in his throat.

Horda shook her head and looked at the People gathered around. "Lena, help us prepare him for the Frozen Wilds." Clearly dismissed, Mach and the others walked away.

Out of the hearing of the others, Thuro asked, "What are we going to do?"

"Do?"

Thuro rubbed his face. "Ryssa must have a place beside a cook fire until she chooses a new mate."

Mach nodded. "We don't have a choice. Do we?"

Thuro sighed. "I'm sorry."

Mach shrugged. "It's not your fault." Then a grin split his face. "Well, actually it is your fault." He sobered. "Has Wilda accepted her pregnancy yet?"

Thuro shook his head. "I don't think so. She still insists she can't possibly be pregnant because she doesn't want to be. I don't know what I'm going to do. She grows rounder every day. And insists she's dying of some unnamed disease."

"I told you once before, Thuro. You're going to have a little one."

"I wish *I* could," snapped Thuro.

"I'm sure it will be all right," said Mach placing a hand on Thuro's shoulder.

"I hope so."

Mach's eyes filled with wonder. "Now, I'm going to have a little one born by my cook fire."

Thuro nodded. "I hadn't thought of that."

"I'm not ready to choose another mate," he said, "but I'm going to hate letting the little one go to someone else after I have it for almost a turning of the seasons."

"There are worse reasons for choosing a mate," said Thuro bitterly.

"Maybe one of the other men will invite Ryssa to his cook fire," said Mach.

"Maybe."

Chapter 15

THE SUN ALMOST TOUCHED the tops of the jagged mountains to the west before Horda returned to her cook fire to prepare for the visitation and Orol's trip to the Frozen Wilds. Mach had already left, but he had helped the children dress in ceremonial clothing. They sat beside the fire waiting for Horda's return.

"My, you look nice," she said.

"Mach washed us and found our clothes, but we dressed ourselves," said Rain Drop.

"I can tell," said Horda tying the thongs at Rain Drop's neck and straightening the fringe on Storm Cloud's tunic. "It's a big help that you're ready."

"Mach fixed my hair," bragged Storm Cloud.

"Mine, too," announced Rain Drop.

Horda hid her smile at the little girl with the warrior's braids. "You both look very nice. I'll be ready in a little time."

"Mach said tell you he was going to talk to somebody," said Storm Cloud.

"He'll see us at the visit," added Rain Drop. "We're

supposed to sit still 'til you're ready."

"Okay, that will be a big help." Horda took a cooking bag of water into the sleeping area. "I have to hurry."

She had washed and was pulling on her ceremonial dress when Mach joined her. "I didn't expect to see you before the visitation."

He leaned down and touched her lips with his. "I have to talk to you."

She nodded and straightened her tunic and tied the thongs at the neck. Reaching up, she unfastened her braids and finger combed the wavy brown mass. When her mate remained silent, she looked at him. "Mach, what's wrong?"

He took her hands in his. "I have to offer Ryssa a place beside our cook fire at least until next Gathering when she can choose a new mate."

She shrugged. "I expected that. It's what leaders do." She rebraided her hair with shells and dyed bone beads.

"Horda, do you mind?" He caught her hands and held them still until she looked into his eyes. "She's breeding."

"I know that." She frowned. "She has to have a place. Her little one is due in two or three moons."

"Horda, can we keep a little one beside our cook fire until next Gathering and then give it up?"

Horda looked at a space beyond his head for a long time before she answered. "I don't know, but we don't really have another choice."

"I don't know whether I'll be able to give the little one up or not," he admitted. "I'm not ready to take another mate, but ..."

"Take another mate?" Tears gleamed in her eyes when she asked, "Are you saying you want Ryssa to be your second mate just so we can keep the little one?"

"I'm not sure." He stared at the toes of his moccasins. "I guess that's what I'm saying."

She pulled her hands out of his and nibbled on her left thumbnail. Then she rubbed her eyes. "Do you think that's fair to Ryssa?"

He shrugged.

"I hadn't thought much about you taking another mate yet." She sighed. "I'm not sure I'm ready to share you."

He hugged her. "I don't want another mate, but I already dread keeping a child for the first winter of its life and giving it up."

Horda arched one eyebrow at him. "Although I personally can't imagine such a thing, what if Ryssa doesn't want you for a mate?"

Mach looked startled then sheepish. "Mother Life, I hadn't considered that."

"Perhaps we should see how she feels about us before we start worrying about her becoming your second mate."

Mach shook his head. "I just wanted to be sure you understand I have to invite her to our cook fire."

"I know," she said. "We'll just have to wait and see what else happens."

He hugged her fiercely and shared her breath. "I love you," he whispered, and then he was gone.

When one of the People departed to walk the Frozen Wilds, the band had a time of visitation. The People came together to speak their regrets and offer memories of the departed one to his or her family. Though a sad time, it also celebrated the life that had ended. Since Ryssa had no other family in the band, the leaders and their mates would stand beside her during the visitation.

Mach and Thuro had taken their places with Ryssa at the head of the ceremonial travois bearing Orol's remains when Horda arrived. She looked around, but Wilda was nowhere in sight. With a mental shrug, Horda walked to Ryssa and took her hands in her own.

Looking into the young woman's haunted eyes, Horda remembered the terrible pain she had felt at her mother's visitation. An icy dagger twisted in her heart, and she shivered imagining Mach lying in Orol's place and herself standing in Ryssa's. In that instant she realized comparing the pain she had known at her mother's departure to the torment Ryssa suffered would be like comparing the prick of a thorn to the pains of birth. "He was a good man, Ryssa. He will be missed." Impulsively, she drew the smaller woman into an embrace.

Tears streaming down her face, Ryssa leaned against Horda drawing from her store of strength and comfort. Then she took a deep breath and pushed herself upright "Thank you for coming and for ..." A sob tore at her throat. Horda watched Ryssa chew the inside of her cheeks while she fought for her composure. Finally, drawing a deep breath through her mouth, Ryssa managed to finish. "... helping — me — today."

"You're welcome," said Horda formally taking her place beside her mate.

All the adults of the band except Wilda filed past. Sometimes Ryssa spoke calmly; other times she battled tears.

Mach and Thuro kept close watch on the young woman offering silent support when she wavered. Sometimes she accepted it for a brief time; others she rejected it and fought her grief alone.

When all finished filing past and speaking, Thuro took a deep breath and lifted Ryssa's left hand in his. Surprise rounded her eyes, but she did not protest.

"Ryssa, it is with great sadness we gather here to take Orol to the Frozen Wilds. I do not pretend to understand his death." Thuro paused and fought for words. "Orol was a good man who suffered much in the short time he walked the earth. Please be comforted to know you brought him great happiness this last turning of the seasons." Thuro released Ryssa's hand and took a step back.

Horda sensed the battle raging inside her mate. He turned to face Ryssa and clasped her right hand in his left. He stared at the young widow for a long time before he spoke. "Orol was a man who suffered deeply before he found happiness," he said. "Orol was my friend. We traveled the Rituals of Manhood together, and we fought Bear Claw and the People of the Tall Grass together."

Horda knew Mach longed to curse Father Death and spit in his face, but she also knew he would not.

He continued in a soft, firm voice. "Orol walked a lonely path from that battle until he chose you. Then he found joy in his life once again. He basked in the warmth of his love for you and yours for him. Your coming little one made his satisfaction complete. Perhaps Father Death felt jealous of such perfect bliss." Mach paused and fought tears of his own. "I can think of no other reason for Orol being called away."

Tears streamed down Ryssa's face, but she made no sound nor did she move. Mach placed his right hand on their clasped hands before he continued. "Horda and I offer you a place beside our cook fire for as long as you choose to use it. Though we promise to teach Orol's little one about the brave warrior who was his father, we will care for him or her as we would care for a little one of our own." He loosed his grip on her hand and took a step back.

Ryssa took a deep breath and stood up straight. She looked at the assembled People then Thuro, Horda, and Mach in turn before she spoke in a quiet but steady voice. "Thank you for your words. They do bring comfort into the cold place where my heart once was. Thank you, Mach and Horda, for offering me a place beside your cook fire, but I cannot accept it. Though I still walk the earth, Father Death came for me today. I will walk the Frozen Wilds this night with my mate."

Gasps went through the assembled People. Women whose mates died had three choices. They could take a place beside the cook fire of a friend who offered until they chose another mate. They could occupy a place beside the cook fire of a grown son or daughter. Or they could walk the Frozen Wilds with their departed mates.

Few women chose to walk the Frozen Wilds with their departed mates, and those who did were usually older women who neared the ends of their own lives. Seldom did a young woman make that choice and never in Horda's memory had a breeding woman made it.

Horda reached past her mate and took Ryssa's hands. "You can not walk the Frozen Wilds," she whispered. "Think of your little one."

"I am thinking of my little one," said Ryssa, "and my mate and myself. We will walk the Frozen Wilds together."

"It's wrong of you to destroy your little one before it has a chance to live," insisted Horda.

Ryssa stared at her. "My father departed before I was born. My mother departed when I had three winters. I don't really remember either of them though I was taught they were both wonderful. My father was a brave warrior who departed on the biggest bison hunt in anyone's memory. He tried to kill the biggest bison anyone had ever seen single-handedly, and it charged him and stomped him into the dirt with the biggest feet anyone ever saw on a bison.

"When I was old enough to really think about it, I wondered why any warrior — brave or cowardly — would be stupid enough to challenge the biggest bison alone. I still wonder." She stared into Horda's eyes as if she dared her to speak.

"My mother was the sweetest, kindest, gentlest woman in the history of the tribe. At least according to the people of the band who raised me. I have a hard time believing their words when all I remember of my early life are cold and loneliness and hunger." Horda gasped against the naked pain in the young woman's eyes and voice. Ryssa shook her head and continued, "I admit I don't really remember my mother. I wish I could remember the sweet, kind, gentle woman I was told about. I can't remember her ever holding me or comforting my tears. I can't even remember her face, but I can remember her telling me to be quiet and go to sleep. Then she would cry for my father."

"But the people wanted to give you good memories of your parents," protested Horda.

"They gave me good stories of my parents. They could not give me memories I did not have." Ryssa frowned. "The only memories I have of growing up are of not belonging anywhere. I was adopted, but I never truly belonged. I didn't have any relatives. The band leader and his mates took me in. They really tried, and I never needed food or clothing or shelter, but I never felt like one of theirs because they always told me stories about my real parents.

"I wanted to belong, but I never did until I mated with Orol. With Orol, I finally belonged somewhere. Our child belongs with us. Father Death won't be so cruel as to separate us. We will go together to the land beyond the stars and dwell with the ancients." Tears still sparkled in her eyes, and the afternoon sun cast shadows on her face when she nodded at Horda. "It will be all right."

Horda shook her head, but she argued no more.

Mach and Thuro took their places at Orol's feet. Four men lifted the ceremonial travois to their shoulders, and the procession started toward the Frozen Wilds. Ryssa turned to Horda. "Will you help me?"

Horda nodded and picked up a share of the treasured possessions Ryssa had chosen. Lifting the cradle board and cooking bags in her arms, Horda wondered how she could have been so blind. These were not the possessions of a warrior; they belonged to a family. She clenched her jaws against the protests and walked beside Ryssa. Together they followed the travois out of the cave and down the shadowed path into the bitterly cold afternoon. The rest of the People walked close behind.

When the trip was almost finished, Ryssa looked at Horda. "Please understand. I don't want to go on without Orol. I cannot stand to walk this earth without him." Fresh tears welled in her eyes, but she blinked them back and continued. "And I can't leave my little one behind. We'll be together this way. It's for the best."

Horda believed in her heart she would make the same choice if Mach departed, but she could force no words past the lump in her throat. She nodded and watched a look of peace settle over Ryssa's ravaged face.

When they entered the mouth of the Frozen Wilds, the sun had reached the jagged teeth of the mountains. Its last rays painted dark shadows across the land. There the men placed the travois on the stones already prepared as its final resting place and stepped back. The People who had helped carry the young couple's possessions placed them conveniently around the travois. Ryssa fussed a little bit placing the cradle board exactly as she wanted it. She straightened Orol's burned hair and gently touched his eyelids.

Mach and Thuro spoke quietly with the young woman. Horda knew they offered her the chance to change her mind, but she wasn't surprised when Ryssa shook her head and seated herself beside her mate. There was nothing more they could do. Watching her, Horda longed to scream at Father Death for being so thoughtless, but she clenched her teeth and held the angry words inside.

A strong gust of cold wind ruffled Orol's hair again and caused the People to shiver. Everything was done except the ceremony. They could delay no longer so Mach and Thuro prayed the prayers and led the People in the singing of the songs of goodbye. Then each person touched Ryssa's hands once more before they turned and made their way through the crystal clear cold back to the cave.

Waiting until last, Horda hugged the young woman. She doubted Ryssa would survive the cold night. Taking a deep breath of the bitter air, she managed to say, "I understand what you are doing." Tears spilled from her eyes and ran down her cheeks, but she forced herself to continue. "I don't like it, but I believe I would do the same thing if I were in your place."

Ryssa swayed in Horda's embrace, but when she looked up at the taller woman, she was smiling. "Thank you, Horda. I needed your words. Go. I'll be all right. Orol is waiting for me." She gestured toward the desolate area the band had chosen as their Frozen Wilds. "He's waiting for us. Just beyond the shadows." Horda clung to her — the bereaved became the comforter. Finally Ryssa took a deep breath and spoke again. "Go. We will be fine."

With a sob, Horda turned and walked away.

Chapter 16

AFTER THE PEOPLE'S RETURN to the cave, life went on as life always does. The People sat down to their evening eats then shared stories in the dancing shadows of the assembly fire while they did their winter night work. No one spoke of Orol and Ryssa though they dominated Horda's thoughts, and she felt sure they hovered close to all the others as well. The People soon sought the warm furs of their winter beds.

Tucking Rain Drop into her bed, Horda leaned down to press her lips to the little girl's forehead. "Why?" asked Rain Drop.

"Why what?" asked Horda.

"Why did Ryssa stay in the Frozen Wilds? Father Death hadn't took her."

Horda rubbed her forehead seeking an answer for the little girl. "Ryssa loved Orol very much. She wanted to be with him."

Rain Drop frowned. "You love Mach very much."

"Yes, I do."

"If he goes to the Frozen Wilds, will you go with him?"

Mother Life, give me words. "Mach is strong and healthy. He is not likely to go to the Frozen Wilds for a long time."

"Orol was strong and healthy."

"Yes, he was." Horda closed her eyes. "But Father Death called him today."

"What if Father Death calls Mach? Would you go with him and leave me?"

Relief washed through Horda. She could deal with this little one's fears. "Not if you needed me."

Rain Drop smiled and threw her arms around Horda's neck. "Good, 'cause I don't want to go to the Frozen Wilds."

"You?"

"I'd go with you if you went with Mach. I wouldn't want to walk the earth without you."

Memories of the abuse and terror this little one suffered in her first three winters with the People of the Tall Grass flooded Horda. She gathered Rain Drop into her arms and hugged her tightly. She knew her tears dropped on the little girl's head, but she couldn't seem to stop them. Horda fought to keep her voice steady. "We'll just have to trust Mother Life will grant us a long time to walk the earth together."

Rain Drop reached up and brushed the tears off Horda's cheeks before she wrapped her arms around her neck and pulled her face down so she could share her breath. "I do trust her," the little girl said. "We will all walk together until I am old and bent like Unna."

"I hope so."

"And you and Mach will have many more little ones grown big and strong before we go."

"I hope so, Rain Drop."

"And Mach will be the chief of the entire band."

Horda nodded and laid Rain Drop back on her bed of furs.

"And —"

"And I want you to sleep now."

Rain Drop nodded and closed her eyes. Horda stood looking at the little girl for a short time. One eye popped open, and Rain Drop grinned impishly. "Horda?"

"Yes, Rain Drop."

"I'll always need you."

"Thank you, Rain Drop." Horda was surprised to find she meant her words.

⊛

"Horda? Horda, please wake up. Wilda needs you." Thuro's whisper rumbled outside the door covering of their sleeping area.

Horda fought off the blessed oblivion of sleep and slipped out of Mach's embrace. Mach muttered, "What's wrong? Do you need me?"

She smiled watching him fight to focus his eyes in the dim light of the night fire. "No, Mach. Go back to sleep. I don't need you." She stuck her head out of the sleeping area. "Yes, Thuro. What's wrong with her?"

"I don't know. She just cries and cries and says she's dying."

Horda fought to keep from rolling her eyes. "I'll be right there."

Not bothering with moccasins, she pulled on the ceremonial tunic she had worn with Orol and Ryssa to the Frozen Wilds. She entered Thuro and Wilda's sleeping area on

Thuro's heels. Her eyes widened before she could stop them. She'd never seen such chaos before — except in the camp of the People of the Tall Grass. More tunics and moccasins and leggings than she owned were scattered about, and the sleeping furs were matted and tossed haphazardly over the area.

Horda forced her eyes to Wilda who sat in a forlorn heap on the sleeping furs. "Wilda, what's wrong?"

Wilda's eyes flashed. "I'm sick. I'm probably dying, but you don't care."

"Tell me what hurts," said Horda in her best healer woman voice.

"Why? So you can tell me I'm breeding?" Wilda glared. "I am not breeding. I am sick."

"Tell me about your symptoms."

"My joints ache. The bones in my arms and legs feel like some one is pounding stakes into them and pulling the pieces apart." Wilda rubbed her right wrist and sniffed pitifully.

Frowning and making sympathetic noises in her throat, Horda examined the wrist but found no swelling or other visible damage. "What else?"

"My legs." Wilda sobbed. "When I stand up, it feels like a grizzly bear is pulling them apart — and it feels like someone built a fire in my lower belly."

"Lie down," said Horda ignoring the suspicion in Wilda's eyes. When Wilda did as she was told, Horda probed her slightly rounded lower abdomen and felt the reassuring pressure of the placenta cushioning the growing child. She almost allowed herself to smile at this affirmation of new life, but a look at Wilda's frightened, angry face stopped her. "What else?"

"What else?" squeaked Wilda. "What else? Every morning I throw up. It's terrible. I feel like my toenails want to come out my mouth."

Horda nodded remembering that same terrible feeling during her dark days as Bear Claw's captive.

"And ..." Wilda cast a glance at Thuro and motioned Horda closer so she could whisper in her ear. "I have to relieve myself more times each day and night than I can count on all my fingers — twice sometimes."

Horda could sympathize with Wilda's complaints.

Wilda leaned close so she could whisper once more. "The two moon cycles before this one were just a few spots, and this one has not appeared at all though it's almost time for another. I must be very sick."

Horda did smile then in spite of herself.

Wilda shrieked, "You're going to say I'm breeding. I tell you I'm not breeding. I refuse to be breeding. Thuro promised I didn't have to breed, and I'm not going to. You're wrong."

Wilda put her hands over her face and cried with huge tears dripping on her lap. "Go away," she squawked. "I knew that was what you'd say, but Thuro insisted on calling you. I told him you didn't know what you were talking about. You let your own mother die of the same disease I have before you even realized she was sick."

White-faced, Horda took a step back as though she had been struck by more than Wilda's words. Thuro reached out to comfort Horda against the false accusation, but before he touched her, Wilda threw herself into his arms. "You have to take me to Nuroo. He'll know what's wrong and he'll help me. He won't tell me I'm breeding."

Horda swallowed her hurt and said stiffly, "Perhaps it would be wise for you to see Nuroo."

Thuro frowned. "The blizzards? It's past time for them to start."

Horda shrugged. "A small party could move quickly to the Inner Band. There are places along the way you can shelter if a blizzard strikes. It's not good for Wilda to be so upset."

"See," said Wilda rubbing her tear-stained face against her mate's chest. "I told you she didn't know what was wrong with me. She admits it."

Horda stepped out of the sleeping area and sat beside the banked cook fire. She could hear Thuro soothing Wilda and settling her for sleep. Questions buzzed through Horda's mind like angry mosquitoes swarming in a strong breeze. Was she wrong? Was Wilda really ill? She didn't think so, but she didn't know for sure. Did she?

What if Wilda died — like Meiran? Was it Horda's fault her mother died? She really hadn't noticed Meiran was ill and losing weight until it was too late. Meiran hadn't wanted her to notice, but shouldn't she have noticed anyway? Nuroo said she shouldn't have. Treema and Zaaco said she shouldn't have. But was Wilda right? Should she have?

Horda closed her mind against the pain of the memories and forced herself to concentrate on Wilda's symptoms. She'd suffered all of them herself, and she'd tried to deny them much as Wilda was, but she'd known too much. She'd finally had to accept the fact she was breeding and unmated, a captive of the brutal Bear Claw. She clamped her teeth into her lower lip hoping real pain would stop the remembered pain of her lost little one.

Thuro's hand on her shoulder caused her to jump.

Flustered, she sat up and straightened her hair. "I'm sorry. I must have fallen asleep."

Thuro did not mention the tears still wet on her face. "I didn't mean to be so long."

"Don't worry about it."

"Does Wilda need to see Nuroo?" he asked.

"It would probably be for the best," said Horda. "She doesn't trust my judgment."

"I do," said Thuro. "What's wrong with her?"

Horda smiled. "She's breeding. She's going to have a little one in a little more than a hand of moons."

Thuro nodded. "She didn't mean what she said about Meiran. Everyone knows Meiran hid her illness."

"Yes, she did," said Horda without commenting on whether Wilda meant her cruel words or not.

Horda watched Thuro fight a battle with himself before he asked, "Are her symptoms anything like Meiran's?"

"No, Thuro, they're not." Taking a deep breath, she told him, "Unlike Wilda who is not bleeding, Meiran bled too much."

She watched relief erase the fear in his eyes. "I didn't think they were. I'm sorry, Horda, but I had to ask."

She nodded. "I've seen her symptoms before." He looked at her and waited for her to continue. "I experienced them, and I can sympathize with her because I tried to deny them myself."

"I know, Horda."

Once more Horda was the lonely, frightened captive waiting to see whether she would be beaten to death by the brutal Bear Claw or taste the Wrath of Fire for her unsanctified mating. She clutched her knees and closed her eyes waiting for the waves of pain and grief to subside. "I'm sorry, Thuro. Sometimes it all comes back, and I have to fight to keep from screaming."

"Horda, you don't need to apologize to me. I was there. I saw some of what happened to you." He paused and rubbed his face. "I'm just sorry to bring it all back, but I didn't know what else to do. Wilda's sure she is dying. She won't even consider the possibility that she's breeding. She's never going to forgive me."

The misery in his voice pulled Horda back to the present. She became the competent healer woman once more. She reached out and touched his hand. "Did you force her?"

"Of course not."

"Then there's nothing for her to forgive you for."

"She's not going to see it that way." Bitterness laced Thuro's laughter. He looked into Horda's eyes. "All of you tried to warn me without words, but I ignored you. I love her. I know she's difficult and spoiled, but she's little and sweet and she needs me. I don't always like her, but I love her very much."

"I know you do."

He shrugged. "What am I going to do?"

"Thuro, I think you should take her to the Inner Band and let Nuroo examine her. I'm almost positive he's going to tell her the same thing I've told you, but there's a slight chance I'm overlooking something."

He nodded. "That's probably a good idea."

"Since the storm yesterday, it should be clear for a few days."

"Probably."

"I'd like to see my father, but it's probably better if Mach and I don't go."

"Probably."

"Maybe one of the other couples will accompany you."

"Maybe." He frowned. "Horda, what are we going to do if she doesn't believe Nuroo?"

She smiled. "Endure the next moons and deliver her little one when the time comes."

She slipped away to her sleeping furs for the short time that remained before the morning eat.

Chapter 17

SHORTLY AFTER THE SUN pushed its light into the cave opening, Thuro called for an assembly of the band. Mach frowned at his bowl of porridge. "What's going on?"

"I'm not sure," said Horda.

"Did I dream it or did Thuro call you last night?"

She yawned. "You didn't dream it."

Mach waited. When she didn't continue, he said, "Well, what did he want?"

"Me to check Wilda who is certain she is dying of some dread disease like my mother."

Mach shook his head. "I'll never understand why he mated with that woman. She is nothing but tr—"

"Because he loves her."

Mach snorted. "What makes you say that?"

"He told me so," said Horda.

Mach closed his mouth and studied the bottom of his eating dish.

Once again all the members of the band except Wilda assembled. Thuro stood and cleared his throat. "Thank you for coming," he said. "Most of you know my mate Wilda is ill."

A small sigh almost like laughter made its way through the People, but Thuro's sad look quieted it. He continued, "Horda says and I believe Wilda is breeding. But Wilda believes she is dying of some dread disease. She wants Nuroo to examine her. Since there is a small chance my mate might be ill, I am taking her to the Inner Band to be examined by the Medicine Man."

"Horda agrees this is the best action to be taken right now." Horda nodded. "I expect to be gone two hands plus two turnings of the sun, but the weather might delay us. I would appreciate it if one or two of you warriors would accompany us."

Mach jumped to his feet. "I will—"

"No, Mach," Thuro said, "we can't both leave the band at the same time."

Mach frowned and sat down. Trefo spoke softly to Lija and Jozsa before he rose. "I will accompany you. Would you like one or both my mates to come with us?"

"Thank you, Trefo," said Thuro. He seemed to be considering Trefo's question before he answered. "I think one of your mates would provide company for my mate on the trek."

After another whispered conference, Jozsa stood. "I will accompany you, Thuro."

Dyson stood. "I will accompany you, but my mate does not wish to make the trek."

Thuro smiled at Marmah whose dislike of trekking

was well-known in the band. "That's all right, Marmah. I appreciate your indulgence in allowing Dyson to join us."

Marmah smiled back at Thuro. "I don't care if the rest of you trek around all winter," she said. "Just don't expect me to go; I have done more than enough trekking for three lifetimes. I am perfectly content to stay in this camp for the rest of my life. I'll stay here instead of going to the summer camps too if it's okay with you."

Laughter rippled through the assembly. All the women who had been held captive shared Marmah's feelings though none of the others were quite so vocal as she.

Thuro nodded. "Then it is decided. I've checked the weather. Yesterday's storm seems to have cleared it for a while. I'd like to begin the trek today. If you could be ready by the time the sun shines fully into the cave opening, I would appreciate it."

The volunteers nodded and hurried off to pack. The other People remained carrying on quiet conversations.

Mach clapped Thuro on the back. "Congratulations."

"What for?"

"You just conducted your first assembly without help from anyone."

Thuro flushed a dark red. "It didn't seem right to ask for your help since Wilda is my problem."

Mach held up his hands. "Hold it. I didn't mean to embarrass you."

"You didn't," snapped Thuro.

"I really was impressed."

"Don't be."

"You did a good job."

Thuro whirled and glared at his friend. "Are you through

making jest of me?"

"Thuro, I am not making jest of you." Mach glared back. "You always said you couldn't talk before a crowd. I never doubted you could, if you could just overcome your nervousness. I'm sorry Wilda is sick, but I'm glad the circumstances showed you not only can you talk in front of an assembly, but you can work them to do what you want."

Thuro refused to acknowledge the compliment. "Wilda is not sick. She's breeding and refuses to accept it."

"Horda said she might be sick."

"*Might be* are the important words here," said Thuro.

Mach opened his mouth to protest but closed it without speaking when he saw the expression on Thuro's face. "I'm sorry I can't go with you."

"You offered. I refused. It's one of the drawbacks to being leaders. We can't both leave the band if we can help it."

"I know," said Mach. "Sometimes I wish I wasn't leader. It was easier being a follower."

"You have that right," agreed Thuro, "though I don't think you've ever been a follower in your life, Mach."

"I was too."

Thuro shook his head. "Your body followed, but your head and heart always led. You were born for this. I, I still feel like an imposter. A little boy playing at being leader."

"Thuro, that's not so. You're a thinker. You plan things well. Until today, you wouldn't share your plans with the group unless someone forced you to. You planned and told me. I stood up and told your plans with a few additions and changes of my own and sounded knowledgeable and smart because I listened to you."

"Right," said Thuro.

"You know I'm telling the truth," said Mach.

"If I'm so smart, why's my life such a mess right now?"

Mach shrugged. "For the same reason, my life was such a mess a while back." He shot a half grin at Thuro.

In spite of himself, Thuro grinned back. "We do better when we think with our heads," he muttered.

"I imagine men have been saying that forever."

"They'll probably keep saying it too."

"Probably," agreed Mach. "Seriously, Horda does think Wilda should see Nuroo."

"I know she does, but Wilda said some awful things to her. Now, I'm afraid Horda's doubting herself."

"I don't think so," said Mach. "She just wants Nuroo to reinforce what she's said."

Thuro looked at the sunlight streaming through the cave opening. "Well, I guess I'd better get Wilda. It's almost time to go."

"I meant what I said about your conducting the meeting."

"I know you did."

"I feel like I should go with you."

"We've discussed that. You can't."

"You went with me."

Thuro grinned. "That was different. We were still children then. I could go without leaving a band leaderless."

"We're still children."

"Seems like. Doesn't it?"

Mach clasped his friend's arm. "Be careful. I need you back."

"We will be."

Thuro and his group had been gone since late morning. The sun's evening rays smeared the shadows of the landscape. The People put away their day's work and finished their evening eat. As night settled, they gathered around the assembly fire telling stories of long ago. Bran came to stand beside Horda.

Mach said, "Zeek, tell us a story."

Zeek's voice rumbled deep in his chest. "Oh, do you want to hear about when I walked with First Man and First Woman?"

"Ah, I knew you were old though I didn't realize you were quite that old." Mach laughed. "But I would be glad to hear any firsthand stories."

Bran caught Horda's hand and held it against his face. She laughed. "You don't have a fever anymore, Bran. You look like you're about well."

He frowned at her without speaking and turned toward his father in the center of the group.

"Now, I didn't really see this with my own eyes." Zeek included all the People. "So it's not really a firsthand story, but when I was just a boy with no more than a hand of winters, the old chief, who has walked the Frozen Wilds for hands hands of winters, shared this story at one Gathering."

A gentle murmur made its way around the People. Zeek was the oldest in their band. They knew it, but to be so reminded of it produced feelings of awe and respect. Mach opened his mouth to apologize for his thoughtless remark, but Zeek waved his words away.

"Mother Life made all the animals for First Man and First Woman to hunt. Some like rabbits were small and ran fast, but they were willing to give themselves that People might eat. Some like the buffalo were big and mean, and the People had to hunt carefully so they wouldn't be injured.

"But one animal was particularly vicious. Huge. He was bigger and meaner than the bison and the bears. He was bigger than any of the other animals." He raised his arms and made his voice big. "He was … he was a squirrel."

The firelight made his shadow loom over the People. Bran hid his face in Horda's skirt. She patted his back.

Zeek continued, "This animal had a huge voice, and he scolded and chattered at the People 'Chuk chukka churr! Chit churra chee!" Bran raised his face but did not laugh at his father's words. "And this animal particularly did not like the First People. He refused to give his life for them. He actually told Mother Life he didn't care if the entire Band of First People starved to death."

"Nooooo." The People were appalled by this animal's cruelty.

"Now this made Mother Life a little angry because she had told the animals their purpose on the earth was to provide food, clothes, and shelter for her People. And this animal was the biggest. He could have been the most help to the People, but he was selfish and self-centered. He refused to help them. He ran in circles around them and scolded and made fun of their efforts.

"This was the first long cold season when the first Moon of the Long Blizzards walked the land. First People were starving. They went to Mother Life and said, 'We're hungry. It's cold, and we need food. We need shelter, but we are having trouble. We don't know what to do. You must help us. We're hungry, but we aren't very good hunters so please help us until we learn. Please, Mother Life, our vessels of time are filling rapidly. Soon we will all walk the Frozen Wilds with Father Death.'" Zeek's voice sounded pitiful.

"Mother Life felt sorry for her People, and she was angry at the squirrel. This was a volatile combination. She waved her arms." Zeek waved his arms, and his huge shadow danced and hovered over the assembled People. Even though this was a serious part of the story, Bran giggled at his father's antics. That little giggle frightened Horda more than anything else that had happened during the child's long illness.

"So do you know what Mother Life did then?" asked Zeek.

Everyone except Bran gave the appropriate answer though all but the smallest children had heard the story hands of times. "No, what?" they all called.

"She called all the squirrels in her land to come to her shelter. Some of the squirrels came — not because they honored the Mother — but because they wanted to make fun of her. They were bigger and meaner and louder than she, and they didn't believe she could make them do her will." Zeek grinned. "Those squirrels stood around laughing and making fun of the First People because they were cold and sad and weak because they were not successful hunters — yet."

The People all looked at each other and asked the children what they thought the Mother would do. Eyes were round, and even the ones who knew the answers looked worried and wondering. Zeek drew himself up to his tallest height and looked down his nose at the People around him. Then he said in his most regal voice, "I am ashamed of you!" Everyone jumped back in fear even Bran who must have sensed the power behind his father's words.

"They pretended to ignore her because they told themselves she couldn't make them do anything they didn't want to do. She looked at them for a long time in the way of disappointed mothers." The silence grew loud as the People thought about Zeek's words.

"Finally the squirrels began to wonder if they were wrong, if there was something the Mother could do to make them do her will. But they wondered too late, and soon they found out Mother Life can force us to do her will. She leaned back and waved her arms causing a flash … Suddenly the huge, mean, menacing squirrels were little, tiny, cute animals no longer able to defeat any of the other animals. Left only with their mean dispositions and their scolding voices, they were destined to an eternal hunt for food so they wouldn't starve as they intended First Man to starve." Zeek folded his arms and bowed his head. "We must always remember this lesson so we do not anger Mother Life and Father Death as we fill our vessels of time."

Zeek nodded his thanks for their appreciation of his words and sat down. Storytelling was over for the night. The People would spend the rest of the time working and talking among themselves until the fire burned down and it was time for sleep.

Bran watched Horda work beads onto a pair of moccasins. "Are you ready for your bison hunt with Mach?" she asked.

The little boy stared at her. She tried again. "Why don't you tell Mach you're ready to hunt with him?"

He frowned and touched her lips but still remained

silent.

Cold fingers of fear traced her spine, but she pushed them away with rationalizations. Bran wasn't really well yet. He was just tired. He'd talk when he felt like it. It was really too soon. He was sick for almost a moon — it would take at least that long for him to regain his strength and be his old self. She pushed the thoughts away and enjoyed the feel of the warm sturdy little body leaning against her.

The fire burned down. It was time to sleep. Reeme called, "Bran, come here."

Bran continued staring at the dancing flames and didn't respond. Horda touched his shoulder. He looked at her, and she pointed to his mother beckoning from their shelter area. He smiled at Horda and ran to his mother. The cold fingers found her heart and twisted, but still she refused to acknowledge her fears.

The sun was rising for the third time since Thuro and the others left when, with her hands full of wood, Horda looked around the shelter and frowned. "The only thing we haven't planned well is storage for our fuel," she muttered.

Mach looked up from his porridge. "What?"

"We have enough fuel for a hand's turnings of the sun, but what if there's a really bad storm? We'll freeze because we can't get down to collect wood. We haven't even stacked it beside the cave opening like we usually do."

Mach looked around the shelter. "I guess with everything else going on we all forgot."

She sighed. "I guess we did."

"We'd better get together and bring in fuel now. The storms aren't likely to wait much longer." He scraped the last bit of porridge from his eating dish and stood. "I'll call the People."

Soon everyone was assembled. "We have a challenge," said Mach.

Horda shook her head. *Challenge? Ha!* This certainly seemed like a problem to her.

"My mate realized when she was preparing our morning eat we have overlooked the collection of winter fuel."

Dismayed gasps met his words.

He grinned. "We have to get busy. First, we must decide on the safest storage place. Then we have to gather the supply." He looked to the cave opening where the thin winter sunlight peeked in. "Fortunately, she noticed on a sunny day."

Zeek said, "There is the area at the back of the shelter where we stored the wood we gathered. We didn't fill it before, and it's nearly empty now. It's far enough away from all the cook fires that it isn't dangerous."

Mach nodded. "That will be good for the short term, and we can also stack wood on each side of the shelter opening, but we need to find a place close to the cave to store the rest."

Lucza, Zhrul's second mate, said, "There's a nice wide space near the last curve before we enter the cave, and it's already clear."

Urscia, Zhrul's first mate, sniffed. "Lucza, that space is cleared because we use it for the necessaries."

Lucza huffed. "Fuel is certainly necessary."

Unseen by the assembled, Horda rolled her eyes at her mate and smiled. He grimaced, but interrupted. "One suggestion has been to use the space beside the last curve for wood storage instead of necessaries. Now, I believe that area is protected enough the snow won't drift in it too badly. I also agree this large area would be good for wood storage."

Lucza raised her eyebrows and smiled at Urscia.

"But if we use this area for the wood, we'll have to find another convenient area for the necessaries."

"Humph!" snorted Urscia with a pointed look at Lucza.

Reeme raised her hand. "Mach."

"Yes, Reeme."

"Right now, there aren't that many of us using the necessaries."

Horda swallowed her laughter watching Mach fight to keep his face impassive at this seemingly useless comment.

"So ..." coaxed Mach.

"Well," said Reeme with an embarrassed titter, "the other day one of the little ones was in a rush, and I was too. We found another area. It's smaller, but it's nearer the cave."

Horda watched Lucza grin triumphantly at Urscia. There was going to be trouble between them. *Mother Life, I don't want to be the leader.*

Mach waited for Reeme to continue, but she didn't. Zeek finally poked her in the ribs. "Go on, woman," he muttered.

"Oh, you want me to tell you more about it?"

"Yes, Reeme, that —" Horda's raised eyebrows moderated Mach's sarcastic tone. "— would be very helpful. Perhaps you'd like to show us so we can judge the suitability of the area for ourselves." Horda smiled at him, and he looked at the ceiling in feigned innocence.

"I could do that," said Reeme without moving.

Zeek shook his head. "For the Mother's sake, Reeme. Let's go."

"Oh, you mean now?"

"Yes, now, please," said Mach in a artificially pleasant tone.

Horda stood. "We'd better get our winter furs. It's still cold out. Hurry, everyone.".

"That woman," Mach muttered to Horda. "This is probably a wild bison stampede to nowhere."

"Be nice," chided Horda.

"Nice?" he hissed. "Nice? I was nice. I didn't shake her until her teeth rattled trying to get the words out of her."

"No, you didn't." Horda smiled at him. "And I'm very proud of you."

"The area is probably totally unsuitable. I doubt she would know —"

"Now, now ..." Horda looked meaningfully at Rain Drop and Storm Cloud, who already had their leggings on and were struggling into their parkas.

Mach subsided with a grimace and went into the sleeping area for his own parka and leggings.

Horda shook her head at the knotted thongs of the children's leggings and said, "Let me help you."

"Don't need help." Rain Drop declared tying the thongs of Storm Cloud's parka in a knot.

Horda caught the little girl's hands before she pulled it tight. "It's much easier to get off if you tie it this way." Horda quickly tied the thongs in a double bow.

"Can't," said Rain Drop working on her own thongs. "Mine won't stay that way."

"Then let me help you until you learn to make them stay."

Horda pushed her hands away. Rain Drop glared but didn't offer any more resistance. Horda tweaked her nose. "I want you to stay close to me while we're outside today."

"Why?" asked Storm Cloud.

"It's time for the blizzards, and I don't want to lose you."

"Oh."

Horda laughed and touched each child's mouth with her own. "There's nothing to worry about. I just don't want to have to look for you if there's a storm. Okay?"

"Okay."

Mach came out of the sleeping area dressed for the outdoors and carrying Horda's winter wear. Dropping her clothes beside her, he frowned. "Please, hurry up. The others are going to be waiting." He headed for the shelter opening with the two little ones on his heels.

She shook her head and hurried.

When she joined the others, Mach looked around. "Is anyone missing?" When no one protested, he turned to Reeme. "Now, show us the way."

She smiled vacantly but led the People out of the shelter. Just beyond the opening, she made a quick right turn. Horda was tempted to join the grumbling. Anyone could see the mountain dropped off sharply just a short distance away. Reeme turned to Mach who smiled encouragingly. Horda was proud of him. She knew he was frustrated, but she didn't think the nervous Reeme could tell.

The grumbling quickly turned to appreciative comments. The path opened into a small clearing just before the cliff. "This is perfect," said Mach with a genuine smile. "Even better than the other area because we have the cliff. It's a good place to empty the night jars and everything. And it's big enough to make a separate area for the men and women."

Zeek hugged the blushing Reeme while everyone except Urscia congratulated her.

Mach looked at Zhrul. "Do you think it would be easier to bring the screens from the other area up here or should we just build a new ones?"

"Build new ones," Zhrul answered. "The path's too narrow to bring the others without tearing them apart. Then it would be hard to get them back strong enough to withstand the wind."

Mach nodded. "Take a hand of People and build the new screens. The rest of us are going to gather fuel." He looked at the sky. "I don't think a storm's coming, Zeek. Do you?"

Zeek sniffed the air and grinned. "Nope."

"Good." Then Mach raised his voice. "Men, get your axes. Let's range out a goodly distance and chop deadwood. The women and children can carry it back."

Laughter and talk filled the air even though the work was long and difficult.

Chapter 18

THAT NIGHT MACH, STILL chilled from bathing in the river, wondered why he hadn't accepted the offer of warm water for his bath. Horda had heated water for herself and the two little ones to wash inside in the sleeping shelter. Now he sat on an antelope skin beside the cook fire drying his hair and watching Horda.

Though she had tied her hair back to keep it out of the cook fire, it hung down her back in a mass of dark honey-colored waves and curls. Mach watched the firelight flash in his mate's hair. "The storage area of the cave is full of wood, and we should have the clearing filled by sunset tomorrow," he said.

"Will that be enough?" Horda stirred the stew for the evening eat.

Mach stared at her. "Horda, every person in this band — except Zakon — has cut or carried wood all day today. We'll do the same tomorrow. We're going to have enough wood to last at least a moon, maybe longer."

She sighed. "Good. That means we don't have to cut or carry for half a moon. So —"

He raised his eyebrows. "Why do I know you're planning another job for me?"

She grinned. "Because you're smart."

"Or stupid," he muttered. "So what do you have in mind?"

"A bath pit?"

He groaned. "That will be harder than cutting wood."

"But think how nice it will be to have our own bath pit. It's getting too cold to bathe in the river."

"Then bathe in a water basket."

She poked him in the shoulder. "You said it yourself. They aren't big enough."

He laughed. "Not for you and me maybe, but they're plenty big for the little ones."

She massaged his shoulders, and he sighed. "Think how nice it would be to soak your tired body in hot water," she murmured. He groaned again when she kneaded an especially sore muscle. She leaned down to blow gently in his left ear. "Think how much you like to have me wash your back," she whispered.

Twisting he caught her in his arms and pulled her down on his lap. "All right, Horda. We'll work on the bath pit next." He gently tugged the masses of her hair over her shoulder and buried his face in the shiny waves. He planted tiny kisses along her jaw bone. "How come your hair always smells like flowers?"

"How come your hair always smells like sage and cedar?" she countered.

"Because I rub my scalp …" She giggled when he paused and glared at her. "There aren't any flowers to rub on your scalp during this season."

"My mother taught me to dry blossoms to use during the seasons when no flowers bloom."

"Umm, smart mother." He traced her mouth with his tongue. "Isn't it time to sleep yet?"

"Nope, we haven't had the evening eat."

"I'm not hungry — for food."

"Rain Drop and Storm Cloud will be," she reminded him.

"Forget them. Run away with me." He drank her breath until she felt she was melting in a puddle at his feet.

"Okay, you win. Where are we going?"

"What you doing?" asked Storm Cloud joining them beside the fire and eying Mach and Horda.

"I'm fixing Horda's hair," muttered Mach setting Horda up and straightening the wavy hair hanging down her back.

"No, you weren't," said Rain Drop. "You were stealing her breath." She scowled at her beloved Mach. "Why were you doing that?"

"I wasn't stealing her breath. I was sharing it," said Mach defensively.

"Sharing it?" Storm Cloud looked him in the eye. "Why?"

Mach's eyes widened. "Why?"

Both Storm Cloud and Rain Drop nodded. "Why?"

Horda stood to tend the cooking bag in an effort to hide her smile. Mach pretended to glare at her. "That's right. Run out on me."

"I have no idea what story you're telling the children so I can't possibly help you."

"Mach's not telling us a story," said Rain Drop. "He's 'splaining."

"Oh, yes," said Horda with another grin.

"Why were you sharing Horda's breath?" repeated Storm Cloud.

"Because ... because ... because Horda was tired and didn't have enough breath of her own so I gave her some of mine."

Rain Drop ran over and took Horda's hand. "Are you real awful tired, Horda?"

"Well, I am tired."

Mach's glare relaxed into a smile.

"Horda says she's not real awful tired, Mach. Tell us why you really were sharing her breath," said Storm Cloud.

"Because I was dumb enough to think I could talk to my own mate beside my own cook fire without having to answer so many questions about what I was doing."

"You weren't talking," said Storm Cloud. "You were sharing her breath."

"We don't share breath like that," said Rain Drop sticking out her tongue and rubbing her lips. "I want to try it." She reached for Storm Cloud.

Mach picked her up and sat her on his knee. "Horda, you'd better help me," he said.

Horda sat on the antelope hide with Mach and Rain Drop and invited Storm Cloud to sit on her lap. "I'm not sure what all the fuss is about, little ones," she said. "You've seen Mach and me share breath before."

Storm Cloud shook his head. "Not like that, we haven't. And you said you were going to run away. Are you going to leave us?"

"I only wis—" Horda's elbow in Mach's ribs stopped the rest of his reply.

"No, we're not going anywhere. Mach was teasing me."

"Teasing?" echoed Storm Cloud doubtfully.

"Yes, teasing. If we ran away, we'd be all alone."

"And you wouldn't like that. Would you?" asked Rain Drop.

Mach's eyes said he would like that very much, but his mouth said, "No, we wouldn't like that at all. We'd miss you." Then he smiled and hugged the little girl. "We'd miss you very much."

"Good," said Storm Cloud. "We'd miss you too."

"Well, I'm glad that's settled," said Mach. "Do you think we can eat now."

Rain Drop shook her head. "Why not?" asked Horda.

"Because you haven't 'splained about sharing breath." She ran her tongue around her mouth once more.

Horda said, "When you are older and all —"

"How much older?" asked Storm Cloud.

"Three hands plus three fingers of winters," said Mach promptly.

"That's when I'll complete my Great Travel," announced Storm Cloud.

Rain Drop, not willing to be outdone, said, "I'll be a woman of the Frozen Earth then."

"Are you going to listen to me?" asked Horda.

Both children nodded.

"When you are grown up, you will meet someone and fall in love. Then you will mate with them." Horda paused and looked at the children.

"Like you and Mach," said Rain Drop.

"And like Thuro and Wilda," added Storm Cloud.

Horda forced herself not to comment and nodded before

she continued, “When you love someone very much, you want to be as close to them as you can. Sharing breath like we were is a way of being very close.”

Rain Drop turned in Mach’s lap and eyed his mouth thoughtfully. “I love you very much,” she said.

He replied, “I love you too, Little One.”

She traced her lips with her tongue. “Will you share my breath like that?”

Watching Mach’s eyes widen, Horda fought to keep from smiling. “No, that’s for your mate and you.” He pressed his closed lips to her forehead, the tip of her nose, and the corner of her mouth. “This way is for us to share.”

“Okay,” said Rain Drop pressing her lips against his cheek. “I like this way too.”

Storm Cloud frowned at Mach. “Do *you* like that other way?”

Mach nodded. “Very much.”

“Will I like it?”

“Someday with the right woman.” Mach smiled at Horda. “I’m sure you will like it as much as I do.”

Storm Cloud looked doubtful but then his face brightened. “I’m hungry. Can we have our evening eat now?”

Mach breathed a sigh of relief. “I certainly hope so.”

The next evening, shadows lengthened, but they still bore the hard edges of day when Horda handed Mach a water bag. “The clearing is almost full of wood,” she said.

Mach poured water over his sweating face. “Good, this is hard work.”

She laughed. “Carrying wood up here from the river bank isn’t exactly the easiest thing I’ve ever done.”

He hugged her. She struggled. “You’re all wet.”

His rich laughter rumbled across the little clearing. “This wood will warm us twice.” He crushed her against his chest. “Today and again when we burn it.”

“Well, if you put it that way, I’d better get the full benefit.” She hugged him and stood on tiptoes to share his breath.

“Maybe three times if we can find a nice secluded spot.” He raised his head and looked around. “Where are Rain Drop and Storm Cloud?”

She grinned. “Helping Lena carry wood.” Hand in hand they slipped away into the shadows.

Mach shed his breechclout and removed Horda’s tunic. He stood and admired her body in the smudgy shadows of the afternoon sun. “You’re beautiful,” he whispered.

She smiled and looked at him. “You are too.” She traced the outlines of his muscles with one finger. He shuddered and lowered her to a bed of pine needles. His tongue traced the line of her jaw.

Zeek called, “Mach, where are you?”

Horda bit her lips to keep from screaming in frustration or laughing at Mach’s thunderous expression. He muttered a curse under his breath and put his hand over her mouth to silence her.

“Mach?” Horda heard Zeek in the clearing. “His axes are here. He can’t be lost too.”

At the word lost, Horda saw fear flame in Mach’s eyes. They stood up and dressed in a hurry. Holding hands, they walked back to the clearing. “Who’s lost, Zeek?” he asked in an almost-normal voice.

Looking at their joined hands and the leaves in their hair, Zeek said, "I'm … ah … sorry … to … ah … bother you."

Horda felt her cheeks turning red, but Mach seemed unaffected. "Who's lost?" he repeated, this time in a normal voice.

"My son," said Zeek. "Bran is lost."

"No," cried Horda, embarrassment forgotten. "He can't be lost."

Zeek nodded. "Reeme says she left him in the clearing with me, but I didn't know it. Now we can't find him."

Mach threw back his head and gave the sharp, staccato calls that would bring his People on the run.

"When did you see him last?" asked Horda.

Zeek shook his head. "I don't remember seeing him since the sun was directly overhead."

Horda looked at the long shadows and shivered. So many things could have happened to Bran since then.

Mach counted the People with his eyes. Everyone was in the clearing except Bran. He took a deep breath. "Bran is lost."

"Oh, is that all?" Urscia took her children by the hands. "I thought something was really wrong."

Reeme shrieked and grabbed for Urscia who by then was out of her reach. Zeek caught Reeme and held her until she quit struggling. "Shh, shh," he said. "You don't want to hurt the children."

Reeme opened her mouth.

"Words cannot be unsaid," cautioned her mate. "Do you really want to make this worse?" She snapped her mouth shut. Her face was flushed before she finally shook her head. Then he released her. "We will find Bran, and everything will be all right."

Reeme dashed the tears from her face as she took a deep breath. "Will it?" she asked. "Will anything ever be all right for my little one again?"

Horda knew her own anger had painted her face a fiery red. Her fingers curled into claws, and she wished she could throttle the cruel Urscia.

Mach's hand on Horda's arm stopped her furious words. "Fighting with her won't find Bran," he said out of the side of his mouth. She nodded and forced her hands to relax.

Mach pointed to Aiyana. "Aiyana, I want you to choose four more women to help you take the rest of the children back to the shelter. You all can feed and care for them there because we don't want to lose any more in the coming darkness."

Aiyana nodded and moved to do his bidding. As she started up the path to the shelter, he called again.

"Yes." She turned back.

"Please prepare some small torches. We may need them. Someone will come for them soon." She nodded and followed the others.

Mach asked Reeme, "Can you show us exactly where you saw Bran last?" She nodded. "Good," he said. "Then we spread out in one long line with the place Bran was last seen in the middle and search in a circle. He's probably just fallen asleep, and our calling will wake him up."

Horda's conscience twisted in her chest. *I don't know anything for sure. He probably was just tired. It will take time for him to get back to where he was before he got sick. I don't know that he can't hear.*

Zeek said, "Ah, Mach."

"Yes, Zeek."

"Yes, Zeek."

"We're — ah — going to have to stay close enough together to see each other."

Mach frowned. "Why?"

Horda watched Zeek's Adam's apple bob as he swallowed, and she saw a tear in his eye glisten in the late afternoon sun. She watched the old warrior fight for composure and knew he wouldn't be able to say the words.

She took a deep breath. "Because Bran can't hear us," she whispered. She watched the tear trace a lonely path through the shadows on Zeek's face.

"What did you say?" asked Mach.

She swallowed her own tears. "I said Bran can't hear us. The fever demons stole his hearing."

"How do you know this?"

"I suspected when his fever broke. I didn't admit it until now though I think I realized the night Thuro and the others left. Bran sat with me during the storytelling, and he didn't say a word, but he kept touching my lips when I talked to him. When Reeme called him to sleep, he didn't respond until I touched his shoulder and turned him toward her. Then he acted like the Bran we used to know."

"I was so afraid of that," Reeme cried. "Urscia is right. He will never be of use to this band. Oh, my little one. Mother Life, why did you spare him for this?" Covering her face, she keened and sobbed hysterically.

Zeek caught her once more and held her against his chest. Then he scolded, "Shh, shh, don't say such things. The Mother didn't spare him to let him be worthless. Our boy will be fine. I'm sure of it."

Mach caught Horda's hand and warned her to silence

with a dark look. Then he drew himself up to his fullest formidable height and spoke to the entire band. “You are entitled to your opinions. You may help us search or not. Most of you do not know the little boy well. I do. I knew him before his illness. He was bright, inquisitive, and very smart for his age. I know him now. The Mother spared him for a purpose. I’ll search for him if I have to search alone.”

Horda stood beside him. “I’ll help you.”

One by one the others joined him until Urscia stood alone. She scowled and joined the rest.

Mach said, “Now, Reeme, if you’ll show us where to begin our search before we have to prepare torches, we’ll spread out four arm spans and begin.”

The shadows of night had almost claimed the land, but the line had completed half the circle when Aiyana brought an armload of torches. “The other women are watching the children. I thought I could help you.” She struck a fire and lit each torch before handing it down the line to the searchers.

Taking a torch, Horda wondered what they would do when they completed the circle, but then she heard Urscia’s call followed by Bran’s frightened cries. She and everyone else ran toward the cries. She thought she saw the woman slap the little boy’s face. She heard her angry voice, but she couldn’t make out the words over Bran’s screams.

Zeek reached them before Horda did and snatched his son from Urscia’s arms. The little boy screamed and flailed and fought his father.

“Turn him so he can see it’s you,” said Horda, “then hold him against your chest and talk to him.”

“What?” asked Zeek trying to calm the hysterical child.

"Hold his arms and tuck him against your chest. Like this." Horda took the screaming child, wrapped her arms around him, and cuddled him against her chest while she crooned to him. His cries lessened, and his terror faded.

"Why talk to him if he can't hear me?"

She smiled down at Bran. "He can feel your words in your chest and be comforted."

Zeek took his son and held him against his broad chest making soft wordless sounds of comfort. Bran snuggled against his father and hiccupped, sniffled, then smiled and touched his father's mouth. "Fa," he croaked in a strange, hollow little voice.

Horda didn't have time to rejoice over Bran's word before Urscia's strident voice intervened. "That child was curled up asleep." She spat in the dirt at her feet. "He is of no value to this bamd."

Zhrul stalked to his mate's side. "Be careful what you say."

She slitted her eyes and glowered. "Here we were endangering ourselves searching for him, and he was sleeping."

"That's what I was hoping he would do," said Mach.

"Sleep?" screeched Urscia. She turned to Zhrul. "Did you hear him? He said he hoped he would sleep. Is he crazy?"

"No," said Zhrul. "I don't think so."

"Then what was he thinking?" she snarled.

"He was thinking," said Zhrul, "that if the child fell asleep, he would stay in one place so we could find him."

Urscia opened and closed her mouth a few times like a fish fighting for life, then she turned on her heel and stalked up the path to the shelter.

Zhrul watched her go before he turned to Zeek. "I'm glad Bran is all right." He hurried up the path after his mate.

The rest of the People followed more slowly until only Mach, Horda, and Zeek remained in the clearing with Bran.

Horda waited until she could contain herself no longer. "Zeek, did you see that woman hit Bran?"

Zeek looked startled then shook his head. "No, I don't think so. It was nearly dark when I heard him crying. I didn't really see anything until I took him in my arms."

"She hit him. I saw her. That's why he was crying."

"Are you sure, Horda?" asked Mach. "He could have been crying because it was dark, and he was scared. Are you sure you saw her hit him?"

Horda scrunched up her forehead and closed her eyes. "I'm not sure."

"You must be very sure before you accuse her of such a thing," Mach said. "It isn't enough that she is selfish and rude."

Horda chewed her lips and frowned. Then she shook her head. "I can't say for sure that she hit him."

"Then you mustn't say any more about it," he cautioned.

She nodded. Looking troubled Zeek reached out and touched her arm then Mach's. "Thank you once more for giving me back my son, but ..." His voice trailed to silence.

"But what?" asked Mach.

"But is Urscia correct? What will become of him? What are we going to do? He can't hear. He doesn't talk anymore. How will he survive?"

Looking sadly at the bright-eyed little boy in his father's

arms, Mach said, “I don’t know.”

Horda spat one of the oaths Bear Claw taught her and stamped her foot before she took Bran into her arms. Mach and Zeek jumped like she had poked them with a hot stick. “Bran is deaf. He’s not stupid. He knew how to talk when he got sick. We have to help him remember how to talk. Then we’ll teach him just like we teach the other little ones.”

“But he still won’t be able to hear our words,” said Mach with exaggerated patience.

She looked daggers at the two men. “He’s smart and we’re smart. We’ll teach him to hear without using his ears.” She smiled at Mach. “You said yourself the Mother spared him for a purpose. She’ll help us.” Horda rubbed her chin on the child’s head.

Zeek looked at Mach and smiled. “She’s an unusual woman.”

“I know,” said Mach. “And so is her colorful vocabulary.”

Zeek laughed out loud. “Sometimes we need that colorful vocabulary to get us back on the right path.”

Mach nodded his agreement.

Blushing, Horda started up the path with Bran in her arms. The men followed close behind.

Chapter 19

THE BAND HAD WORKED together and prepared all the foodstuffs they could find. With them and the supplies they had brought from their other bands, the food caches were nearly full; they had hides and furs to work into clothing and shelters during the Moons of the Long Blizzards. They were ready for the storms to begin, but the days remained mild and sunny. The snows were late.

Horda, Mach, and Zeek used the relatively free time to work with Bran. They had decided all of his waking time would be spent with one of them. Though Bran called each of them by name, he made no other efforts to speak.

Every morning one of them would set the little boy where he could watch as they went about their daily chores. Constantly they talked using simple one or two word phrases to tell him what they were doing. They repeated the same words over and over until some of the other members of the band avoided them whenever possible.

Bran watched their mouths as they worked. Sometimes, if they were close enough, he touched their lips and frowned. Other times he would move his mouth almost like he was repeating their words silently. One time he pulled on his ear and rubbed the side of his face with a puzzled look.

On that day, Horda stopped and scooped him into her arms. She spoke slowly in front of his eyes. “Yes, Bran. You remember. You used to hear. You remember.” He frowned again and put his hands on her face, but still he remained silent.

Reeme tried to help, but she could do little more than cry. Mach and Zeek sometimes had to walk away to keep their frustration and discouragement from showing, but Horda never faltered in her work with the small boy. Nor did she relent as she cajoled, threatened, kidded, shamed, and sometimes cursed the other adults back to work with Bran.

Three hands turnings of the sun had passed since Thuro and his group left for the Inner Band. “It’s time for them to return,” muttered Mach looking out at the cloudy sky. “We need to bring more wood into the cave. There’s going to be a blizzard soon.”

Horda lifted her hair off the back of her neck and looked at the dirty grey clouds. “It certainly feels like a blizzard,” she said. “Though it doesn’t look like one.”

“You can’t see what’s coming over the mountains,” he said shortly.

She shrugged. “Maybe they’ll return by the time we get the wood and before the blizzard hits.”

When the cave storage area had been filled to capacity, everyone searched for tasks that would keep them outside but close. Mach leaned down to Bran and said, "Let's find Horda."

Bran smiled and readily took his hand but made no sound. Placing the little boy's hand on his lips, Mach repeated, "Horda."

They joined Horda in the wide space just inside the shelter where she worked a bison hide with a mixture of deer brains, ash, fat, and bracken. Mach shook his head and touched Bran's shoulder. "That stuff stinks," he said.

Bran scrunched his face so tightly his eyes were almost closed. Mach laughed and stuck his finger into the mixture. Waving it beneath the little boy's nose, he said, "Stinks, Bran."

Bran took a step back and Mach followed. "Say stinks, Bran."

Horda laughed. "Don't tease him, Mach."

Mach touched Bran's nose with his dripping finger. "Stinks, Bran."

Bran glared and rubbed the gunk off his nose. "Nassy, Mach!" His voice sounded flat and hollow, but it was music to their ears.

Mach lifted the little boy and twirled him around. "That's right, Bran. Nasty!"

Bran laughed as Mach danced around chanting, "Nasty, nasty, nasty.

Finally Mach scooped a handful of the deer brain mixture and brought it toward Bran's face. Bran's eyes widened and he cried, "No! Nassy!" He struggled in Mach's arms and commanded, "Down."

Mach set the little boy on his feet. Bran looked up at the disgusting stuff and repeated, "No. Nassy." Then he turned and stalked outside where his father worked knapping points.

Mach looked at Horda. "He can still talk."

"And he still has a mind of his own."

"Now what do we do?" he asked.

"Keep trying to teach him new words." She sighed. "And maybe we could get him to talk when he's not angry."

"I'm going to tell Zeek," said Mach.

Horda smiled. "I hope Bran already told him."

Mach found Zeek sitting on the ground with Bran in his lap. Bran's face was scrunched up, and he was repeating, "Mach nassy. Mach nassy," in much the same fashion they had repeated words and phrases over and over to him.

Zeek looked up and asked, "What have you done to him?"

Mach told him. Zeek smiled and shook his head. "That stuff is disgusting. Did you really put it on his nose?"

"Yes. I probably shouldn't have, but it got him started talking."

Zeek laughed out loud. "It surely did."

Reaching up Bran caught his father's chin and pulled his face down until they were eye to eye. Then he pointed to Mach and frowned. "Mach, bad," said Bran clearly

"No, Bran," said Zeek. "Mach's very good."

"No," argued Bran, "nassy."

Mach held out his arms, but Bran refused to go to him. "Nassy," he declared.

Mach drew his flint knife from his belt. "Knife," he said slowly.

Eyes sparkling Bran held out his hand for the knife.

Mach held it out of his reach and said, "Knife."

Bran glared and reached again. Mach kept it beyond his grasp and repeated, "Knife."

Stubbornly silent, the little boy reached again. Mach shrugged and put the knife back in his belt. Bran said, "Kniif."

He placed the knife in Bran's hands.

"'Ank you."

Mach's eyes widened, but he tipped Bran's face up until the child looked at his mouth. Then very carefully he said, "You're welcome."

Bran smiled and went back to examining the knife. Then he looked up at Mach. "'unt?"

Mach frowned. "What?"

Taking a deep breath, the little boy sighed. "'unt bis'n, Mach?"

Mach swung him around in a mighty bear hug. Then he looked directly in Bran's eyes and spoke slowly. "Yes, Bran, we certainly will hunt bison."

"Now?"

Mach thought fast. The bison had gone further south for the Moons of the Long Blizzards, but he didn't really want to find any with the little boy. They were just going out to track. He looked at the shadows cast by the setting sun. The air was oppressive, but only a few clouds were visible. Shaking his head, Mach said, "I think it's too late today. Don't you?"

Bran stared. "'unt now."

"After the morning eat tomorrow if it isn't snowing," said Mach.

Bran looked puzzled. "Not now?"

Mach closed his eyes and pretended to sleep then he opened them and pretended to eat. "Tomorrow," he said.

❂

It seemed Horda had been right. From that day Bran talked almost as much as he had before he fell victim to the fever demons, but it would be a long time before he progressed beyond the words and phrases he had as a small child.

❂

The sun cast smudgy shadows through the morning haze above the edge of the prairie, and the air felt heavy with the promise of a storm when Bran found Mach alone in the shelter opening. "'unt, now." The little boy held up two tiny spears.

"Hunt, now?" echoed Mach with a yawn. "I haven't had my morning eat."

Bran solemnly handed the spears to Mach who took them and examined the blunted points and feathered shafts. He held them on the palm of his hand and checked their balance. "These are fine spears, Bran."

Bran smiled. "Fa."

"Your fa made them?"

The little boy nodded.

"For me?" Mach peered down the length of the small shafts. "They are nice and straight."

Bran's smile was gone. "No, Mach, mine."

"I thought you were giving them to me."

"No, fix 'em." Bran turned around and Mach slipped the

two spears into the braided leather harness and patted the little boy on the shoulder.

Bran wiggled his shoulders and reached up to feel the spears. The he said, “Let’s go.”

Mach squatted down. “What about the weather?” He pretended to shiver in the warm air. “What if it snows?”

“No.” Bran narrowed his eyes and shook his head. “’unt now.”

“I’m hungry,” said Mach pretending to eat.

“No. Let’s go.” Bran pulled toward the shelter opening so Mach picked him up and carried him back to the cook fire.

Horda added hot water to the yampah root flour and pemmican she had prepared for porridge. Then she poured a horn of the rose hip tea Mach had brewed earlier.

“’unt,” demanded Bran.

“Ohh, the little cub shows his teeth,” said Mach.

“Stop teasing him,” said Horda. “Next, you will be punishing him for being rude.”

“No, I won’t,” said Mach. “I’m glad to hear him talking. And anyway I’m going to take him out after I eat.”

“What about the storm?” Horda prepared a horn of the tea for the little boy.

Bran shook his head.

“We won’t go far,” said Mach.

Bran watched Mach’s face as he spoke. “’unt?”

“Later,” said Mach sitting on the ground.

“I wan’na go, too,” announced Storm Cloud.

“Me too.” Rain Drop caught Mach’s hand. “Where are we going?”

“We are going out to carry wood.” He lifted the little girl onto his lap. “Can’t you feel the weather? There is going to be a storm. It may be very cold."

Rain Drop's eyes rounded, and Storm Cloud frowned. He muttered, "I don't wan'na do that."

"Perhaps you should find out what people are talking about before you join in the conversation." Mach laughed and gently poked the little boy on the shoulder. "Don't you think that might be a good idea? We will be on our way as soon as we finish the morning eat."

"I don't want to gather wood," said Rain Drop climbing out of his lap.

"Me either," announced Storm Cloud. "I wan'na hunt bison."

"'unt," said Bran.

Storm Cloud looked at the little boy and then at Mach. "Are you really going to gather wood today?"

"Horda?" Storm Cloud moved to stand in her path. "Is Mach going to gather wood today?"

She shrugged and waited. "Why don't you move so I can prepare the morning eat?"

He sighed but stepped aside. "Is he?"

"Don't ask me. Ask him."

"I did, but he didn't answer me."

She touched her cheek to the little boy's head. "Ask him again." She looked at Mach. "He will tell you."

Storm Cloud climbed into Mach's lap and caught his face between his hands. "Mach, what are you going to do today?"

"I'm going to pay off a promise I made a long span of time ago."

Rain Drop climbed into his lap too. "What does that mean?" she asked.

After eying the three, Bran stood by Mach's knee. "'unt, Mach, now."

Storm Cloud said, "I knew you were going hunting. I want to go too."

"I do, too," chirped Rain Drop.

"Move, little ones. Everybody has to eat before anyone goes anywhere," said Horda.

Reluctantly they climbed out of Mach's lap and sat down beside him. Bran stood at his knee looking bewildered. Speaking directly to the little boy, Mach said, "Sit down, Bran. We are going to eat." He rubbed his stomach. "I'm hungry. I want to eat first."

"Me, too," echoed both Rain Drop and Storm Cloud taking the food Horda had prepared for them.

Bran frowned though he obediently sat down. Horda offered him porridge and rose hip tea, but he shook his head and said, "'urry and 'unt, Mach."

"When I finish eating." Mach made a show of blowing on the hot tea before he drank some.

Bran watched patiently, but both Mach and Horda could feel his excitement. Mach knew he had to talk to the other children. What was he going to say? He hated to disappoint them, but he had promised Bran this "hunting" trip a lifetime ago when the little boy was so sick and before he lost his hearing.

Mach took the last bite of his porridge. He took a deep breath. "I'm sorry, Rain Drop and Storm Cloud, but this is Bran's hunt. You know Bran cannot hear. I feel he needs all my attention today."

"I'll give him my attention," declared Storm Cloud. "I will help you."

"Me too," echoed Rain Drop.

"No," said Storm Cloud. "I will go along and help him."

"I'll go and help too," insisted Rain Drop.

"I just told you neither one of you can go," said Mach firmly.

"I'm going because I will help you," said Storm Cloud. "She can stay here. We don't need her."

"Apologize," said Mach sternly. "Now."

"But—"

"Do not argue. You must not be disrespectful to Women of the Frozen Earth."

"She's not a Woman of the Frozen Earth." Storm Cloud glared at Rain Drop. "She's a lil' girl."

Mach picked Storm Cloud up and placed him on his knee. "Now, listen to me very carefully because I am only going to say this one time. Do you understand me?"

Storm Cloud's voice shook. "Yes."

"Little girls grow up to be women. Do you know what that means?"

Storm Cloud's eyes were swimming in tears, but he managed not to let them fall. "Not 'zactly."

"Well, it means they are Mother Life's emissaries on earth."

"Huh?"

Mach smiled. "It means they stand in Mother Life's place on the earth. They have little ones and take care of us and help us as we fill our vessels of time."

"Bear Claw used to say the women were worthless," said Storm Cloud. "He beat them. He used to hit H—"

"He did. He always hit anybody who got in his way or

made him angry." Rain Drop nodded solemnly. "He hit us all the time, Mach."

"Bear Claw was wrong. He was very wrong." He lifted Rain Drop up to sit beside Storm Cloud. "Listen to me."

Both little faces turned up to watch him. "The People of the Frozen Earth do not hit another."

"Sometimes the little ones get swatted," said Storm Cloud.

"Is that the same as a hit?" asked Mach. "Is the person who hits them trying to hurt them?"

"No, they want their attention." Rain Drop grinned. "Horda swatted Storm Cloud because he wouldn't stay away from the river, but she didn't have to swat me."

Storm Cloud scowled at her, but he didn't contradict the truth.

"Okay, Little Ones," said Mach. "Storm Cloud, you said Rain Drop couldn't go with us because she was a girl, and we didn't need her."

"I 'pologize, Rain Drop. I didn't really mean it." He looked earnestly at Mach. "I know she is important too. I know someday she is gonna have little ones like Aiyana and all that. I know women are 'portant, Mach. I promise I won't ever say she isn't again if you will let me go and help you."

Mach shook his head. "Storm Cloud, are you listening to me? You cannot go because this is Bran's hunt."

"But I really really want to go, and it's gonna come a storm. So, please, won't you let me go and help you?"

"I said, 'no.'"

Storm Cloud closed his mouth. He knew Mach's answer was final.

Rain Drop put her arms around Mach's neck. "I'm not

arguing."

"No, but when you point out what you aren't doing, you had just as well do it."

She frowned. "Am I in trouble like Storm Cloud?"

"What makes you think he's in trouble?"

"I don't know, but he is. Isn't he?" Rain Drop looked worried.

Mach fought to keep a straight face. "Not yet, but keep it up. You'll both make it before you know it." He set the children on their feet. "Do whatever Horda tells you to do today." He stood up and lifted Bran.

"'unt, Mach?"

"Yes, we are going to hunt, Bran. Tell Zeek he's with me." He touched Horda's cheek. "Keep the little ones busy. We really may need some wood." He laughed at the scowls they gave him and strode toward the shelter opening.

Chapter 20

IT WAS LATE AFTERNOON when Mach and Bran returned. Thick snow clouds darkened the sky, and the wind blew in harsh gusts. Horda and the women scurried around lighting more lamps and stoking up the fires. Mach and the men secured the bearskin covering the cave opening before reinforcing it with woven brush mats.

Soon everything was taken care of, and everyone was snug around their own cook fires waiting for the evening eat and listening to the howling storm. Horda looked across at Thuro's deserted area, thinking of all the things that might have delayed their return. She pushed the frightening thoughts away. They would be fine. They were fine. There were plenty of small caves where they could find shelter.

All thoughts of Thuro and his party flew from her head at Urscia's strident voice. "Leave my things alone!"

Lucza shrieked, "Your things? Your things? You selfish bison cow. How dare you say —"

Zhrul's low rumble silenced both women.

Horda looked at Mach. "What are we going to do?"

He shrugged. "I wish it was time for Gathering so I could

turn them over to Zaaco."

She smiled because her father would surely know how to handle the fighting family. "Zaaco isn't here, and it's a long time until Gathering. We have to handle them."

"You go right ahead."

"You have to help." She squared her shoulders. "Do you think Zhrul causes some of the trouble?"

He shrugged again. "Who knows?"

"You need to know. You're the leader."

"Co-leader," he reminded her.

"Leader," she said. "Thuro's not here to help you."

He looked to Zhrul's area where quiet had returned. "Should I go over there?"

She sat lost in thought until he poked her and repeated his question.

"I'm trying to think what Zaaco did in a case like this."

"I'll save you the trouble. You don't know because there weren't any jealous mates in the Inner Band."

"That's what you think. I remember one time. I wasn't very old. Xyla was still alive." A soft dreamy look suffused her face as she thought of her father's first mate. "Fa sat beside the jealous People's cook fire so often Ma got jealous. Xyla told her he had to see for himself what was causing the trouble." She nodded. "Yes, you should go over there."

He looked at her. "When were there jealous mates in the Inner Band?"

"Go over there and give Zhrul a chance to talk to you."

"When were there jealous mates —"

"Several times I know about." She glared at him. "Are you going?"

"Not until you tell me who."

"Who what?"

"Who had jealous mates?"

"Mach, it's over."

"This isn't. Maybe it will help me to know."

She frowned, but finally answered. "Elko."

"Elko?" Mach's eyes widened. "The second chief?"

"Yes."

"Recently?"

"No," she admitted. "They weren't actually in the Inner Band when it happened, but my father had to deal with the problem at Gathering one time."

"What happened?"

"If I tell you, will you go?"

"Yes."

"Elko took a third mate because it was expected of him. The second had accepted the fact he loved Suka more than he did her. She was satisfied to be the mate of a leader, and he did take good care of her and her children. The new woman was jealous of Suka, and she resented being lumped in with the other. She caused trouble around Elko's cook fire. Elko didn't have the wisdom to make each mate feel special in her own way. My father helped him."

"Special in her own way?"

Horda nodded. "I heard my father explain to Elko that his love for his mates was much like his love for his children. The more love he gave the more love he had." She smiled at the memory. "I wasn't sure I'd like to be a mate compared to a child, but then my father asked Elko if he loved each child in the same way.

"Elko said, 'Of course, not. They're all different.' My father laughed and told him each of his mates was different and special in her own way. Then he said it was up to Elko to find how each mate was special."

"And that solved the problem?"

"Not completely, but it helped. My father said when a man has more than one mate he must be sure each feels most important to him in some way."

"I need to remember that."

"I won't let you forget it." She nodded toward Zhrul's area.

Standing, he touched his mouth to hers, squared his shoulders, and walked across the open area.

By sunrise the second morning, the storm moved on leaving bitter cold. A dusting of clean white snow frosted the fiery colors of the land to the river and beyond. Here and there the footprints of animals marked the snow in paths to and from the water's edge.

Tired of being cooped up in the cave, the People bundled up to replenish the wood supply and carry water from the river. Working together, those simple chores were quickly finished, but most people remained outside in the crystal clear morning.

Horda watched Mach stand silently looking down the path Thuro had taken so many days before. Walking up beside him she placed her hand in his. "It won't be long now."

Looking down he forced a smile. "I know," he said. "I'm turning into a worrying, old woman, but I wish they'd get back."

"Perhaps Nuroo found something really wrong with Wilda."

"Do you believe that?"

"No, but I believe he might have kept her to help her accept her pregnancy."

Mach's face brightened. "I didn't think of that."

"I did. I hope he's successful. I hate to think of the coming moons if he isn't."

Mach sobered. "They're not going to be easy. Are they?" Urscia's harsh, scolding voice silenced the laughter of the children playing in the snow.

"No, but Wilda's not our only problem."

"I know she isn't." He gestured with his chin toward the silence. "What are we going to do about them?"

"I don't know."

"I watched them last night beside their fire."

"I did, too," she said. "He's really partial to Lucza and her little one."

"I know," said Mach, "but when I mentioned partiality, he told me he treated both his mates and their children exactly the same."

"He does not."

"I know he doesn't, and you know he doesn't, but he doesn't know he doesn't." Mach pulled off one of his mittens and rubbed his face. "I wish Thuro was here to help me deal with Zhrul. He's sure I'm too young to help him with Urscia. He told me I didn't understand the problems of older men."

"The very idea. You are the leader of this band."

"Co-leader," reminded Mach gently.

"Co-leader. Anyway, he's not even the second leader."

"Maybe I'll sic you on him. I'll bet you can straighten him out."

Horda rolled her eyes. "He'd pat my hand and tell me not to worry."

"Probably," said Mach. "He certainly has funny ideas. Doesn't he?" He laughed at her stormy expression.

"This isn't funny. He's blind to the way he really behaves, and some of his ideas are downright stupid. He and his mate are threatening the peace of our band."

"Calm down. I know this isn't funny. I'm trying to find some way to help him and us, but I haven't found it yet."

She sighed. "I know. I'm frustrated. You could help Zhrul if he'd let you. Zaaco never had this problem."

"At least not that you know about. He had almost two hands more winters than I do when you were born."

"You're the leader of this band."

"Co-leader," he corrected again. "At least Bran is talking now."

"Stop trying to change the subject."

"I thought we'd talked this one out."

She shrugged. "Bran talks to us, but we can't talk to him. We have to make him understand us so we can teach him new things."

"I've been thinking about using the hand signs we use on hunts," said Mach. "You know the other day when I was rubbing my stomach; he knew I meant I was hungry."

She stared at him until he began to doubt the value of his idea. "I know the hunter's signs don't cover everything, but we could make up signs for the everyday things they don't cover."

Chewing her lip, she continued staring at her mate

without speaking.

"It was just an idea," he said. "I know it probably won't work.

"Yes, it will! You are so smart." She threw her arms around his neck and hugged him. "We've been trying to teach him words he can't hear, but he could see the signs. Mach, I think you've solved our problem."

She started off, but he caught her hand. "Hold it," he cautioned. "This isn't going to be easy. You have to learn the hunter's signs."

"I know."

"And we have to agree on all the signs so we don't confuse Bran."

"I know." She grinned. "There's a lot to be done so why don't we get started."

He looked down the path at the gentle shadows playing on the melting snow before he followed her into the shelter.

Chapter 21

HORDA AND MACH STOOD outside the cave opening watching the last rays of the evening sun smudge purple, pink, and blue shadows across the landscape.

"Look," Mach shouted. "There they are. They are almost home." He stared across the distance. "They're pulling something on a travois."

"But there's still a hand of people walking." She squinted. "Oh, Mach, is that Unna with them?"

"I think so."

"Oh, I'm so glad." She leaned forward as if she could hurry the travelers' return.

Mach smiled at her happy face. "Tell the others. I'll go help them."

She stepped inside. Premo, Zeek, and Imad immediately put on their outer wear and hurried down the icy path after Mach.

Horda struck the fire Mach had already prepared in Thuro's area. When it was burning merrily, she went to her cook fire and dipped two portions of the stew from the cooking bag. Then she carried the remainder to Thuro's fire and set it to simmering. She'd already straightened the sleeping area and placed dried herbs to freshen the air, but she checked it once more. Satisfied, she took the twig broom and swept the area around the fire free of her footprints. Then she returned to her own cook fire.

There she added four horns of water to the little bit of stew she had kept and shredded two double handfuls of dried venison into the thin broth. She ground four medium-sized yampah roots into coarse meal and stirred it into the mixture. She tasted it, chopped in a wild onion, crumbled in a few leaves of dried sage and cow parsnip, and tasted it once more before she added a bit of the precious salt. There. Not as good as the original, but hot and filling. She'd make fry bread while she waited.

The new stew was boiling. Two baskets of frybread set near the fire keeping warm. The food was ready. She walked to the cave opening and looked out. The travelers were halfway up the icy path.

She hurried back inside and found one of the small shelters hunters used. It would give Unna privacy and help keep her warmer in the cave. Horda would look for a more permanent solution tomorrow, but this would work tonight. She set up the shelter with the opening away from the cave entrance and lined it with her extra sleeping furs. With the ones Unna brought, she was sure to be comfortable. Horda nodded and smiled to herself. Everything was ready.

Not quite. She took one of the baskets of frybread to Thuro's cook fire. She smoothed away her footprints once more. Finally she sat down to wait. Only then did she admit how worried she had been about the travelers' delayed return. *Thank you, Father Death for sparing them, and Mother Life, for keeping them safe. And for sending dear Unna back with them. She'll help me handle Wilda and Urscia and Bran. Oh, thank you, Mother Life.*

All the People gathered around to greet the returned travelers as they entered the shelter. Horda watched Thuro touch the People's hands in greeting. Seeing Horda, his tired face forced a grin, and he saluted her. "We're so glad to be home." She read shadows of despair in his dark eyes when he reached out to touch her hand.

Unna formally greeted Horda before they shared a fierce embrace. "I've missed you, Unna," Horda whispered. "I need you."

Unna barely had time to smile at Horda before Rain Drop and Storm Cloud landed in her arms. Hugging and scuffling like young wolf cubs, they almost knocked the old woman down. Holding them by the necks of their tunics, she held them away so she could look at them. "By the Great Mystery! What are these People feeding you little ones? Growing seeds?"

Rain Drop giggled. "I'm 'most tall as Storm Cloud now."

"Yes, you are." Unna hugged her again.

"And I'm 'most as tall as you," declared Storm Cloud eying the wizened woman's stooped back.

Unna cuffed him gently on the shoulder and laughed. "Yes, little one, you are, and glad I am to see it."

Lija threw her arms around Jozsa first then Trefo. "I missed you," she said. "I worried when you didn't return. Horda told us you were all right, but Mach and I were about to come looking for you."

Trefo grimaced. "We were delayed."

Marmah was wrapped in Dyson's embrace. "Next time, I'm going with you," she announced. "I hate being alone more than I hate trekking."

Dyson laughed at her sour face and hugged her again. "I'm not going next time," he snapped.

Horda watched Thuro listen to the men's words and sensed a new sadness in his manner. "Come," she said. "Your cook fire is ready. Unna, I've set a place for you beside our fire. The little ones will show you the way. Wilda, may I help you walk?"

"No, the pain makes walking impossible." Wilda's voice was little more than a sigh.

Horda turned to Unna for an explanation. The old woman looked at the ceiling of the cave and shrugged.

Thuro and Mach lifted Wilda and carried her to the cook fire seating her on a buffalo robe Horda provided. "Thank you," whispered Wilda. "You are too kind." She lifted one hand and let it drop as if she were too weak to hold it up.

Horda frowned and positioned herself to watch Wilda while serving Thuro stew and frybread. Wilda had the gently rounded look of middle breeding, and her face bore the soft glow many carrying mothers wore. Horda watched her fluff her hair and smooth and straighten the buffalo robe to suit herself with no sign of the weakness she earlier exhibited. Then Wilda half-closed her eyes and lolled back against the robe allowing one hand to trail to the ground. Anger built in Horda. What was this woman doing?

Horda took Wilda a dish of stew and frybread. Wilda struggled to sit up then eyed the food distastefully. "I'm sorry. I can't eat this." She fell back on the robe with a sigh. "I've been longing for ..."

Thuro set his dish aside and rose to his feet He took Wilda's hand and asked gently, "What are you longing for?"

Wilda's fingers fluttered in his big hand. "Nothing. It's too much trouble." Her eyes closed. "I'll just rest for a time. It was such a difficult journey." Wilda appeared to sleep.

Horda looked at Thuro who shrugged tiredly and went back to his eat.

Mach sat talking with Thuro. Horda gave Mach Wilda's dish of stew then sat to observe her a little longer. She thought Wilda watched her from beneath half-closed eyes, but she couldn't be sure. Finally, giving Thuro and Mach a wave, she left.

Back at her own cook fire, Horda accosted Unna. "What's wrong with Wilda?"

"Besides being as rotten as fresh meat left in the summer sun too long?"

"What did Nuroo say about her illness?"

Unna rolled her eyes. "She's breeding."

"I thought that," said Horda. "Why is she so weak?"

"Because she wants to be."

"She wants to be? You mean she's not really that weak?"

"No, she's not weak. She's angry she's breeding, and she's found a way to punish Thuro and everyone around her. The trip back was one long nightmare. First, the pains in her legs became too bad for her to walk so Thuro rigged the travois. Even then, there were some days she couldn't travel at all because the jolting ..." Unna paused and placed one aged hand delicately against her wrinkled forehead in a perfect parody of the affected Wilda. "... just caused her too, too much pain."

"Are you serious?"

Unna nodded. "One time we stopped for four turnings of the sun while Thuro and Dyson hunted antelope."

"Antelope?" Horda frowned. "There aren't many around here in this season."

"Everyone, even Thuro, knows that," sniffed Unna.

"Then why was he hunting antelope?"

"Because Wilda's delicate stomach couldn't tolerate any of the traveling food we had, but she thought perhaps, just perhaps, she could eat a little fresh antelope steak." Unna's stubby eyelashes fluttered in the wrinkles of her face. "The fool girl wouldn't even try to eat anything else. And her dumb mate nearly killed himself until he finally found an antelope for her."

"It's going to be a long time until she gives birth."

"Gives birth?" Unna threw up her hands. "The Mother protect us. I'm going to knock her over the head with a heavy bison jawbone club when the time for that comes."

Horda leaned close to Unna and whispered, "I almost hoped Nuroo would give her some of the herbs to end her pregnancy."

"He offered. Thuro didn't want him to though he wouldn't have stopped him." Unna gazed across the camp. "Then Wilda figured out she'd give birth ending the pregnancy, but without any chance of a little one. She bravely refused." Unna sighed. "Nuroo sent me to help you with her, but I don't know how much help I'm going to be." Unna glared in Wilda's direction once more. "Unless I strangle her for you."

"Do you think we could get away with it?"

Unna raised one eyebrow. "If she doesn't straighten up soon, I'm willing to take the chance."

The two women sat in silence until Unna clapped her hands and looked at Horda. "Enough about her. That stew smelled good when I served the little ones."

"Where are my manners?" Horda laughed and jumped up to serve the old woman. "I'm sorry it's kind of traveling stew. I gave the other to Wilda and Thuro though she didn't eat any of it."

"You tried, Horda. That's all you can do." Unna smiled at her young friend. "Now, tell me how you like being number one mate of the co-leader of the band."

"Are you sure you want to hear about more problems now?"

"It'll keep us from talking about Wilda. Won't it?"

Horda told her about the troubles with Urscia and Zhrul and trying to teach Bran in spite of his deafness.

"Umm." Unna chewed a bit of frybread. "Those are real problems. Let me think on them. What else?"

"Else?"

"You talked like you had a lot of problems. That's only two."

"I'm still not breeding."

"But you're still working on it."

"Yes, but sometimes ..."

Unna smiled gently. "... things or people or life get in the way. That's why you have to give it time. That's not a problem."

"It doesn't seem f—"

"Fair?" sputtered Unna. "Neither the Great Mystery nor Mother Life ever promised to be fair, Girl. Give it time. It'll happen when it happens. What else?"

Horda thought then shook her head. "The other problems are just little daily things the People resolve themselves."

Unna sopped the last bit of her stew with a piece of frybread. Old eyes twinkling, she took a bite and chewed thoughtfully. "Tell me the good things," she commanded.

Horda looked startled. "There are so many problems," she protested.

"Only two," said Unna, "three counting wonderful Wilda. That leaves lots of room for good things."

"I don't know. I haven't thought about them in a long time."

"Then it's time you did." Unna stuck the last bit of frybread in her mouth and chewed patiently waiting for Horda to speak.

"Well, everyone worked together to fix us a bath pit. It's even better than the one in the Inner Band." Horda's eyes sparkled.

"Tried it out with that handsome mate of yours lately?" asked Unna with a saucy grin. Horda blushed and Unna laughed. "You don't need to answer that. I haven't always been old. What else?"

Horda was surprised to find once she started telling Unna good things, the list grew longer and longer. Some were simple, personal things like how glad she was to see Rain Drop and Storm Cloud growing normally and talking and even fighting between themselves. Others were bigger like the bounty of stored food the band had, the way Bran had remembered how to talk, and Mach's idea about using the hunters' sign language to communicate with him. Then Mach joined them and added his share of good news.

The fire burned low and Storm Cloud and Rain Drop cuddled sleepily in Unna's lap before the list ran out. Horda looked around the quiet cave. "Oh, my, I didn't realize it was so late."

Mach stretched. "This was good. And there's nothing important to do tomorrow."

Unna rubbed her eyes and yawned. "Wouldn't matter if there was. You both needed that more than you needed sleep."

"You're probably right," said Horda. "I feel better than I've felt since Mach was named co-leader."

Mach took her hand and helped her up. "It's nice to feel like we're doing some things right. Isn't it?"

"Yes, it is," said Horda.

Mach lifted a sleepy child in each arm, and Horda helped the old woman to her feet. "Unna, I'm so glad you're here. Thank you for coming."

Unna hugged Horda. "I'm glad I'm here too."

Mach smiled down on the old woman. "You can't imagine how glad we are that you are here."

Sounds of a fire being built pulled Horda from sleep. Sitting up she muttered, "It doesn't seem like I closed my eyes. It can't be time for the morning eat."

Mach grumbled and rolled up in the sleeping furs. Horda stumbled out into the cave where she found a sleepy-eyed Thuro feeding wood to his cook fire. "What are you doing?"

He yawned. "I'm cooking."

"Cooking what?"

"Antelope." He rubbed fat on the flat baking rock and pushed it into the flames to heat.

"Thuro, it's the middle of the night."

Giving another jaw-cracking yawn, he shrugged. "Wilda's hungry. She thinks perhaps she will be able to sleep if she eats a little fresh antelope." He unwrapped an antelope haunch and cut several thin slices. "Ah, Horda?"

"What?"

"Do you have any fresh cow parsnip?"

Horda's eyes widened. "Fresh cow parsnip?"

"Yeah. She says it tastes so much better sprinkled with fresh cow parsnip."

Horda shook her head. "Thuro, it's the middle of the winter moons. There is no fresh cow parsnip."

He sighed. "I didn't think so, but I just thought I'd ask."

"I have some of the trader's salt."

"She hasn't acquired a taste for salt. Says she doesn't like it. She's always asking for fresh cow parsnip."

"Well, I have some dried parsnip."

He dug in a large parfleche by his side. "So do I, but she doesn't like it as well. Says it doesn't taste the same."

"It doesn't. We'll soak some. That helps a little."

"Huh?"

"We'll soak some while the stone heats." She poured a small amount of warm water into a flat wooden bowl. "We'll dip the meat in the water and the cow parsnip will stick to it. It looks more like fresh."

"Good idea." Thuro pulled out a packet of the dried herb. He started to pour it into the water.

"Just about a handful."

"She likes lots. She wants it to taste salty."

"That's enough. Don't use all of it. You'll need some later."

"I don't understand why she doesn't like real salt," he said. "Do you remember when the trader Thunder Eagle brought salt to Gathering?"

"I remember the first time. It is one of my earliest memories. He had salt and shells. My father wanted shells for his mates, but they wanted the salt. He didn't understand. It was so expensive.

"My mother argued with him. He kept telling her how pretty the shells were. They were, but they weren't that different from the ones we get from the river. Finally she stopped arguing and gave him some frybread and water lily tubers cooked with a few grains of the salt the trader had given them to sample.

"My father quit arguing and tried to trade for all the salt the trader had in his pack. The trader said, 'Man, you are rich, but you aren't rich enough to afford all my salt.'"

She laughed at the memory of her father's angry face. He managed to get three packets about the size of a double handful for each of his mates. They hoarded the salt for three turnings of the seasons."

Thuro nodded. "My father tasted your ma's cooking and traded most of his trade goods for one of those packets. My ma and his other wives had a fit," he paused dramatically, "until they tasted the frybread he brought from your ma. They decided it might be worth it."

"It was delicious. I'm sorry Thunder Eagle missed this past Gathering, but I'm glad he brought us salt."

Thuro asked, "Do you remember when he was at Gathering without salt?"

Horda nodded. "I had just begun my training with Nuroo. Thunder Eagle was one of the first people I sewed up."

"We weren't in the Inner Band then. I never knew exactly what happened to him. Was he attacked?"

"By a flood. He was washed down a river and lost all his supplies and got his face gashed. It must have been frightening."

"Someone should have told us what happened." Thuro paused. "I remember some of the People were upset he didn't bring any salt that time."

"He didn't want to talk about it. In fact, if he had been able, he would have left before Gathering."

"He's a strange man, isn't he?"

"Yes, he is," said Horda.

Thuro counted back. "He was more than three years late. He was due at the Gathering Meiran — ahm ... ah, I mean Bear Cl— ah— I— ah — mean the one when we chose mat..." Thuro's face flamed, and he finally sputtered into silence.

Horda smiled sadly. "That wasn't the happiest Gathering was it?"

"No. But it didn't sound like too happy a time for Thunder Eagle either."

She shook her head in memory before she continued the litany of disasters the People had suffered. "My mother went to walk the Frozen Wilds. Bear Claw rattled his arrows and spears. The fever demons consumed my brother's friend Brash because he didn't tell us he had been hurt. Rattlesnakes, drownings." She shook her head to dispel the gloomy thoughts. "It was not a good time."

Thuro shrugged. "Mach doing the Dance of the Sun. Tyson saved from drowning. Mach and me declared heroes of the People. Choosing mates. I don't think it all turned out badly. Do you?"

"No, Thuro, it didn't all turn out badly for us, but in that time Thunder Eagle lost his mate and little one."

"Yes," said Thuro. "He did. It must have been awful."

"Thuro," whined Wilda. "I'm really hungry."

Horda rolled her eyes and swallowed a grin as Thuro grimaced. He dripped water on the stone where it sizzled and danced.

She nodded approvingly. "It's ready. Do you want me to cook the meat?"

"No." Thuro was already dipping one of the pieces of meat into the little bowl. "I'll do it, but I still wish I had some fresh cow parsnip." He spread the meat on the stone and dipped another piece.

"Me, too." Horda watched him lay the pieces of meat on the stone and reach for the wooden tongs. When he had turned the first slice, she yawned. "Since you don't need me, I'm going back to sleep."

"Sleep well, Horda."

"Sleep well."

"I was."

"You're a good man, Thuro."

He shrugged and finished turning the meat.

Horda crawled back into her sleeping furs and snuggled her cold feet against Mach's legs. He grumbled and turned over pulling her into his arms. "Whatza matter?"

"Thuro's cooking antelope."

"Huh?" He squinted at her in the near darkness of the

sleeping shelter.

"Wilda's hungry."

"Itza middle o' tha night."

"Yes, it is, but she's hungry and he's cooking."

Mach muttered under his breath.

She poked him in the ribs. "Will you cook for me when I'm breeding?"

"Huh?" he sniffed and snorted.

She poked him again and repeated her question.

"Prob'ly not," he said and began snoring once more.

Horda smiled burrowed her head into the hollow of his neck. *Mother Life, help all of us get through this pregnancy.*

Chapter 22

TWO MORE MOONS OF cold winter days dragged past. Mach stood looking out of the cave one morning and announced, "There's not enough snow."

Thuro looked at him. "What?"

"There's not enough snow."

"There's plenty for me."

"No," said Mach, "The Moons of the Blizzards have almost passed, and there is hardly a covering of snow."

"So what?" Thuro shrugged. "It has been easier for us to get by this winter without having to deal with the snows and storms. Can't you just be thankful the Mother has spared us?"

Mach shook his head. "I don't think you understand. The snow makes water for the earth and the river. It will be dry next summer unless we have more snow."

"I don't doubt you, Mach, but where do you get these ideas?"

"I don't know," he admitted. "But I just realized usually the whole earth is covered in snow — some places deeper than I am tall. In the spring when it melts, the earth and streams are filled with water. Now the snow doesn't even reach my knees anywhere. That can't be good for the earth." Mach frowned up at the soft puffy clouds floating across the pale blue sky.

"I'm sure you're right." Thuro gazed at the mottled landscape. "Maybe it will snow soon."

"Maybe." Mach kicked several small stones before he asked, "How's Wilda?"

"The same," Thuro grumbled.

"Does she even try to walk?"

"No, I keep telling her the women say she needs to move around, but she just sits and cries." Thuro muttered an oath. "She's sure she is going to die."

"To die?"

"Yes, she insists she will never hold her child in her arms." He rubbed his face. "I wonder if she believes her own words. Sometimes I think she just wants to see us upset. She made Horda cry yesterday."

Mach hoped his anger did not show in his voice. "She did?"

"I know she says things she doesn't mean because she is sick and frightened, but sometimes she says such cruel things."

Now Mach fought to keep his opinion of Wilda's cruelty from showing on his face. "What happened?"

"Horda and Unna were trying to get her to walk and Wilda was refusing like she always does. Horda told her fresh air and moving around would help make the sickness go away. Wilda got angry and told her she didn't really know anything about this sickness since she had never been pregnant."

Mach sucked in his breath and scowled. He knew how

terribly sick Horda's unsanctified pregnancy had made her all during her captivity. He'd even told Thuro one day trying to reassure him nothing was really wrong with Wilda.

"Horda is the strongest woman I know," said Thuro. "She looked like she'd been slapped, and I saw tears in her eyes, but her voice never changed. She just kept trying to get Wilda to do what she needs to do. I couldn't have done it. Even though I love her, I know I would have slapped Wilda or kicked her or something. I know I would have forgotten everything I have been taught and let her have it.

"I don't think I've ever been so angry at Wilda. I almost told her to keep her mouth shut about things she knows nothing about, but Unna pinched me, and Horda's eyes told me to keep quiet. Sometimes I just want to shake Wilda and tell her to grow up."

"But you can't." Mach shook his head wondering at the problems his friend was having. "She is suffering even if it's in her own mind."

"I know. Just like Urscia is suffering even if she won't admit it, and we can't get through to Zhrul." Thuro sighed. "That's what makes it so hard."

"I sympathize with her and with them, but I just wish there was some way to make them do what needs to be done instead of making all of us suffer," said Mach.

"I am sorry," said Thuro, "I wish I'd never let her make me promise she wouldn't have a little one. Maybe she wouldn't behave so badly if I hadn't foolishly promised."

"Do your really think it would have made any difference?"

"I don't know." Thuro closed his eyes. "We'd been mated for so long without a little one. I had no idea."

Mach put his hand on Thuro's shoulder. "I wish I could help you."

"I've learned my lesson," said Thuro. "As Mother Life and Father Death are my witnesses, I will never mate with Wilda again as long as I live."

"Be careful making vows you can't keep before the Mother and Father," Mach cautioned.

"I will keep this vow. Mating was never worth one finger of what we are going through now."

Mach's eyes widened. He'd found mating with Horda worth everything he had suffered. "Perhaps she'll change when the little one is born."

"Perhaps," said Thuro, "but I won't. I'll never go through this with her again."

Four blizzards came in quick succession. The snow in the flats reached up the tree trunks and covered the brush that grew near the path. After struggling out the shelter opening, Mach pushed sheets of snow from the path to the wood clearing. *Thank you, Mother Life.* He smiled behind the leather snow mask that protected his eyes.

The thirsty earth would drink — not as well as some years, but well enough. Now, if Wilda would have her little one, Bran would learn to use the signs, and Urscia would quit being such a problem everything would be wonderful in the band.

He cleared more snow from the steep path. He leaned on the handle of his snow pusher, took off his mask and rubbed his face then looked up at the sky. *Mother Life, I'm just asking for three things.* He grinned. *Three small miracles.* He laughed out loud. *Make that three very large miracles, please.* He put his snow mask on and went back to work.

The sun had dropped behind the teeth of the mountains leaving the snowfields tinged dusky pink when Mach sat in the grey dust of the cave's open area drawing pictures for Bran. Zeek made the sign naming each of the things Mach drew. Reeme sat a short distance away beside a small fire and worked red and yellow quills into the yoke of a shirt for Zeek.

Suddenly Bran laughed and pointed to one of Mach's drawings. "Bis'n," he chortled.

Zeek caught his shoulder and made the sign. Bran frowned. "Bis'n," he repeated pointing to the picture in the dust. His father signed "bison" once more.

"Hunt?" said Bran hopefully.

Mach shook his head. Once again he spoke slowly and signed, "Too much snow."

Bran demanded, "Hunt."

Mach led the child to the cave opening. Picking up a handful of snow, he leaned in front of Bran's face and said, "Too much snow." He dropped the snow and made the signs. Bran frowned and picked up some snow. Mach lifted him up and showed him the wide expanse of white tinged with the pinks and purples of the setting sun. "No bison," Mach said shaking his head.

Mach went back inside and met Urscia leaving the cave.

Anger burned on Zeek's cheekbones.

"What'd she have to say this time?" Mach asked.

Zeek glared at her and said, "She was muttering about the leader wasting his time playing in the dirt with the dummy."

Mach took a deep breath. "I can think of nothing I need to do more. Can you?"

"No," said Zeek, "but what if she's right? What if he is a dummy and never learns?"

"He isn't a dummy and you know it," said Mach. "He will learn. We just have to keep working with him."

Bran said, "Down." When Mach set the little boy on his feet, he caught Mach's hand. "Draw," he commanded.

"He's communicating with us," said Mach taking up his pointed stick once more. "Someday we'll be able to communicate with him."

Bran caught Zeek's hands and pulled on them. "Sit." He turned his father's hands loose and waved his own hands in the air.

Zeek stared at his son.

"He's trying to tell you to sign," said Mach in a low voice.

Blinking back tears Zeek reached out and hugged Bran who said, "Sit," and waved his hands once more.

"He's going to learn," Zeek said. "He's really going to learn."

"I never really doubted it." Mach began to draw a bear in the dust. *But thank you for giving us hope, Mother Life.*

The morning eat was finished, and the gentle sun climbed

the pale blue bowl of the sky while the People went about their winter work. The sun had passed its zenith when several of the women pushed back the entrance covering and sat down to sew.

Horda and Unna spoke as they used the natural light for their work. Unna smiled at Horda. "The morning porridge was delicious with the pemmican. I still can't believe how well it keeps, or how much we have to eat. My people were always told meat would ruin, and we had to eat it when the first blizzard came."

"I'd never heard that until Bird Wing told me," said Horda.

"That has to be one of the stupidest things I ever heard," said Urscia. "I can't imagine anyone would believe such a thing."

Unna closed her eyes and took a deep breath. "When I tried to save meat, I never realized I had to put it out to dry more, and it soured. I had no reason to doubt what I had been told."

"No, I'm sure you didn't," said Horda.

"Everyone knows meat must be thoroughly dried to keep." Urscia shook her head. "Even my son knows food needs to be dried completely if it is to be kept for the winter."

"I know that now," said Unna. "But we had never prepared for winter like the People of the Frozen Earth do. Whatever was prepared before the first blizzard walked the land was what we had. I never thought to question.

"The time you call the Moons of the Long Blizzards were the Starving Moons for us." Unna chewed on her lips and blinked quickly to keep her tears from falling. "And many of my people starved during that time. Everybody got sick, but the very young and the very old suffered most. It was a bad time for us. I never did learn to figure out how much food I needed for the winter, and I never managed to put enough away."

Urscia sniffed but a warning look from Horda kept her quiet.

Reeme smiled. "I never seem to know either. Lena is in charge of how much we need. I just keep gathering and drying and slicing and pounding until she tells me we have enough. Then I quit."

"We have counted how much each person usually eats during a moon. We always try to put aside enough to last through the Moons of the Blizzards and well into the first Moon of the Growing Plants," said Lena. "I add a little more than we estimate to be sure there is enough, and we usually have some left over."

Unna shook her head. "I tried to count and measure, but even before the bad times, my people never tried to save food until it was scarce. Then we suffered and many died. Most seasons we ran out and had to scrounge long before now."

Horda could almost feel the pain emanating from the old woman.

"That is really stupid," said Urscia. "I cannot believe you would admit grown men and women didn't know how to prepare for winter."

Anger flashed through Horda, and she spoke before she thought. "You know absolutely nothing about what Unna's people did or did not know, Urscia, and until you do, it would be better if you keep your mouth shut."

"Yes, Urscia, it was stupid." Unna touched Horda's hand. "But, you see, that stupidity is only one of the reasons my people are no more."

Urscia had the decency to blush and stammer an apology as she fled the sewing circle.

Aiyana joined them with baby Zakon in his cradle board. He waved his arms and looked at the world with large brown eyes. The women stopped their work to comment on how big and alert the little one was becoming. He happily cooed and gurgled to remind them he was still there after they went back to their work.

The afternoon sun had crawled toward the jagged teeth of the mountains before Urscia returned. Soon another disagreement broke out.

"If I couldn't quill better than that, I wouldn't waste my time." Urscia fingered her own fine quillwork and looked down her nose at Unna's work. "I look forward to finishing this shirt for my Zhrul because I so enjoy doing things well. You know, I have been recognized for my needle work at the last hand of Gatherings."

A red flush tinted Lucza's cheeks, but she didn't comment as she folded the small tunic she was making for her child.

Unna glowered at Urscia and continued to pull her stitches as tightly as her hands would allow.

Mother Life, will that woman never stop? Horda said, "I'm certainly glad it's not snowing today. We can go outside if we want."

"Yes, Horda, that's just like you." Urscia waggled her finger at Horda and pretended to smile. "Always ready to leave work for play."

Horda's eyes widened at the insult. "I have every intention of finishing this pair of moccasins after I go outside to collect wood for the fires and see if any plants have started growing in the places where the snow is melting."

Baby Zakon fussed from his cradle board. Aiyana made soft crooning sounds which quieted him.

Urscia glared at her. "Aiyana, you need to care for that little one. When my children were little, I never allowed them to fret. It isn't good for them. I'm sure he needs his swaddling changed. He's going to get a red bottom if you don't take better care of him than you are."

Aiyana answered, "I know he's hungry. I just want to pull this stitch so it doesn't unravel."

"It isn't right to allow a little one to fret for our own pleasure," said Urscia. Then she sighed. "At least your stitches are tight and true." Urscia looked from Aiyana's work to Unna's. "I still don't understand why she's wasting our good dyed quills on such an ugly piece. Her stitches are so loose the design hardly shows, and the next thing the threads will be catching on things and breaking."

Horda smiled her apology at Unna. Then she spoke politely to Urscia. "Perhaps Unna's using the quills because they are *her* dyed quills."

"Her quills?" Urscia blinked. "What do you mean? Her quills? I thought they belonged to the Band."

"Well, yes, they do belong to the Band now, because Unna made the store of quills and gave them to us. She knows how to treat them so they don't become brittle after they are colored. She had a large store, and she was kind enough to share them with us so we could decide if we wanted to learn the new way to treat them."

"Well, it does seem like she would allow us to do the quill work for her. She's old and her hands don't have the strength they —"

Unna said, "It's my tunic as well. I will finish it for myself."

Though Horda cheered silently because Unna was no longer afraid to stand up for herself, she had to stop the confrontation.

Urscia opened her mouth to reply, but Horda stopped her. "Since you're finished, why don't you find something to do somewhere else?"

"Well, I never," sputtered Urscia.

"Perhaps you'd like to bring in some wood or start your evening eat," suggested Horda.

Urscia shot her a murderous look, but she lumbered to her feet and stalked away.

"Good job," whispered Aiyana. She moved the fretting Zakon into his carrying strap so he could nurse. His contented snuffling and smacking soon had the women smiling.

Unna smiled her gratitude to Horda who nodded. *I didn't help anything. I just delayed it. Mother Life, help us help Urscia stop being so cruel.*

CHAPTER 23

THE COOL PINKS AND purples of twilight had faded to the navy blue blackness of night. Tiny pin pricks of stars twinkled in the sky, and a bright winter moon had just climbed above the plains when Mach returned for his evening eat.

"You must talk to Zhrul again tonight," murmured Horda as Mach took his first bite.

He choked. His eyes rounded, and he hacked and coughed. She pounded him on the back. "Don't make such a fuss," she admonished.

"What are you talking about?" he asked when he could speak again.

"I'm talking about Urscia."

"What did she do now?"

In a voice not much louder than the sighing of the night wind, Horda recounted all the afternoon's events.

Mach frowned. "What do you want me to do?"

"I don't know, but you must do something. She is so very unhappy all she does is complain about everybody and everything in the band. If this keeps on, someone will strangle her," she sighed, "and it might be me. You must do something."

"Why shouldn't it be you who does something?"

"Me?"

"Yes, you. Strangling sounds like as good an idea as any of mine. I've talked to Zhrul until I'm blue in the face. I even tried talking to Lucza and Urscia. Neither of them admits there is a problem." Mach took another bite of stew.

"I know," she grumbled. "Unna and I have talked and talked and talked. Now we just want to shake all three of them." She sat down with her own horn of stew. "What are we going to —"

A huge commotion arose from outside the cave. "Help me. Help me!" Lucza's screams pierced the night air as she stumbled into the cave. "Zhrul, Zhrul, someone," she screeched. "You have to come quickly. Hurry." Tears streamed down her face, and she looked like a mad woman. "Oh, Mother Life! Help her. Please! Don't let Father Death have her!"

Mach was the first to reach the frightened woman. He caught her flailing arms and looked her over. "What is wrong? He examined her with his eyes. "Are you hurt?"

"No, I'm not hurt. She is," she cried. "Help her, please." She tried to pull him through the cave opening.

By this time, Zhrul had reached his mate and held her in his arms.

"It's terrible," she babbled. "There is blood on the snow. Oh, Zhrul, I'm scared. I know she's hurt. What if she wa —"

"Who is hurt?" he demanded. "What is wrong, woman?"

Gasping, Lucza finally said, "Urscia. It's Urscia. She's fallen off the cliff where we stored the wood."

Pausing only to grab two of the torches burning beside the entrance to the cave, Mach followed Zhrul down the path while Thuro raced to the storage area of the cave for the braided lines of sinew the band kept there.

"Be careful," screamed Lucza. "The cliff broke."

Horda's heart seemed to stop in her chest. "Mother Life, she hadn't really meant to wish Urscia ill." Her mind told her this was not her fault, but little fingers of guilt and doubt tickled the base of her spine as she followed the others to try to help the fallen woman.

Mach and Zhrul stood at the edge of the broken cliff looking down on the crumpled body lying in the shadows of the silvery moon. "I can't tell if she is breathing," said Zhrul.

"Neither can I."

"We have to do something." Zhrul's voice shook with unshed tears. He took a step down the cliff.

"Wait, man." Mach caught his arm and pulled him back. "You falling down on top of her won't help her one bit."

Zhrul jerked away. "I have to do something. I can't just leave her lying down there like some piece of garbage."

Horda had feared he was going to say something bad, but he didn't.

"We are not going to leave her down there like a piece of garbage, Zhrul, but we have to decide the best way to help her."

Zhrul began to sob, and Mach placed a comforting hand on his shoulder. "Why would she do this?" he asked. "Why? I loved her and Lucza just the same. Why would she do this terrible thing?"

Cold fingers gripped Horda's spine. *What did he mean? Did he think Urscia had meant to take her own life?* She watched Mach comfort him, but she also heard the silence. *What could Mach say? We have failed. We knew Zhrul believed he loved each of his mates equally, but we also knew he did not treat them equally.*

This looked like an accident, but they had just been talking about how unhappy Urscia was. Was this more than an accident? Looking up she met Mach's dark gaze and read his question. She shrugged ever so slightly. She had no idea whether this woman had slipped or jumped.

Suicide except after the loss of a beloved mate or when a person was no longer able to care for themselves and help the band was virtually unknown to the People of the Frozen Earth. They worked too hard to stay alive to purposely fill their vessels of time. But what if Urscia's life had become so intolerable ...

Guilt wrapped itself around Horda like a dirty fur. *What if? What if my angry words drove her to do this terrible thing?*

Horda watched Mach lean over the edge to peer at the woman. She forced herself to swallow her words of caution. He would not appreciate them. When loose pebbles and dirt slipped over the side, she turned her back and closed her eyes. Mother Life would have to take care of him. Horda couldn't take a chance on causing more trouble.

Mach stood and said, "I believe she is breathing, but I will have to climb down to see."

"I will climb down." Zhrul rubbed his eyes and squinted into the shadows of gathering darkness.

Mach and Thuro looked at him. A strong gust of wind

blew dry snow in swirls around them. "Do you really want to try to climb down the embankment in the dark?" Mach knew Zhrul's eyesight was not as sharp as it had once been.

Zhrul scowled while the torches smoked and flickered. He stared over the side of the cliff. He rubbed his eyes and looked at the younger men. Finally he admitted, "No, I can't see well enough to climb down there in the dark." He sighed. "And even if I could, I wouldn't be much help to her when I got there."

Mach nodded. "Nor will I. If Urscia does not walk the Frozen Wilds, I'll have to call on the healer woman."

Horda watched the three men and pretended she couldn't hear the words about calling her down. *Mother Life, please don't make me climb down that cliff.* Immediately after she prayed, guilt flooded her. *No, I don't mean that. I will climb down if need be. Please, let me be needed because that will mean Urscia is still alive. Please don't let her walk the Frozen Wilds. Please. And give me strength to climb down and don't let anything happen to me.*

She turned back as Thuro and Mach fashioned the climbing seat from the braided sinew and leather stripping and secured it around Mach's body.

"We will wrap this around that sapling." Thuro pointed to the tree whose trunk was about the width of Mach's arm. "It will be easier if you can use your feet to climb down." Now Thuro looked over the side. "If we try to lower you, you may get caught on the roots and rocks. If you climb, you can clear the face of the cliff so you can reach Urscia. We'll hold you so you don't fall while you guide her up."

"We will probably use a travois for Urscia." Mach peered into the darkness.

"And bring her up the path?"

"I think it will be easier on her injuries even if it does take much longer."

Thuro's look told him he didn't think Urscia would care whether the trip was bumpy or not. "Get down there and see what needs to be done before we send anyone down the icy path in the darkness."

Mach nodded. "Do you have more sinew?"

Thuro lifted two more braided coils.

"Good. How about a hide or robe?"

Thuro shook his head, but Horda said, "I'll get a robe back here by the time you need it."

"Thank you." Mach started the descent. Thuro and Zhrul guided the line and helped him make his way to the bottom.

Horda rushed up the path trying to outrun the questions buzzing in her head. They kept pace as she entered the shelter, where she faced the questions of the women. There they found a buckskin hide that had been tanned but not yet cut, and a warm sleeping fur. She quickly folded them together, secured them to her shoulders, and hurried back down the path. All the unanswered questions still buzzed. *Oh, please Mother Life, don't let it be my fault Urscia is hurt,* she pleaded.

Mach's feet touched the ground at the bottom of the cliff just as Horda looked over the side. She watched him touch Urscia's neck checking for the beating of her heart. Horda didn't realize she was holding her breath until he said, "She is alive."

Horda heard the People's collective sigh of relief. *Thank you, Mother Life. Thank you, Father Death, for sparing her. Thank you, Both.*

Then Mach's behavior interrupted her prayers of thanksgiving. He walked around the woman. His face was grim as he looked up. "Horda, can you climb down here? Thuro and Zhrul will help you with the harness."

"Me," she squeaked. *No, no, no, I can't,* roared in her mind. *My moon cycle has not come. I may be breeding. Climbing down that cliff is not easy. I might hurt my little one.* Her hands moved to her flat stomach. *My moon cycle has been late before. It is probably nothing. I am the healer woman of the band. But, Mother Life, I want to take care of myself for once.* "Yes," she said. "I will come down to examine her."

Thuro pulled the line up, and Zhrul helped Horda secure the seat around and under herself. Slowly, gently, carefully, they lowered her down the face of the cliff. She collided with one small outcropping, but the robe took the brunt of the impact. Even so, tears filled her eyes. The trip seemed farther than it was. She was shaking when her feet touched the broken ground beside her mate.

He unfastened the lines and helped her stand. "I don't like this," he whispered.

Horda felt her eyes round. Urscia's legs were twisted and turned almost as if they were braided. They were bruised and discolored. The bones stuck through the skin and blood dripped from the wounds.

Horda ran her hands over the woman's neck and back and was pleased to feel the straight column of Urscia's spine. But her legs? What could they do with such legs? Horda looked at Mach and found her dismay mirrored in his eyes.

"What are we going to do?" he whispered.

Taking a deep breath, she squared her shoulders. "First,

you will call up for Unna, our medicine packs, and more warm furs. Then tell the men to prepare a travois and come down the trail to get Urscia." She shivered as a gust of wind pulled at her furs. "Next, we need small fires for light and heat, and we need to wrap Urscia so the cold doesn't harm her more than the fall. After Unna gets down here, I think we must try to straighten her legs and brace them for the trip up."

He called her instructions up to Thuro and Zhrul who hurried to do her bidding. Mach rigged a small windbreak while Horda covered Urscia without moving her. Then Horda collected snow to melt for water while Mach found wood for the fires they would need. Soon two small fires crackled providing sporadic light and meager warmth, and Horda had prepared a third slightly larger fire.

Thuro called, "Unna is ready to descend."

Mach reached up and lifted the old medicine woman down the last part of the cliff with her and Horda's packs.

"Brr!" Unna stamped her feet and blew on her hands as she huddled over one of the fires. "It is not a good night for sleeping out." She turned to their patient who was starting to fret. "Shh! Shh! Urscia, you must lie still," soothed Unna. "Fix a tonic of lobelia and willow. Quickly."

Horda opened her pack and pulled out the leaves and bark.

Unna looked at Urscia and thought for a brief span of time. "Also add some bugleweed. She must not move."

Relieved to have someone else take charge, Horda added another scoop of snow to the small water basket on the fire. Still holding the leaves and bark, she blew on the flickering flames. They crackled and sputtered without growing larger or stronger.

Unna looked at the ice and snow in the basket. "We need hot water soon."

Urscia moaned and thrashed.

Pleased their patient showed life, Horda knew the woman had to be still to avoid more damage.

Mach called up, "Thuro, send someone to get us hot water. We need it now." The rustle of running feet provided the only answer.

Uncovering Urscia's feet and legs, Unna sucked in her cheeks and shook her head.

Horda watched her. "It's bad. Isn't it?"

Unna nodded. "You can see that. Why did you need me?"

"I have never dealt with such extensive wounds alone," said Horda. "I guess I wanted your knowledge."

"You are kind to an old woman," said Unna.

Horda shrugged and tears filled her eyes. "Not so, but thank you."

"Thank you." Unna touched one of Urscia's legs. "I am here to help, but you will tell me what we should do."

"I am afraid to try to move her. What if we do more damage?"

"We can't leave her lying on the ground outside until she heals." Unna moved to the other side of the injured woman. "Think, girl. What are we going to do so we can move her?"

"We have a water bag," called Thuro. "How are we going to get it down there without spilling it?"

Unna glared at the perplexed Mach. "You had a good idea sending for hot water. Why don't you go up and get it?"

Mach frowned. "Just like that? Climb back up?"

"We need the hot water right away," said Unna. "Do you have a better idea?"

Mach took a deep breath and glowered at the rough face of the cliff. He rubbed his cold hands together over the fire and chewed his lips. Finally he said, "No." He secured the lines around himself once more.

Unna smiled. "We really do need hot water as soon as we can get it, and you really are one of the most able climbers in this band."

He sighed. Already in harness, he took some of the wood and fashioned a small stand to hold the water bag near the fire. Then he called up to Thuro. "Help me. I'm coming up."

Horda and Unna discussed various plants they might use to treat Urscia's torn and mangled legs. When they had pulverized bugleweed, lobelia leaves, and willow bark with some wild tansy leaves, they placed them in a stone cup to wait for the hot water.

In a short span of time, Mach had gone up the side of the cliff and returned with a large bag half full of hot water. "Do you want me to help you pour the water into the horn?"

Without speaking, Unna held out the horn, and he poured a small amount of the steaming water into it. She stirred the mixture, then stared into the horn. She stuck her finger into the concoction and felt the leaves and bark. She frowned. "We ought to let it steep so we can strain it." She stirred some more.

"I used a lot of the leaves and bark," said Horda. "It should be strong enough by now."

"Maybe."

Horda spoke to the injured woman. "Urscia, this is Horda. You have had an accident." *At least I hope it was an accident.* "Unna and I want you to drink this tea. It is for fever, pain, sw—"

"She doesn't need a full accounting of what we are doing, Horda. Just tell her enough we don't frighten her and make her choke." She strained the strong-smelling liquid into another drinking horn as she spoke.

Horda shook Urscia once more and whispered urgently, "You have to wake up a bit so you can drink this medicine. It is to make you feel better."

Urscia regained consciousness long enough to cry out she was falling. She grasped Horda's arms while she babbled. "Help! Help! The snow slid behind me. I couldn't stop!" Her eyes showed rings of white around the dark irises. Panic raised her voice to a breathless screech. Then she twisted away.

Horda breathed a sigh of relief — almost. It didn't sound like the older woman had been trying to kill herself. But even so, Horda had no idea whether the fall had been an accident or not.

Urscia grumbled and fretted while they prepared the tonic, but she swallowed the first bit and did not speak again as they fed her the brew.

"Now," said Unna.

"Now what?" asked Horda.

"Now, we will make more tonic. The plants we used are still strong enough to use again." She took a small water bag and more leaves and bark from her pack. She bruised the plants and shredded the bark before placing them in the bag. Then she poured the left-over tonic and plants from the horn into the water bag. Finally she added a measure of water and hung the small bag beside the larger one at the edge of the fire.

"Now, we wait, and collect more fuel for the fires and the splints." She looked at the young man. "Mach, while you are collecting fuel, look for straight pieces of wood — not too thick and near the length of your leg."

Mach did not hesitate. He hurried to collect more fuel for the small fires and also found four small straight limbs, which he trimmed before he gave them to the women. After feeding the fires, he went for more fuel.

Unna searched through her medicine pack — fingering, smelling, and occasionally tasting the bark, leaves, seeds, and resin she found there. "You, Horda, you need to cut the buckskin into strips to use as the wrappings for the poultice."

Taking a sharp obsidian knife from her belt, Horda slashed the leather before she rolled the strips. She wondered if she would ever have the same kind of confidence Unna displayed in such difficult circumstances.

The next thing she knew a sharp cramp twisted her lower body. A gasp escaped before she could swallow it.

Unna looked at her sharply. "What's wrong?"

"Nothing." Horda bit down on her lip and rolled the last strip of leather. Another pain lanced through her, and she couldn't stop the tears that filled her eyes. It's nothing but my moon cycle, she told herself. *It always hurts some. It hurts more today because I am out in the cold. It's nothing.*

Unna shook her head. "Are you sure?"

Horda whispered, "It's just my moon cycle."

"I'm sorry." said Unna.

Horda shrugged. "It's normal."

"I know you were hoping."

"Am I that clear?" Horda glowered. "Can everyone see my thoughts?

Unna shook her head. "You are only clear to me, Dearest. Only to me."

Horda dashed the tears from her face as Mach returned to the fire.

"Are you all right?" he asked.

She forced a smile and said, "Of course, I'm all right. I'm just kind of cold."

He added the wood he had in his arms to the fire nearest Horda and reached for more.

She laughed. "Mach, stop. You're going to singe the furs off Urscia's coverings."

"Are you sure you're all right?" He looked at her. "Do you need anything? Can I help you?"

Unna snapped, "Find us a large smooth, flat stone."

He did not tarry.

Horda's pain had faded, and she was left with only the familiar dull ache that often accompanied her moon cycle. She chewed the inside of her lip as she lectured herself. *Do not be upset. It was nothing. You know it was nothing that hasn't happened more than a hand of times before. Your moon cycle comes when it wants to. If there had been a little one, there would have been more pain. Much more pain. You know that.*

"The ointment must be prepared." Unna placed a quantity of resin on the ground. Next she pulled out balsam poplar leaves, twigs, and seeds. "These are good for swelling," she said to no one in particular. Finally she found a bunch of speckled alder leaves. She pursed her lips and looked at them. "Horda?"

"Yes?"

"Are speckled alder leaves good for swelling? I can't seem to remember."

"Yes, Unna, speckled alder leaves are good for swelling." Horda smiled. "Her legs are torn and bruised. Do you need some more wild tansy?"

"For the ointment?"

Mach placed a flat rock about four hands square into the flames of one of the fires. "Will this do?" he asked.

"No." Unna frowned. "It should be fine." She placed the resin on the stone and waited for it to heat.

"If it won't do, why are you putting the resin on it?" asked Mach.

"I was talking to Horda, Mach." Unna waved her hands like she was shooing away a pesky fly. "The rock is fine. No, Horda, I don't want wild tansy in the ointment, but you could put a little more in the tonic for Urscia to drink before we try to move her."

Horda bruised the leaves and bark and dropped them into the bag over the fire.

Unna used an obsidian knife to chop the leaves and bark into small pieces and placed them in separate stone cups. Then she took a portion of each and ground it into a powder with her pestle. She worked the warm resin into a soft ball before she mixed the ground balsam poplar leaves and twigs and the speckled alder into it. Soon she had a glob as large as two fists. She inspected it. "Do you have more resin, Horda?"

Without a word, Horda handed her a ball of resin almost twice as large as the one she had fashioned.

"Good," said Unna. "I trust you also have more of the leaves and twigs I need."

Smiling, Horda handed her bunches of dried plants.

"Thank you." Unna chopped and ground the plants. "Would you choose the wood for her splints?"

Still silent Horda found the suitable pieces Mach had prepared. She approved the way he had trimmed and smoothed the limbs. They would stabilize Urscia's legs for the move to the shelter. Horda counted two hands plus two fingers of rolled strips of leather and two larger pieces she had prepared to hold the poultices against the flesh of Urscia's legs and protect them from the splints. She hoped it would be enough. Should she have Thuro send down more?

Then she saw the bobbing torches as the men made their ways down the trail from the shelter. She wondered if anyone was at the top of the cliff who could help her if she needed them? Her back hurt. *Did Urscia fall or jump or was she pushed? Would they ever know?* She blew her warm breath on her cold fingers. It would be better if they could soak the leather wrappings to make them more sturdy, but the cold made such an action impossible. *Please, Mother Life. Please.*

Mach came back to the fire with still more wood. "Thuro and Zhrul and the other men will be here soon. We should have Urscia in the shelter before sunrise."

"I cut up the buckskin. The wrappings are ready," said Horda. "I hope there are enough strips."

"I don't remember needing this much of the ointment at one time before. I hope it is strong enough," muttered Unna.

She gave the mixture another stir and frowned. "I'm going to add some of the skunkweed leaves to the packing."

Horda considered for a short while. "I don't see how they could hurt, and they might help. Do you need some more resin?"

"I don't think so." Unna rummaged in her pack. "You did mix one part lobelia with three parts willow and bugleweed leaves for that tonic. You did add the extra tansy — didn't you?"

Horda took a deep breath. "Yes, it's exactly like the first we fed her except for about twice as much tansy. It's steeping so she can drink it before we begin the climb. I even mixed some of the dried goldenrod blossoms in the water bag to wash her wounds."

Unna nodded. "I'm sorry."

"No, I'm sorry. I didn't mean to snap at you. I'm worried."

Unna smiled. "And I'm not? Remember what she thinks of my hands and my age."

"I suspect she is going to have to rethink many things before this is over." Horda looked at Mach who had returned with still more wood. "Mach, I think we have enough wood to last us. Do you think it's time to bandage her legs?"

He watched the lights moving along the path before he answered. "Yes, they will be here shortly."

"Why don't you see if you can help them?" suggested Horda.

Unna uncovered Urscia's left leg. Horda shook her head as she sponged the wounds with the goldenrod water. Then she slipped a length of leather under the left calf. "I've never seen such breaks."

"Nor have I." Unna molded the leg until the broken bones were almost straight before applying the resin poultice to the torn skin. "They appear to be shattered." She loosely folded the leather around the damaged limb. "We have to leave some room for her legs to swell."

Horda asked, "Do you want to finish this one before we start on the other?"

"No, let's do both while we have our hands in the poultice."

Horda washed the right leg before slipping the leather beneath it. Urscia moaned but did not waken. Unna straightened the bones, packed the poultice around the leg, and folded the leather over it.

"Do you think they will heal?" Horda fitted the smoothed splints to the sides of Urscia's left leg.

"Only the Mother knows that, Horda." Unna took a strip of the leather and loosely bound the splints to the leg.

Horda smiled at the old woman. "I thought you believed in the Great Mystery. When did you start to believe in the Mother?"

"Don't be fresh." Unna frowned at the young woman she loved as a daughter or a granddaughter. "I have been a Woman of the Frozen Earth for more than two turnings of the seasons. It is time I embraced the religion of my new People."

"I'm glad," said Horda.

Chapter 24

URSCIA'S LEGS WERE BOUND, and she had been dosed once more with the strong tonic before Mach and the other men returned to the place at the bottom of the cliff.

"Are you finished?" asked Mach.

"Yes, we are ready to put her on the travois."

The men looked frightened when Urscia moaned. "How are we going to get her on the travois without hurting her?" asked Thuro.

"I don't ... think ... we can," said Horda. "But I think she has been given enough tonic she won't really feel the pain."

Zhrul looked doubtful. "She sounds like she's hurting."

"I'm sure she is though I don't believe she's conscious of her pain," said Unna. "But we have to get her inside or she will be hurting even more."

Thuro nodded. "If two of us take her body and two take each leg, maybe we can at least move her quickly."

Horda said, "We'll help."

They lifted and transferred Urscia to the travois in one quick motion. She moaned but did not awaken or struggle.

Horda and Unna fussed over their patient bracing her legs and bundling her into the sleeping furs the men had brought.

"Are we ready?" asked Mach.

Horda looked longingly at the face of the cliff. It would be so much quicker to climb back up than to go around the path. Urscia whimpered in her sleep.

"Is there anyone at the top to help Unna up the cliff?" Horda asked.

Unna looked startled. "I don't want to climb the cliff, child."

"But it's eas—"

"No, I much prefer to walk up the path on my own two feet."

Horda yawned. "We must put out the fires."

"Horda, you and Unna go ahead with Zhrul and the others. Thuro and I will take care of the fires," said Mach.

Horda clenched her elbows to her sides in effort to stop the dull ache. It was nothing she told herself yet again. A small pain twisted through her stomach. A tiny echo of the awful pains she had felt when her little one departed. "I'm sorry, but I must have some privacy."

Unna nodded and extended her hands to the fire.

Mach looked at her. "Can't you wait until we get back to the shelter?"

"What do you think, Mach?"

"No, you probably think you can't, but it is really cold and dark down here, and there might be wild animals."

Horda smiled in spite of herself. "Thank you, Mach, for your reassurance. I needed that."

He looked contrite. "I will go with you."

"I think not."

Unna said, "Put out the fires, Mach. I will keep a watch. She will be fine."

Horda moved as quickly as her cold limbs would allow and took care of her needs. She was back to Unna before Mach had smothered the fire. She straightened and wrapped one of the furs around herself.

Another small pain echoed through her memory. *It is not the same,* she told herself. Then she trudged up the shadowy trail lit by the pale moon and the flickering torches. She could barely see the travois carrying Urscia. All thoughts of herself suddenly disappeared, and she asked, *Mother Life, what are we going to do now? How will we show her that her feet and legs are not her only value to our band?*

Morning slipped gentle fingers around the hides covering the shelter opening. The People slept later than normal after the long night working to bring Urscia home. Because the fires had burned later, the shelter held an unaccustomed warmth, which had encouraged everyone to sleep.

Everyone, that is, except Baby Zakon who woke only a little later and demanded his morning eat. His mother's soft words and actions quieted his cries. Soon his contented snuffling and gentle snorts echoed the sleeping sounds of others throughout the shelter.

"Aiyeeeee!" A loud screech brought all the adults to their feet and had the men grabbing for weapons and the women counting children. "Aaaaa-yah!" Another howl had everyone looking for the intruder. The third blood-curdling cry had all the smaller children except Bran screaming and crying, and all the men and women searching the shelter for the grave danger.

Barely awake, Horda put her hand on Urscia's shoulder. "Shh! You must stop this screaming."

"Why?" Tears streamed down the older woman's red and mottled face as she stared at the bandages and shrieked. "My life is over. I cannot live like this. My legs are ruined. My life! Aaaaa-yah! My life!"

Horda looked at Unna who shrugged and reached for her medicine pack. "I see the effects of the medicine have worn off. You stir up the fire and heat the tonic we have from last night. I will prepare more."

Horda stirred the embers and added kindling before placing small limbs on the fire. Then she filled a drinking horn with the last of the tonic from the water bag. She handed the horn to Unna for safekeeping while she helped the crying woman into an upright position.

"Argh! You are hurting me!"

"I'm sorry," Horda soothed. "You must raise up so you can drink." She lifted again.

"Eeeee-yow!" Urscia's howl nearly deafened Horda as she tried once more to raise Urscia who slapped at her hands. "Why don't you let me die? I cannot stand the movement. Don't you understand? Let me die! My life is over."

Horda bit her lip. Angry words buzzed in her head. *Mother Life, help me. Please … Please.* She said, "I know it hurts, but you must sit up to drink the tonic. It will help the pain go away."

Her soothing words were lost in Urscia's strident complaints. "Nothing will ever help me again."

Unna ground more of the roots, leaves, and seeds. While

Horda struggled to get the tonic down Urscia, Unna placed the powder mixture in a small cooking bag at the edge of the flames. Then she took boiling water and covered the powder leaving it to steep.

"You are in the cave. You are alive though your legs are broken. Your lungs are in fine shape. I see no reason to think you will not heal. I don't think your life is over yet," said Horda.

"You are being flippant," snarled Urscia.

"No," said Unna, "she is not. She has stated the facts as we see them."

"My life is over."

"What are you talking about?" asked Horda.

"It is the way of the People," wailed Urscia. "When a person is no longer useful, it is time for them to walk the Frozen Wilds."

"Oh," said Unna. "Like you wanted Bran to walk the Frozen Wilds because he cannot hear?"

"I don't want to go to the Frozen Wilds, but it is the way of the People. I told you he should go, and I should …" Urscia's sobs soon stole her breath.

Horda put a hand on the woman's shoulder though she would have liked nothing better than to shake some sense into her head. "I think it is a little early to say you are of no value to the tribe."

"But if I cannot —"

"You fell yesterday. Who knows what damage was done? Who knows how much you will heal?"

"I lied. I know I am hurt, but there is no pain." Urscia struggled to sit up. "Did you take my legs off?"

"No," Unna said. "We have kept you dosed thoroughly

because we want you to lie still so your legs have a chance to heal themselves."

"I won't be able to hunt."

"Neither can I," said Unna matter-of-factly.

"Humph," said Urscia.

"But there are many other things I can do." Unna stirred the herbal mixture.

"Do you think that will be true of me?"

"Probably," said Horda. She felt guilty, but she was still angry at the woman who had tried so hard to send Bran to the Frozen Wilds. She would not try to have her abandoned, but she hoped Urscia suffered just a little bit so she would understand life is a gift not to be taken lightly.

"What can I do?" cried the frightened woman.

Horda mentally rolled her eyes and straightened the wrappings on Urscia's legs. "As you told us yesterday, you are an excellent seamstress."

"Yes, I don't suppose my hands will be affected."

Unna nodded. "I am well able to walk the drying racks for the meat and fish. If you cannot walk, perhaps we could work a trade."

"I would love to do your beading for you."

"No," said Unna. "I still like to do my own beading, but my seams don't hold as well as they once did."

Urscia looked startled, and Horda swallowed a grin.

"Oh ... well ... I guess I could sew seams for you." Urscia said.

Unna laughed. "I know you don't like my bead designs, Urscia, but it really doesn't matter too much if they are somewhat loose, and I still enjoy working with them. You can't tell it now," she looked at her large knuckles and gnarled fingers, "but I used to be known for my intricate bead work." She sighed. "The beads may be a little loose without any real damage to the garment, but the seams must be sturdy. I would appreciate your help with them."

Urscia chewed her lips and looked around before she spoke. "I think my mate will provide food for me," she said, "but I still believe in the old ways. When everyone did their part, we were stronger because each of us had responsibilities."

"Oh, Urscia," Unna said, "I do understand what you are saying, but I don't think you understand what I'm saying."

"I don't think I could stand to be a burden to the People." Urscia finished the horn of tonic. "I believe it is my duty to walk the Frozen Wilds if I cannot do my part like I always have."

Unna looked into the younger woman's eyes for a long time before she spoke. "My life has changed as I grow older. My part has also changed, but I am still valuable to the tribe. Your life changed in the blink of an eye when you fell, but is that really different? Can't your part change? Just as I am more than strong hands and a strong back and Bran is more than a pair of ears, you are more than your legs." Unna sighed and squared her shoulders. "I am finished speaking. I will leave you to think on my words." She turned and walked away.

Horda watched silent tears slip down Urscia's face. Advice, questions, suggestions clamored in Horda's chest. Urscia's pain touched Horda much as her own pain in the captivity had touched the others. She remembered well-meaning advice sometimes made the pain worse. She reached out and hugged Urscia who did not resist but did not welcome the touch.

Finally Horda could keep silent no longer so she gave Urscia the same advice Unna had given her so long ago. "Wait, Urscia. Do not make any decisions now. Wait and see."

The tears left silvery tracks down Urscia's cheeks. Anguish etched new lines on her face. A sob escaped before she shook her head and pretended to sleep.

Zhrul walked into the sleeping area while Horda and Unna still tidied. He sat beside Urscia and watched her face before he took her hand. She opened her eyes, and he asked, "How are you?"

"How do you think I am?" More tears rolled down Urscia's face before she snarled and tried to pull her hand free. "I fell and ruined my legs. I will never walk again, and you ask how I am. Are you stupid?"

Horda winced at Urscia's angry words, but Zhrul did not release her hand though he gently wiped the tears from her cheeks with his fingertips. "No, Love, I'm not stupid. A little slow, but not stupid."

"I am going to walk the Frozen Wilds."

"I hope not for a long time." He patted her hand.

"Well, it is my duty. I can no longer do the things that are my responsibility."

"Urscia, do you really think the only value you have to us is your legs?"

"No, but they are m—"

"You must forgive me," he said. "I have wronged you. I did not understand what Mach and Thuro tried to teach me."

Horda was pleased by Zhrul's words. Though she was

embarrassed to witness the private conversation, she wanted to hear the warrior make amends. But out of the corner of her eye, she saw Unna motion with her chin. Horda followed Unna away from the fire.

When they were a safe distance, she whispered, "Unna, do you think he's going to be able to convince her?"

"Not today. That would be too easy, and that one does not do anything easily."

Horda stared at Unna.

"Well, you asked me," Unna said. "Stop staring."

"Are you serious?"

"Yes, I'm serious. I don't know what it will take, but I don't think one conversation is going to convince her of anything.

"I hope you're wrong," said Horda. "I don't know what we are going to do with her."

"We'll deal with her the best we can. Right now she is going to sleep for a while. Let's have our morning eat."

"Shouldn't we feed her?" asked Horda. "Or do something?"

Unna shook her head. "We did something. We checked her bandages and gave her enough tonic to put her back to sleep until the sun is high. Zhrul will be telling us she's asleep soon. Then the next time she wakes we will help her relieve herself and feed her, but for now, the best thing is to let her rest."

Sure enough, Zhrul found them beside the cook fire. "Thank you for helping Urscia."

"You're welcome," said Horda.

"It was very dangerous. You could have been hurt," he said.

"Yes, we could have," said Unna. "But the Mother was gracious. She helped us save Urscia and ourselves."

"I am glad no harm came to either of you."

Fighting to keep her face blank, Horda bit down on her cheeks. *I will never know for sure. I'm sorry, Mother Life, but you are going to have to help me. It doesn't matter how many times I tell myself it was nothing. I will always wonder if I was expecting a little one for a brief span of time.* She pressed her elbows against her sides and said, "Thank you, the Mother helped us."

"Yes, she truly did help us in our time of need." Zhrul looked back toward the sleeping area. "Is she all right?"

Unna answered, "No, Zhrul, she spoke truly when she told you she isn't all right. Her legs are badly broken. We put them back together as best as we could. But no one can say how well they will heal until time runs its course."

He looked embarrassed. "I know she isn't all right now." He shrugged. "But will she eventually be all right?"

"I'm sorry, Zhrul. I cannot answer that question. Horda, what do you think?"

Horda considered her answer before she spoke. "Zhrul, sometimes I wish I could look into the future. I cannot. She is strong and healthy. I do not know whether her legs will heal or not. I believe she will recover, but I don't know whether she will ever be able to accept herself and her limits."

"She seems determined she must walk the Frozen Wilds." Tears shimmered in his dark eyes. "I ... I ... I just want to know if you think that's necessary."

Horda watched the smoke drift to the ceiling of the cave and out the fissure in the rocks. She took a deep breath to allow time to formulate her answer, but before she could speak, Unna answered, "Zhrul, do you think I should walk the Frozen Wilds?"

The man looked startled. "Of course not," he snapped.

Unna nodded. "Then I seriously doubt there will be any need for Urscia to walk the Frozen Wilds as the result of this accident."

Zhrul was confused. "What does your not walking the Frozen Wilds have to do with Urscia?"

"I am old. I cannot do all the things I once did. I am not of much value to the tribe. You could easily put me aside."

He glared at her. "I do not understand why you say such a thing."

She glared back at him. "Zhrul, you are kind, but you know exactly why I say such a thing."

They stared at each other. Finally Zhrul said, "You saved Horda and Suka and the others from Bear Claw's wrath."

Unna chuckled. "You are certainly too kind. I could not save myself from Bear Claw's wrath. He believed it was time for me to walk the Great Beyond which is what my People called the Frozen Wilds. He was going to put me out in a storm. According to him, I had outlived my usefulness to the tribe. I could not keep up on hunts nor could I walk or sew as well as I once did. The younger members of my tribe thought the food I ate was wasted."

"Then they were wrong," declared Zhrul. "You are correct. Your steps are slower than they once were, but you have traveled many paths. You have lived through many turnings of the seasons and have dealt with many problems and challenges and successes. You can share your knowledge and wisdom with us to help us on our journeys."

"Do you hear yourself?"

Zhrul nodded. "I have answered my own question. Urscia

does not need to walk the Frozen Wilds."

"No, she does not." Unna took his hand. "Life is a series of challenges, and she has met many of them. She may no longer be able to run from the challenges, but she can still face them bravely and help us as we journey."

"Agreed." Zhrul clasped the old woman's hand in both of his. "Thank you, Unna, for helping me see clearly."

Unna nodded. "Now, we will have to help her see clearly."

"Yes." Then he disappeared into the shadows toward his own area.

Chapter 25

IT WAS ONE OF those wonderful days that sometimes come near the end of winter. Breezes blew across the snow and melted the top layers. Soft puffy clouds cast shadows on the earth as they sailed across the pale blue skies like dandelion fluff on the river. A few hearty birds flew overhead playing chase and calling their delight like the young children of the band. The sunshine called the People and encouraged them to throw off their heavy winter furs and enjoy the hints of spring.

By unspoken agreement, the women accepted the invitation and moved their sewing where they could bask in the warm sunshine and keep watchful eyes on the little ones who were racing and tumbling.

Though Urscia's legs had almost healed in the three moons since her accident, they were not strong enough to support her weight. Zhrul had carved wooden braces much like the splints, but lighter and more flexible so they supported her legs without immobilizing them. He had earlier carved crutches with protective animals and signs on them. At first, Urscia had refused to even attempt to move about. Though her mate did all he could to help her recover and to make her happy, she insisted all she wanted to do was go to the Frozen Wilds.

One day Zhrul's patience snapped and he said, "If that is what you want, I will not stop you."

Mach and Horda heard the exchange and wondered what would happen next. Urscia whined, "Then help me. I knew you did not want me before I was crippled. Now, I am useless, and you will be happy I am gone."

"By the Father's dirty teeth! Woman, why can't you understand? I accept that I was wrong!"

Horda held her breath and looked at Mach. What was going to happen?

Urscia cried. "I know you never wanted to mate with me!" She struggled to stand, and Zhrul lifted her to her feet.

Holding her close against his chest, he spoke, "Look at me."

Tears still streamed down her face.

He hugged her. "For once, look at me and listen to me. I am tired of you putting words in my mouth. They are not my words. They are the words you think I'm going to say, but you do not know my heart. I'm sorry. I didn't know my heart very well either."

She sobbed, but she stopped struggling and raised her face to Zhrul. "What can you tell me I haven't told myself? I was careless. I fell because I was angry. It was my fault." Her voice sounded as desolate as the Frozen Wilds.

Horda bit her lips. At least she knew for sure Urscia had not been pushed nor had she tried to end her life. What were they going to do? How could they help her?

Because the People of the Frozen Earth lived in such close

proximity, hearing other People's business was a fact of life. They were careful not to comment on things they should not know, but knowing them was often helpful. Now Horda wracked her brain. What could they do to help Urscia and Zhrul?

Zhrul tilted Urscia's face up so she looked him in the eyes. "It was not your fault," he said gruffly. "It was my fault."

"Why do you say that?" sobbed Urscia. "You had nothing to do with my carelessness."

"Yes, I did."

"No, you did not."

"Oh, yes, my love, I did." Zhrul smoothed her hair back from her face and dried her tears. "You see, I was blind."

"Blind?" Urscia almost shrieked. "Blind? You are not blind. You have perfect eyesight! What are you talking about?"

"Mach and Horda talked to me and talked to me, but I did not understand what they were saying. I managed to blind myself to the situation. I told myself your unhappiness was your problem and no fault of mine." He patted her back and hugged her. "I was wrong."

"I am afraid I have no idea what you are talking about."

"Urscia, you do know what I am talking about. You have been unhappy for a long time."

"Yes, I was." She sighed and squared her shoulders. "But I have accepted it. It is my lot in life as the second mate. You cannot help it. I should not complain. I should walk the Frozen Wilds. No one needs me anymore."

"No, you are wrong. I need you very much." He leaned down to share her breath. "I did not realize how important you are until you were no longer there, and I didn't know if you would ever be back." He smiled at her. "Urscia, you deserve to be loved for yourself. Not just for the things you did for me. Not just because you could walk around — not just for any one reason. I love you because you are you."

Urscia began sobbing again. "It's going to be much harder to go to the Frozen Wilds since you are telling me these things. You are very kind, but I don't believe you anyway."

"I don't blame you," said Zhrul.

"What?"

"I said, I don't blame you," he repeated. "I was so very wrong. I told Mach and Horda I treated you and Lucza exactly the same. I believed I did."

Urscia sobbed. "But you didn't. I've always known you only chose me because you thought you had to. I know you didn't want to choose me."

Zhrul frowned. "What ever gave you that idea?"

"You ignored me and my little ones."

"I didn't mean to."

"You didn't care for us."

"No, that is not true!" insisted Zhrul. "I have always cared for you. I thought I treated you and Lucza exactly the same. I intended to, but that was wrong. I'm sorry. You are different people."

"It doesn't matter," she said in a small voice. "I am no longer of any consequence to you. I was important when I could help with the work, but I can't even do that now." She sighed. "Let me go."

"No."

Biting her lips, she managed not to sob. "I am useless."

"No."

"Let me go."

"I won't stop you."

She closed her eyes and cried, "Take me to the Frozen Wilds."

"No, I will not. I won't stop you, but I will not help you either. I love you. I do not want you to go to the Frozen Wilds for a long time. Our children need you, and I need you."

He lowered her to her seat, then turned and walked away.

Lucza brought Urscia's smallest child Sepram to be with her. With only two winters, the little one did not walk if he could run. He tumbled and capered following the other children like a healthy wolf cub. But he seemed to understand his ma's injuries. The tiny boy sat quietly and played with the ends of her braids. He never pulled, but he clanked and jingled the little decorations while babbling about baby things. He stood beside her and patted her legs. "Hurt?" he asked.

One day, as the women were sewing, Urscia laid aside her work to hold Sepram,

Lucza looked at the tunic and said, "You know, Urscia, you are a really fine seamstress."

"So what," growled Urscia. "Soon my supply of furs and hides will be gone, and I will be worthless once more. It won't be long until I should walk the Frozen Wilds."

"Oh, does that mean you will be working the leather with

your feet?"

"Of course not, you stupid bison cow!" Urscia's anger burned into Lucza, but she did not blink beneath the onslaught. "It means," spat Urscia, "that when I have no more hides and furs, I will have no way to get more, and it will be time for me to go to the Frozen Wilds."

Baby Sepram whimpered, and Urscia absently comforted him with "Ma's here, Ma's here." He grabbed her and clung to her neck.

After the little one calmed, Lucza repeated, "Do you work the leather with your feet?"

"What are you talking about? You are so cruel. Why would you ask such a thing?"

Lucza looked her in the eye and asked yet again, "Do you work the leather with your feet?"

"Well, no, of course not, but I can't walk."

"I don't usually walk around when I'm treating the hides to make them into leather," said Lucza. "I sit in one place and pull the leather to myself. I don't use my feet either. Do you?"

Urscia had to admit she didn't.

"Do you think we might have found something else you are good at?" Lucza asked.

"I don't know," muttered Urscia. "I still think I should go to the Frozen Wilds, but I can't walk well enough to make the trip."

Mach, who had just joined the sewing women, opened his mouth. Horda burst into a coughing fit. When she caught his eye, she used her harshest glare to stop his words even though this was a tired and oft repeated argument.

Later he asked, "What did you think I was going to

say?"

Horda shrugged. "I didn't know, but I was afraid you were going to offer to help her find her way to the Frozen Wilds."

"Do you have so little faith in me?"

"I'm sorry, but I know sometimes you joke before you think."

"I do, but not about this. It's too serious, Horda. All I was going to do was tell her how much I appreciated the moccasins she made for me out of leather I gave her."

"Oh, I forgot about them."

"See, I was just going to try to help Lucza," he crowed.

"I'm sorry," she said. "I underestimated you."

He smirked, then sobered. ""There are a number of things she does very well that do not require walking. If we can just convince her, she will be all right. But it might be easier to teach a bear to fly."

"I know she does many things well," said Horda, "but she doesn't seem to know that. You should have seen her with Rain Drop and Storm Cloud the other day. Urscia taught them and some of the other little ones to write signs with a burned stick."

"We all make pictures of signs to label foods and things," he said.

She shook her head. "No, they were making signs for things I didn't know had signs. I don't think Urscia even realized we don't all do that."

Mach nodded. "See, there are a number of things like that, but she seems determined to be unhappy."

"She was unhappy before this happened."

"I know, but I believe this is worse."

She nodded before she asked, "Did you see Bran yesterday?"

"No, what happened?"

"Urscia was working with the children again, and I saw him standing by her side. When she noticed him, I thought she would send him away, but she pulled him closer so he could watch her write. He frowned and looked and pointed at one of the signs."

"What did she do then? Scowl and send him away?"

"No, she spoke the word slowly with him looking at her mouth."

"Really?"

"Really. Then he signed it and pointed to another. After he had asked about three or four of the symbols and signed them, she hugged him."

Mach smiled. "Do you think she is finally realizing we all have value?"

Horda shrugged. "I certainly hope so. Have you seen how Zhrul is treating her?"

"Yes, I'm glad he's finally learning. I'm sorry she had to be hurt so badly before he realized his mates are two different people, but he seems to be aware each one is special in her own way. It's almost like he's given himself permission to care about them in different ways."

"Uh-huh. He seems to see each as an individual. Perhaps someday he will have two only wives."

Chapter 26

THE MOON OF THE Wet Snows was nearly past. The Moon of the Early Green would soon begin. Most days the winds gusted instead of blowing fiercely.

Urscia's legs showed slow but steady progress in their healing, but her bitterness still bubbled and boiled beneath the surface ready to burst forth when least expected. Sometimes her anger snapped and snarled worse than before while at other times, it seemed to be gone. Lucza and Zhrul spent time with her and encouraged her about ways she could be useful though she was seldom receptive to them.

Even with the love and support she was receiving, Urscia still spoke of her own worthlessness, and she talked about going to the Frozen Wilds to get away.

One day Zhrul had brought their daughter Zeena who was completing her fifth winter to spend some time with her. The little girl remembered when Orol and Ryssa walked the Frozen Wilds together. She had talked about it and asked questions ever since it happened. Her parents did not seem to realize how much it bothered her, but after Urscia's accident, the little girl woke up screaming almost every night. Lucza and Zhrul tried to talk to her, but she only cried.

As Urscia's condition improved, Zhrul and Lucza encouraged the children to spend time with her. Though Sepram seemed comfortable with their mother, Zeena was not.

Horda and Unna noticed when Zeena sat beside her mother, her fear grew until it was almost a tangible thing. It didn't take long to determine the reason for Zeena's fear.

The little girl had frequently been spending time with her mother when Urscia said to no one in particular, "I still believe I should go to the Frozen Wilds."

Zeena tried to creep away, but her mother caught her and hugged her close. "You are my baby girl," she said.

"No," cried Zeena.

"Yes, you are."

"No, let me go."

Now Urscia was crying. "Please stay with me. I love you."

"No, I don' wanna go with you."

"I'm not going anywhere. I can't walk."

"You said you were." Zeena struggled out of her mother's arms and backed away. "I don' wanna go."

"But, I'm not going anywhere," protested Urscia.

Realization dawned on Horda. She went to the little girl and leaned down. "Where don't you want to go?"

"Fwozen Wilds." She moved into the folds of Horda's tunic.

Horda looked at Urscia who put her hands over her mouth. "Oh, Little One, come here." She held out her arms. "Oh, my baby."

Zeena would have nothing to do with her. Her dark eyes

looked huge in her little pale face as she backed further away from her mother. Tears trailed down her cheeks as she whispered, "I don't want to go to the Fwozen Wilds like Owol and Wyssa and their little one. I'm scared. I don' want you to go either, Ma. I don't."

Horda watched the tears streaming down Urscia's face and realized another stone had been removed from the path of Urscia's recovery.

"Oh, Little One. I'm not going to the Frozen Wilds," said Urscia.

"You said you were."

Urscia took a deep shuddering breath. "I know I did. I have no excuse."

"Why did you say that?"

"I was sad. My legs were hurt. I don't know."

Zeena looked at her mother. "You said it lots of times."

"I was upset and sad. I fell."

"And hurt your legs," prompted Zeena.

"Yes, and hurt my legs. After that I was afraid I wouldn't be able to walk. I thought people would want me to go to the Frozen Wilds."

Horda felt sad for this woman who was hurting so badly. She wondered why they hadn't realized how much she had wanted and needed reassurance that the People of the Frozen Earth didn't want her to go to the Frozen Wilds because she had fallen. It wasn't enough to tell her all the things she could do if no one told her how valuable those things were to the People and how much they wanted her to stay with them.

"I don' want you to go to the Fwozen Wilds," said Zeena. "I think it is enough if you just hol' me in your arms and talk to me."

"I don't want to go either."

"Then stop talkin' about it."

Horda put her hand on Urscia's shoulder. "I think that is good advice. I'm sorry I told you all the things you could do to help the People, but I never stopped to tell you how important you are. All the things have to be done, and you are better at them than many of us. You are still a valuable member of our band because of things you can do, but you are more valuable to us because you are you.."

Urscia sniffed and closed her eyes. She smiled faintly before she spoke. "Thank you. I know you have tried to help me. I know you spoke to Zhrul, and I know he didn't exactly listen to you until after I fell. Then he seemed to understand what you and Mach had been telling him, but I told myself it was too late. I didn't care. I was going to the Frozen Wilds.

"I heard you telling me all the things I could do well without legs, and I knew you were right — about most of them, but I didn't want to accept it. I thought my only value was in doing all the duties of the Women of the Frozen Earth — and doing them better than anyone else. I didn't want to accept other things made me valuable. We don't all have to do everything. I only lost my feet and legs. I can do other things that use my mind and my heart as well as my hands. But I didn't accept the value of those other things. I thought if I couldn't do everything, I couldn't do anything."

Horda opened her mouth, but Urscia waved her words away. "Let me finish or I may not. I watched you working hard doing all the things a leader's wife does, and then I watched you working tirelessly with Bran even when it seemed you were making no progress. You saw he still had value, and you were not going to let it go to waste.

"And Wilda. I don't know how you and Unna have done it, but she is working. Not as much as she might, but she will soon have a new little one. She does what needs to be done, and she's not whining anymore. I thought she would have to be banished, but she didn't. Once more you found value in someone I thought was worthless.

"But me? I didn't think Zhrul loved me. He took care of me and my little ones, but I never felt like he cared for me. I thought I was worthless. If my own mate didn't value me, who did?"

Zeena threw her arms around her mother. "I love you," she cried. "You're not worthless."

"Shh, Little One, I love you too. And I know now I'm not worthless, but I didn't then." Urscia hugged and patted the little girl.

Zeena looked up. "I love you very much, and I don' want you to go to the Fwozen Wilds ever."

Horda closed her eyes. Now they had another problem. How do you explain to a little one everyone will die sometime? You can't lie to them and tell them you will live forever. This little girl already knew that wasn't so. But they had just reassured her, and now they were going to take that reassurance away.

Urscia and Horda exchanged speaking looks. Horda shrugged and said, "Maybe we should call Unna."

"Or Zhrul?" said Urscia.

"Perhaps even Mach," suggested Horda. "Do you have any idea what to say?"

Shaking her head, Urscia lifted the little girl onto her lap. "Zeena, I don't want you to get all upset again. So you are going to have to listen carefully to everything I say. Okay?"

The little girl frowned, but she said, "Okay."

"My words have upset you before, and I didn't even realize it. I'm sorry."

Zeena patted her mother's face. "I was afraid you were goin' to the Fwozen Wilds and not comin' back."

"Yes, I know you were, and I'm sorry. I did think about it, but I don't think I ever really meant to do it."

"Then why did you say it?"

"That's hard to explain." Urscia closed her eyes and thought for a little while. "You know how Marcon pretends he is going to put things in the cook fire?"

Zeena giggled. "He's just aggavatin' you. He wants you to tell him to stop."

"That's right."

"Did you just want us to tell you to stop?"

"No, Little One, I didn't exactly want you to tell me to stop. I wanted you to tell me I didn't need to give up. I wanted you to tell me I am valuable to you even if I can never walk again."

"You are, Ma. You are!" Zeena hugged her again. "Now promise me you won't ever go to the Fwozen Wilds."

"I can't promise that."

Terror filled the little girl's eyes. "Why not? Are you goin' to take me with you? I don' wanna go."

"No, Little One, you must listen to me carefully. I cannot promise I won't ever go to the Frozen Wilds because someday everyone goes."

"No, I don' wanna."

"It will be many turnings of the seasons from now before I go and even more before you go."

"Huh?"

"How many winters do you have?"

Zeena held up five fingers.

"How many is that?" asked her mother.

"A whole hand."

"A whole hand, that's right. How many winters do I have?"

Zeena giggled. "Lots and lots and lots. You are old."

"Yes, I know. How many do you think I have?"

"Hands and hands and hands."

"You're being silly. Ma's ma has a hand plus four fingers hands of winters, but I only have a hand plus a finger's hands of winters."

"Tha's a lot."

"Yes, it is."

"You aren't walking the Fwozen Wilds."

"No, I'm not."

"Unna has lots and lots of hands of winters too," said Zeena.

"Yes, she does."

"She's not walkin' the Fwozen Wilds."

"No, she's not."

"Horda has lots and lots of winters."

"No, I don't," said Horda. "I have four fingers hands plus two fingers of winters."

"Tha's a lot, and you aren't walkin' the Frozen Wilds."

"No, I'm not, and neither is Zaaco or Nuroo."

"Or Mach or Thuro or Zeek," said Zeena. "They are really old."

"Okay," said Urscia, "Now, you see there are lots of old People in our band."

Zeena frowned, "Not lots."

"Yes, there are," said Horda. "Lots."

"You need to listen to me," said Urscia. "I'm trying to explain to you the People of the Frozen Earth usually live many winters before they walk the Frozen Wilds."

"Um-huh," said Zeena.

"I'm planning to live many more winters before I walk the Frozen Wilds, but if I were to promise you I would never walk them, it would be a lie."

"Lies are bad."

"Yes, lies are bad, so I will not promise you I won't go."

Zeena's little face wrinkled as she prepared to cry. "I don' want you to go."

"I promise I will not go voluntarily until you have as many winters as I do."

"Wha's voluntarly?"

"Because I want to."

"Oh. What if you have to go?"

"If Father Death calls me and fills my vessel of time, I will have to go whether I want to or not." Urscia looked into the little girl's eyes. "I promise to be careful and do everything I can to keep Father Death from calling me."

"Okay, but if you go, what about me?"

"I promise no matter if Father Death calls me, I will not take you with me unless Father Death has also called you."

"Okay, Ma." Zeena hugged her and tried to climb out of her lap. "Can I go play now?"

"If that's what you want to do."

"I do." Zeena waved. "I'll see you, Ma."

The two women watched the little girl run off to play. "You did a good job," said Horda.

"Do you think?" asked Urscia.

"Well, she certainly seems satisfied by your answers."

"I had no idea what was bothering her — or me, for that matter."

"Me either," said Horda, "but it makes so much sense. I'm sorry."

"It was silly of me," said Urscia. "Now I realize by telling me things I could do, you were telling me I was valuable, but I didn't understand it then."

"Just don't forget it."

"I won't. Zhrul has been very good to me, and he has been working hard to help me remember."

Horda smiled. "I know."

"I'm a little slow, but I believe I am finally getting the message."

"Finally, and I'm glad for you — and us."

Urscia laughed. "Me too."

Although Urscia was better, not all the bitterness and anguish were gone. Sometimes they pushed her to do more than she wanted to. And sometimes she became angry and did things she had given up hope of doing.

One fine spring day, Horda and Lucza angered Urscia enough she managed to hobble outside on her own feet. Instead of angry when she got there, she was elated and then frustrated. Though she tried, she could not lower herself to the ground so she was stuck standing in the warm sunshine. Horda and Lucza knew Zhrul and Zeek had been working on a seat to give her a degree of independence.

Urscia had been moving around inside, and Zhrul and Zeek had fashioned a sort of chair for her from a tree trunk. She was able to sit by herself, but she usually needed assistance to rise. Now the men had carved another seat with arms she could use to pull herself into a standing position. They had padded the seat with furs, and it was more sturdy and comfortable than the one she used inside.

Zhrul and Zeek brought the seat and placed it in the area of the women's circle.

"What is that?" Urscia asked.

"The new improved leg sparing seat," said Zhrul with a smile.

"Want to try it out?" asked Lucza.

"That's why you pushed so hard to get me outside," Urscia grumbled, but she sank onto her seat and raised her face to the warm sun.

"You didn't want to come out, and Zhrul and Zeek really wanted you to try the seat." Horda adjusted the furs.

Urscia caught the arms of the seat and hoisted herself to a standing position. Then she reached for her crutches and took a few steps. "Thank you."

The four adults hugged her and helped her back into her seat. "Don't overdo it," cautioned Zhrul.

Her daughter Zeena followed carrying her ma's sewing pack. Horda had watched the ornate bag growing empty as the projects were finished, but on that day, she could see new leather in the top of the pack. It was truly a good day.

Though Urscia still complained sometimes, she no longer threatened to go to the Frozen Wilds. Horda wondered what they would do if she asked. It was not the way of the People to disregard another's wishes, but she hoped Urscia was no longer considering it. Horda's heart twisted as she thought about little Ryssa. She missed the quiet young woman and the baby that never had a chance to live. She wondered if Ryssa regretted her decision to walk the Frozen Wilds.

One day they were sitting in the sun sewing when Bran walked up to Urscia. Horda held her breath because she did not know what Urscia would do or say to the little boy. He stopped and looked at the wood braces that held her legs in place. He frowned and patted her calf. "Hurt?" he said and signed.

Horda wasn't sure whether Urscia wasn't paying attention and didn't realize the child spoke to her or whether she ignored him. Before she could decide what to do, Bran tugged at Urscia's hand, and once more signed and said "Hurt?" Urscia glared. Bran drew his eyebrows into an almost perfect imitation of hers and signed and said, "Hurt?" once more.

Urscia laughed at the little boy's face, and said, "Yes, Bran, they hurt."

He watched her lips. Then he shook his head and signed his question again. Horda watched Urscia look around nervously, but she clumsily signed "Hurt."

Bran looked sad and said, "Sow'wy."

Horda breathed a sigh of relief when Urscia signed "Thank you" before she hugged the little boy.

He looked at the splints on her legs and walked from one side to the other. He leaned on her lap. "Did bis'n hurt you?" he asked and signed.

"No," she said frowning. "Not bison." She shook her head, but her hands were still. "I fell over the cliff."

"Sign," commanded Bran.

She shook her head. "I don't know how to sign," she

said.

The little boy looked confused. He did not read lips well so he had little understanding of Urscia's words. Horda wanted to help, but she had decided that the conversation was one she shouldn't join without an invitation.

Bran pulled on Urscia's hands and said, "Sign."

Urscia looked around. "Horda, help me. He wants me to sign, and I don't know how."

Horda signed an explanation to Bran. He cocked his head like an inquisitive bird and looked from Horda to Urscia and back. Then he smiled. "I'll learn her signs."

Urscia looked alarmed.

Horda asked, "What if she doesn't want you to teach her signs?"

He frowned and looked at Urscia. "Want learn?"

After a short time, she said, "Yes, I want to learn."

Soon Urscia, Bran, and all of the children of the band with at least three winters were studying the sign language as well as how to write the signs and pictographs. Urscia was a kind and patient teacher who blossomed with her enjoyment of her new duties. Horda and Mach breathed a sigh of relief as Urscia's problems helped solve Bran's. Now if something would just solve Wilda's problem.

Chapter 27

THE MOON OF THE Wet Snows had ended though the snow so slow to begin had lingered into the Moon of the Early Green. One morning Horda stepped out to gather snow for water and found a snow buttercup had pushed its way through the thin crust of ice near the cave entrance. She stared at the little flower and gave silent thanks they had survived another winter. "Spring," she called. "Spring is almost here."

Mach stuck his head out the cave opening. "What?" he asked looking up at the cloudy grey sky spitting snow flurries.

"Spring is almost here." She pointed to the tiny flower.

"Humph. Those things don't mean anything, Horda. They bloom through the ice crust. Anyway, it's snowing."

Horda refused to allow him to dampen her mood "When they begin to bloom, the worst is over."

Mach laughed. "The worst maybe, but not all by any means. When the primroses and forget-me-nots start blooming, then I'll listen to you hollering about spring being here. That's when winter's almost over."

"The plants begin to grow, and the animals will soon come back. Spring is almost here." A snowflake landed on her nose, and she shivered when a gust of wind lifted her hair.

Mach laughed. "So you say."

"So I say." Horda sniffed and knelt by the flower.

While she was filling her basket with snow, several members of the band trooped outside to admire the little flower. She giggled. Mach might not believe winter was almost over, but he was sure telling about her flower.

Going inside, she met Thuro and Wilda on their way out. "Greetings, Wilda and Thuro. Spring is almost here. Are you going to see the buttercup?"

Wilda fluttered the hand Thuro wasn't holding. "I want to see the early flowers one more time."

Horda swallowed her sharp retort and forced a smile. "It's right out there in the snow. There will probably be more by tomorrow."

Horda's eyes widened before she could stop them when Wilda placed her hand on her swollen stomach. *Mother Life, when did her hands begin to swell so?* Horda looked down at Wilda's ankles and saw they ran into her calves with little definition. *Oh, no. That doesn't look good.* She mentally counted the moons. The end of this one and then the little one was due in the Moon of the Growing Things. *Maybe if she quits eating so much cow parsnip it would help. Does she drink enough water? Oh, Mother Life. Please don't let her really be sick.*

"I hope I get to enjoy the spring flowers one more time before I go," murmured Wilda.

"Oh, I'm sure you'll see the summer flowers too." Horda

ducked past them into the cave. *If we can get the swelling down, you will. Please, Mother Life. Please.*

Though Wilda had stopped insisting on being carried everywhere she went and completed the chores assigned to her, she still played the invalid talking as if her death were imminent. Horda and Unna had given up trying to convince her her pregnancy was progressing normally and would reach its conclusion in its own time.

Now, the swelling made Horda wonder. She hung the bag of snow on the support over the cook fire where Unna was making porridge. "Unna, have you noticed anything about Wilda?"

"Besides she's obnoxious?" Unna chuckled before she saw the fear in Horda's eyes. "No. What have you noticed?"

"Maybe it's nothing, but her fingers are so swollen all the wrinkles on her knuckles are smooth and her legs look like tree trunks."

"Don't worry about it. Lots of women's hands and feet swell when they near the end of breeding." Unna stirred the porridge.

Horda frowned and shook her head. "I hope you're right, but I haven't seen many so swollen. She looks like she is going to burst."

Unna stared at Horda. "You're really worried."

"No, not really." Horda's eyes gave lie to her words. "It's just she's always talking about going to the Frozen Wilds. What if she's right?"

"I don't know," said Unna. "She probably just ate too much cow parsnip."

Horda blew out a breath that fluttered the short hair curling on her forehead. "I remember one young woman

Nuroo treated. She first came to him complaining of headaches and seeing lights. But her hands and feet were so swollen, I thought they were going to burst. He told me she was poisoning herself."

Lost in memory, Horda chewed the tip of her right index finger. "She wasn't as close to delivery as Wilda is. He kept giving her herbs trying to help her relieve herself and get the swelling down so the baby could grow."

Unna frowned. "I've seen such cases a few times."

"One day her whole body swelled like she was already dead and had been lying in the sun too long. Nuroo gave her herbs to bring the little one, but they didn't work. She had convulsions like Bran did, but she didn't have fever demons. She went into a coma and departed before we could get the baby out." Horda's voice was small and frightened. "Oh, Unna, what if that happens to Wilda?"

"You've treated others with the same symptoms, haven't you?"

"Not really."

"Not really?"

"There aren't many little ones born in the Inner Band. Selah, my father's youngest mate was expecting when Bear Claw kidnapped us." Tears roughened her voice. "She was so excited. It was going to be her first. She was certain she was having a little warrior, but she and her little one were gone to walk the Frozen Wilds when we returned." Horda blinked to dry the tears on her eyelashes. "She was beautiful and sweet. She could make the softest leather. Norlon said she bled and bled and bled …"

Unna said, "But did she swell?"

"No, she didn't. Have you treated women who swell so

much?"

Unna pursed her mouth. "A few times."

"What happened?" Horda asked.

"Well, usually they delivered healthy little ones. Sometimes the swelling went away before; sometimes it didn't. I remember one departed or maybe it was two. But I've been a medicine woman for a long time."

"I'm glad you are here. I don't know much about this. I do remember one time, one of Elko's mates swelled — her face and body, though, not just her hands and feet — and Nuroo forced her to deliver." The pain of the memory darkened her eyes. "It was too soon. The little one was too small. But once it was out, the swelling went away, and the mother was fine."

"That's been my experience. We'll watch Wilda carefully. Her time is getting close."

"Are you sure her time is not passed?"

"No, it only seems that way, but I've been here for a hand of moons so she should be near her time. It won't hurt the little one if we have to hurry it along a bit."

"I've never done that without Nuroo to supervise."

Unna said, "I have. Anyway don't borrow trouble. I still say she probably ate too much cow parsnip."

"You'll check her?"

"As soon as I finish my morning eat."

The short days lengthened, and the thin winter sun strengthened. Mottled patches of brown and grey soil appeared near the cave entrance as the snow melted and ran down the mountainside in a gurgling stream. Patches of snow buttercups shined like captured sunbeams. Then tiny pink primroses brightened the sheltered places near the boulders strewn down the slope.

The Moon of the Melting Snows waned when Horda stepped outside to find forget-me-nots joining the primroses and buttercups to form a patchwork of yellow, blue, and pink dotted with their dark green leaves and pale green grass shoots. She hugged herself and turned her face to the early morning sun. *Thank you, Mother Life.*

Wilda's hands and feet still swelled, but not so much as the day of the first snow buttercup. She no longer ate food seasoned lavishly with cow parsnip because no more cow parsnip remained in the stores of the band. Horda thanked Mother Life Wilda had never developed a taste for the precious salt the trader had brought and pushed away the memory of burning one of her last three bunches of dried parsnip. It was worth it she told herself. Soon Wilda's little one would be delivered, and the band would be back to normal.

Bran pulled at Horda's fingers. "Pwetty," he said without signing.

Kneeling down so he could see her mouth and her hands, she signed and repeated, "Pretty."

He reached out and touched her lips before imitating the sign, but he did not speak again.

"Would you like to pick some flowers?" she asked signing *pick flowers*.

Bran's eyes brightened, and he caught her hands almost pulling her off her feet. He raced off before she had time to savor his response. Catching him, she signed *bring rock*.

He frowned at her. She repeated the signs. He shrugged but picked up a rock and handed it to her before signing *pick flowers.* She nodded then signed *for your fa*.

He shook his head. "*For Mama.*"

Together they fashioned a bouquet of the tiny pink, blue, and yellow flowers before she picked him up and carried him inside to the cook fire where his mother worked. Setting him down, she signed *tell her*.

Bran walked to Reeme and tugged on the fringe of her tunic. She smiled down at her son without speaking. He laughed and thrust the crumpled bouquet into her hands. Then he signed and said, "For Mama."

Reeme's eyes filled with tears before she reached down to hug him. "Thank you, Bran," she murmured against his hair.

He shook his head and pushed her back. "What?" he demanded touching her mouth.

Hurt filled her eyes, but Horda said, "Sign for him. He wants to know what you said."

Obediently, Reeme set the flowers aside and signed "*Thank you, Bran.*"

Smiling Bran signed and said, "Welcome."

Zeek looked at Horda across the cook fire. "He's signing and talking just like you and Mach said he would."

She nodded. "Now, the work really begins."

A cloud covered the sun and cast a shadow causing Horda to shiver as she hurried to find Mach and share the news, but Wilda's hysterical whines and screams followed by the sharp counterpoint of Thuro's deep voice slowed her steps. *It's nothing. Some new complaint to punish Thuro. I must find Mach and tell him my news.* Then the unmistakable sound of retching followed by an agonized moan drove all thoughts of Bran and Mach from her head. She ran to the sleeping shelter.

"Thuro, Wilda, it's Horda." She entered without waiting to be acknowledged. "What's happening?"

Thuro stepped back. "She's awfully ill, Horda."

Wilda's eyes were tiny black pinpoints in her bloated face. "Father Death is coming for me. The campfires of the elders flicker on the walls of my shelter."

Lifting Wilda's hand, Horda saw the unnatural smoothness the swelling had produced. She ran her fingers lightly down the arm and felt the puffy tautness where the wrist should have been. Fighting to keep her voice level, she said, "Nonsense. You're getting ready to give birth. Nothing more." Horda's sensitive fingers probed Wilda's stomach, which seemed to have doubled in size overnight.

"Aieeee!"

Horda forced a smile. "See the pains of birth are beginning."

"In my ribs?" whined Wilda.

"Sometimes," lied Horda smoothly. "Thuro, call Unna and get my medicine pack from my cook fire. I need to examine Wilda."

"Don't leave me."

"I'm not leaving you."

"I want him to stay!"

"One of us has to get my things." She built up the shelter fire and washed her hands. "If Thuro goes, perhaps I can help the birth go more quickly."

"Hurry," commanded Wilda.

Horda hid her smile. At least this one wasn't passive —

yet. When Thuro was gone, she stripped the sleeping furs and clothing from Wilda's body so she could see what was happening. Though Wilda's womb was thinning and opening for the birth, it still lacked a great deal of being ready.

Wilda began retching again. Horda held the hide bowl for her and washed her face with the bit of soft leather Thuro had been using. When Wilda cried out against the pain in her ribs, Horda placed her hand on her stomach and knew for sure the pain wasn't caused by a contraction. She made a decision. They'd use the herbs.

Unna bustled into the small shelter with her medicine pack. "What's happening?"

Horda forced gaiety into her voice. "Wilda's going to have her little one. Would you like me to help you wash before you examine her? I'm sure there's hot water by the cook fire."

"Don't leave me," commanded Wilda.

"We're only stepping outside the shelter," said Horda. "We need hot water. We'll be right back."

Outside Horda held the water bag for Unna. "She's swollen."

"I can see that," muttered Unna. "Is she in labor?"

"No."

"Hmm ... the herbs?"

Horda nodded. "She has the other symptoms. We have to do it."

"Are you going to tell her?"

"No."

Thuro and Mach arrived with Horda's medicine pack, two large bags of water and a supply of wood.

"Thank you. I didn't think to ask for the wood and

water."

Wilda cried out, and Unna lifted the door covering.

Horda watched her disappear before she turned to Thuro. "Wilda is very ill."

"Ill?"

"Yes, I'm sure you've noticed how swollen she is. Her body is poisoning itself."

"With something she's eating?"

Horda shook her head. "No, no, it's nothing like that. It's something that happens sometimes. Nuroo doesn't know why, nor do I."

"What do you mean?"

"I'm not sure how to explain it." Horda searched for the right words. "It happens sometimes during pregnancy. The woman's body collects fluid, and she gets so she can't relieve herself. She swells. If it goes on too long ..."

Thuro's dark eyes showed his fright. "What can you do?"

"Deliver the little one," she said. "Once that is done, whatever caused the problem is over. The woman relieves herself, and she goes back to normal."

"Just like that? Deliver the little one." Thuro laughed bitterly. "What do you do lean down and tell it to come out?"

Horda squared her shoulders and stood firm against his unexpected venom. "No, with your permission, there are herbs we can give her to bring on her labor."

Thuro rubbed his mouth. "What about the little one?"

"Wilda's body is preparing itself to give birth. We believe the little one will be fine." She closed her eyes. *Please, Mother Life, let my words be true.*

"If you don't force the birth?" Thuro's dark eyes speared her soul.

"They will both depart to walk with Father Death."

"This is all my fault." Anger and pain painted red slashes across his cheekbones.

Horda touched his hand. "No, Thuro. It's no one's fault. Sometimes this thing happens."

Thuro's glare told her he did not find comfort in her words.

Wilda cried out, and the color drained from Thuro's face. His shoulders slumped, and his body seemed to shrink before her eyes. "Do whatever you must to save my mate."

Horda entered the shelter and found Unna had already prepared the tonic. Silently the old woman showed the young one the herbs she had used.

Horda said, "Wilda, we would have you drink this tonic. It will help you."

Unna looked at Horda but did not speak.

I'm not lying. The birth of the little one will help her.

Horda and Unna struggled to lift Wilda's immense body so she could drink the tonic.

After the first sip, Wilda pushed it away. "It tastes bad," she complained.

"Yes, I know it does," soothed Horda still supporting Wilda's shoulders, "but you must drink it."

Wilda frowned and took a few more swallows. "Enough," she declared and tried to lie down.

"No, it's not enough. Sit up. You must drink all of it."

"I don't want to." Wilda slumped.

Horda closed her eyes and in her mind touched the fingers of each hand. "It will help you." She placed the horn of tonic against Wilda's lips.

Wilda drank a little more and began to gag.

"Take deep breaths," commanded Unna.

Wilda glared before she took a deep breath and shrieked against the pain below her ribs.

Horda peered into the horn. "Just a few more swallows," she encouraged.

Wilda gulped the rest of the tonic and fell back gasping. "It hurts so much."

Girl, you don't know what pain is yet. "The pain will come and go," said Horda. "When it comes, I want you to look into my eyes and breathe like this." She demonstrated short panting breaths.

"Why?"

"Because it helps you rise above the discomfort."

"I want Thuro," fretted Wilda.

Horda stepped to the door. "Thuro, would you come sit with your mate for a time?"

Thuro's face was pale beneath the bronze, but he came in and took Wilda's hand. He talked to her while Horda and Unna prepared the seatless birthing chair, boiled water, and placed the sharp obsidian knives and sinew in a shallow basket of hot water. As she worked, Horda watched Wilda and waited for the pains of labor to begin.

Unna stepped to the door and motioned Horda outside with her chin.

"What's wrong?" asked Horda.

"She needs more tonic."

"More tonic?"

"The pains should have begun by now."

Horda moved inside away from Wilda. She dipped a small

basket of boiling water. Then she mixed another portion of the tonic from the herbs Unna handed her. Sniffing the mixture, she wrinkled her nose. "This is stronger. Should I add mint and camas molasses?"

Unna rolled her eyes. "Do you think it's necessary?"

"I don't know, but if it will get this down her, I'll add cow parsnip."

"We don't have any," said Unna.

"Well, yes, I do. I hid two bunches."

Unna raised her eyebrows.

"I thought I'd pretend I found it in the stores and cook her some fresh meat with it after the little one got here."

Unna shook her head and chuckled. "Add the mint and camas molasses. It tastes better."

Horda crumbled dried mint leaves into the tonic before dropping in two small ladles of thick camas molasses. She smelled the tonic again. "At least it smells better."

Wilda shrieked and Unna said, "Our patient's calling us."

Horda gave the tonic another stir and followed Unna around the fire to Wilda's side.

Thuro's face had paled more than before. Wilda's eyes showed white rings around the dark brown in her puffy face, and her nails dug crescents into her mate's hand. "It's terrible. I'm being torn in two," she babbled.

With quiet confidence Unna said, "Thuro, you may leave now. Go out and pace with Mach or something."

Wilda screeched, "Please, Thuro, don't leave me!"

Torn between his mate and the healer women, Thuro stood beside the fire.

Stepping around him, Horda filled the drinking horn with

the tonic and took a position beside Wilda's head. "We need to help you. Thuro will only be in the way."

"No."

"I need you to drink another horn of the tonic now, Wilda."

"No."

"You must. It will help the little one get here more quickly."

Looking terrified, Wilda allowed Horda to lift her head and help her drink about half of the tonic. "No more," she wheezed. Then she began to scream.

Horda placed her hand on Wilda's swollen belly and felt a reassuring movement from the little one. "Breathe like I showed you, Wilda," she coaxed.

Wilda ignored her and continued to scream. Soon the contractions began, and her screams grew louder and more frantic. Finally the first one faded, and she took a deep breath. Then she cursed Thuro who still stood motionless beside the fire.

Looking an apology at Thuro, Horda made soothing noises deep in her throat and agreed men were worse than snakes. When Wilda calmed, Horda again explained how to breathe and focus to ride the pain.

Another pain began and Wilda clutched Horda's hands and screamed and cursed once more. Horda managed to escape Wilda's grip and rubbed her hands. She looked at Thuro and shrugged. Maybe he could help. This birth was going to take a long time.

Unna, who had been examining Wilda, whispered, "Horda."

What now? "Thuro, sit beside Wilda and help her drink

the rest of this tonic." She joined Unna at Wilda's feet.

"She's opening." Unna motioned Horda to examine Wilda.

The relief Horda felt at Unna's words died when her sensitive fingers told her the little one wasn't in position to be born. *Mother Life, help us!* Taking a deep breath, she said, "Wilda, I want you to walk around the shelter."

"No."

"You must." Horda grasped her shoulders and pulled her into a sitting position.

"I will not." Wilda slumped against Horda's hands. "I can't walk."

"You have to walk. Your little one isn't in position to be born."

Panic sharpened Wilda's whine. "What do you mean?"

"I mean you have to stand up and walk so your little one has room to move into position to be born."

"I can't."

"Yes, you can." Thuro lifted her in his arms until her feet dangled above the dirt floor. He tried to stand her up, but her swollen legs wobbled. He lifted her again. "Stand up," he commanded.

Another pain gripped her. She screamed and fought him. He held on until the pain ended. Then he looked into her eyes. "Don't you want to help our little one be born?"

"No," she spat. "I never wanted a little one at all. You promised I wouldn't have to go through this."

Thuro took a deep breath. "I know I promised, but I promised too late, Wilda. Now, if you want the little one to come out, you're going to have to help Horda and Unna and do what they tell you. You are making this harder than it has to be."

Her lower lip quivered. "I never want to go through this again."

"Neither do I," vowed Thuro.

"You won't make me do it anymore." She looked up at him through eyelashes spiked by tears. "Will you?"

"No, Wilda. I won't make you do it anymore."

She seemed to consider his words. When he set her on her feet again, she stood. "You promise?" she whispered.

"I promise," he said. "I already vowed before Mother Life and Father Death, but I will vow it again at the next Gathering if you want me to."

A half smile curved her lips. "Maybe I can do it this once," she said.

"I know you can." He put a supporting arm around her, and Horda placed one of Wilda's arms around her own shoulder and her arm around Wilda's waist. Together they walked in slow circles around the sleeping shelter. Each time a pain began Wilda panted and focused on her mate's face for a short time before she screamed and cursed again.

Horda praised her. *Maybe it's helping a little bit. Please, let the little one get in position.* From time to time they fed Wilda bits of snow from shady places and sips of white alder bark and dried buckthorn bloom tonic.

Horda knew the sun had set long ago. Her feet felt like they had trekked back to the Inner Band, and her shoulders and back screamed in protest as she took more of Wilda's weight. Now she and Thuro carried Wilda around the sleeping shelter while her feet moved aimlessly in walking motions but supported none of her weight. Wilda's screams had weakened to hoarse moans though the pains came closer together and were much harder. Her skin was stretched to the point she looked like it would split. "Let her lie down," Horda said. "Wilda, I need to examine you."

Lying down, Wilda drew herself into a ball and whimpered. "It hurts so much."

Horda straightened Wilda's legs to examine her. Her womb had opened until her body was ready to give birth. But the little one was not ready to be born. Still it presented its back to the birth canal. Horda sat on her haunches and frowned. Another pain roused Wilda to cry and whimper, but it ended, and she faded into a stupor.

Horda massaged Wilda's swollen abdomen trying to turn the little one from the outside. Unna watched Wilda before she went to the shelter door and called, "Mach, bring me some bear grease." Then she announced, "I'll turn the little one."

Horda's eyes widened. "What?"

"I'll turn the little one."

"I've heard of that, but I've never seen it. How are you going to do that?" asked Horda.

"With my hand." She took one of the flint knives and pared her fingernails away until the tips of her fingers were smooth.

Horda dipped a basket of steaming water.

"If you can turn the little one with your hand, why did we spend all the time walking?" asked Thuro.

Unna scowled at him. "Men have no place in a birth shelter."

"I'm here," he said, "and I asked you a question."

Unna washed her hands with the hot water and soaproot. Then she rinsed them before she answered. "It is very difficult to turn a child. Sometimes ..." she paused and looked at the seemingly oblivious Wilda. "My hands are smaller than Horda's though I don't have the strength I once did."

Now Thuro's eyes widened, and his face turned a definite shade of green. "Are you going to put your hand in —"

Unna stopped his words with a hard look. She nodded. "It's the only way I know."

Mach handed Unna a small wooden bowl of rendered bear grease and stood staring at Wilda. "Is she sleeping?" he whispered before another contraction knotted her stomach and caused her to open her eyes and moan.

Unna greased her hand, wrists, and forearm. "Do the rest of the warriors want to join us for this?"

"No." Mach backed out of the shelter.

Unna looked at Thuro.

Horda touched his hand. "You should leave."

He shook his head and took a place at his mate's shoulder. "This is my fault and I'm staying."

"It's no one's fault," said Horda. "It just happens sometimes."

"Maybe I can help," he said.

Unna muttered something under her breath about bison flying and took a position between Wilda's outstretched legs. "We need to elevate her hips."

Horda hurried to bring the seatless chair they had fashioned earlier.

"Take it apart and tilt her bottom up," commanded Unna.

Another contraction racked Wilda's almost comatose body. The pain ended and Unna said, "Hurry. I have to work between the contractions.

"After the next pain, Thuro, hold her shoulders steady. Horda, you try again to turn the little one from the outside." She pointed to the left side of Wilda's swollen abdomen. "The head is there, and it needs to be here." She pointed again.

Thuro swallowed audibly.

"If you're going to be sick," said Unna. "Leave now."

"I'm not going to be sick," said Thuro although the green shade of his face darkened.

Unna rubbed more of the bear grease on her hand and wrist as another contraction began. Horda looked at Unna who nodded almost imperceptibly.

As soon as the pain eased, Unna pushed her fingers into Wilda's body. Water and blood gushed forth. Thuro swallowed noisily, but his hold on his mate's shoulders didn't waver. Unna slipped her hand farther into the womb. Horda placed her hands on either side of Wilda's abdomen and rubbed it trying to turn the lump into position.

Wilda's eyes flickered open and she moaned, but Thuro soothed her and she quieted.

Unna pushed and turned. "I feel the shoulder," she murmured. "It's moving."

Horda nodded. Unna kept pushing against the little one. Then her eyes widened. Another contraction squeezed through Wilda compressing Unna's arm and hand and causing pain to flare in her eyes.

"Keep trying to turn the little one from the outside." Unna's old eyes narrowed. "I can feel the head."

Thuro held Wilda's shoulders, and Horda massaged her knotted abdomen trying to straighten the little one's body.

Unna pursed her lips, and the tip of her tongue stuck out

the corner of her mouth while her arm moved gently. "Now, that's better."

Horda waited for her to remove her hand. She didn't. "What's wr —"

"Shhhh! I'm waiting for another contraction." Unna didn't have long to wait. The contraction started and she coaxed, "Come on, little one. You can do it." She allowed her hand to be expelled. Then she watched the contraction reach its conclusion. A smile lighted her tired eyes. "We did it. I can see the top of its head. It's coming."

Horda and Thuro sat back to watch, but Unna said, "No. Help her. Put your hands above the little one and help it out."

Cautiously, Thuro placed his hands on Wilda's abdomen.

Horda laughed. "Not like that. Use your strength." She pressed Wilda's stomach and guided the baby.

Thuro took a deep breath and did the same. Wilda moaned but did not fight them.

"I have its shoulders," said Unna cradling the half-born little one. "One more contraction, and it will be here."

The contraction began. They worked together once more. Unna said, "You have a little warrior, Thuro."

Chapter 28

THURO STARED AT THE tiny grey scrap of humanity lying so still in Unna's greasy, blood-stained hands. "A man child?" he croaked.

"A man child," said Horda.

"What's wrong with him?" asked Thuro. "Why is he so still?"

"Nothing's wrong." Unna thrust the child into Horda's hands. "Clear his mouth." She turned back to the father. "He's just not quite ready to breathe air."

Horda used a hollow reed to remove the birth fluid from the baby's throat and nostrils. Then she rubbed the soles of his feet. Pink suffused his tiny body before he gave a lusty yell.

"See, nothing's wrong with him, Thuro." She smiled though tears streamed down her cheeks. "Listen to those lungs." She cuddled the child against her lonely breast little more than an instant before she passed him to his father. "Here, Thuro. Hold him against your chest so he can hear your heartbeat."

"Me?"

Horda laughed. "No, your invisible friend beside you."

"I've never held a baby this new."

"I daresay you've never held a baby before." Horda smiled. "Have you?"

"Horda, I need your assistance," announced Unna.

Horda thrust the little one into Thuro's reluctant arms. "So, it's fitting your son should be the first."

The little one's squawking cries faded to silence as he burrowed against Thuro's chest.

Thuro traced a fingertip along the curve of the infant's cheek. The baby blinked and seemed to stare at his father's face. Thuro looked at the pulsing purple umbilical cord. "What are you going to do about that?"

"Watch." Using wooden tongs, Horda fished a small ball of sinew from one of the boiling bags. She tied the cord in two places. Then she lifted her best obsidian knife from the bag and slashed between the knots. "Wrap him in one of the fawn skins and sit by the fire," she directed. "We'll bathe him after we care for Wilda."

Horda watched Thuro stare down into his son's enormous blue-black eyes. Regret and longing scalded her soul. *Mother Life, why? Why can't Mach and I have a little one of our own?* Taking a deep breath, she swallowed against the burning tears in her throat and turned to help Unna once more. They delivered the afterbirth, and Horda wrapped it in another new fawn skin.

Unna cleaned Wilda's body and nodded. "It's started," she whispered.

Lost in her own regrets, Horda jolted. "What?"

"All that water. It's already draining away."

Horda looked at Wilda and said, "I'll fix her bedding."

Together they cleaned Wilda and placed her on a kind of night bag so her kidneys could wash away the poison without soiling her bed.

Exhausted, Unna leaned back and smiled her approval. "Now, let her drain for a while. Wash your hands and brew a tonic of columbine petals and leaves to help her get rid of the swelling."

Thuro looked at his mate's still form and at the wiggling scrap in his arms. "Will she be all right?"

"I'm certain of it. She never became deeply comatose, and she didn't convulse. Already her body is ridding itself of the swelling." Unna patted his arm. "She should be fine before another turning of the sun."

Thuro blinked. "Another?"

Horda laughed. "A day, a night, and most of another day have passed, Thuro."

"A day, a night, and a day?"

"We were kind of busy," said Unna.

Thuro yawned, and his stomach rumbled.

Unna cackled. "Now that he knows, he's exhausted and starving."

"No, I'm not." Thuro cradled his son against his chest.

"Well, I am." Unna rotated her shoulders. "As soon as the little one is settled, I'm going to eat and sleep. Birthing's hard on old bones."

Dipping her hands in hot water, she scrubbed them with soaproot and fine sand. Horda poured more water over them to rinse away the last vestiges of grease and blood. Unna inspected the purple bruise on her wrist.

"Wilda's still strong, Thuro." She rubbed her aching hands then reached for the little one.

Thuro hesitated, then surrendered the bundle to Unna. The little one jostled and opened his eyes. He glowered while Unna unwrapped him. He fretted until he stuffed his right fist into his mouth. Then he smacked and slurped.

Sitting beside the fire, Unna lowered the little one into the shallow basket of warm water Horda had prepared. He squawked around his fist and glared accusingly.

"Now, now, little fellow," crooned Unna. "You have to have your first bath. It won't take long."

Careful of the knotted umbilical cord, she washed him with soaproot and rinsed away the suds. He blinked and smacked contentedly.

"There," she said patting him dry with the fine fawn skin. "Where's Wilda's birthing pack?"

"I don't know." Thuro surveyed the shelter. "I don't think she has one."

"Doesn't have one?" Unna's eyes narrowed as she looked around the cluttered shelter. "This little one needs clothing and pads of soft leather and combed flax seeds and moss."

Horda said, "I'll get what he needs."

Unna grunted and snuggled the little one against her sunken chest where he made snuffling sounds. "Hurry. We don't want him chilled."

"I'm sorry, Unna," murmured Thuro.

"About what?"

"That the little one doesn't have —"

Unna waved both his apology and her anger away. "He came early. I'm sure Wilda would have been prepared."

Thuro shrugged.

Horda returned with a supply of combed flax, moss, and a tiny rabbit skin sacque.

"Good." Unna swaddled the baby's behind in the flax and moss. She slipped the sacque over his head and pulled his arms through the sleeves. He blinked at her then opened his mouth wide. Instead a full scream, a squeak escaped.

Watching, Horda laughed around the lump in her throat. Her arms ached to hold her own little one.

Thuro jumped and hovered over his newborn son. "Is he all right?"

Unna settled the little one against her shoulder and rubbed his back. "Of course, he's all right. Aren't you, little fellow? Tell your fa getting born is hard work. You're about ready for a sleep."

Thuro looked doubtful. The little one yawned and whimpered. "How will we feed him?" he asked.

"We aren't going to feed him," murmured Unna.

Horda fought to keep from laughing at Thuro's scowl.

"What do you mean we aren't going to feed him? Even I know babies have to be fed — often."

"Calm down, Thuro," said Horda. "We don't have to feed him. His mother will."

"His mother? But she's very ill."

"Actually her illness is pretty much over now that the little one has been born," said Horda.

"Over? Just like that?" asked Thuro.

"Just like that."

"Do you mean the little one made her so sick?"

"It seems that's what happens," said Horda. "Because once the little one is delivered, the swelling goes away, and the mother recovers. She should feel much better in one or two turnings of the sun. She will be back to normal before a moon has passed."

"Normal," muttered Thuro with a grimace.

Horda bit her lips but otherwise ignored Thuro's disgusted look. "She'll be able to nurse him now, but we'll care for him while she recovers." She watched Unna position the little one at the sleeping Wilda's breast.

"Don't." Wilda tried to turn away.

"Your little one is hungry." Unna pushed Wilda's shoulder back.

"My little one?" Wilda's eyes popped open. "You mean my little one has been born?"

"Yes, your little one has been born." Unna chuckled. "Obviously it wasn't too bad if you didn't even know when it happened."

Horda turned to Thuro. "See. We told you."

"It was terrible," whined Wilda. "Unbearable pain that went on and on and on." Her eyebrows drew together and her lips pursed. "It felt like a giant bird was eating my insides. I couldn't breathe. I will never do that again."

"Nonsense," said Unna. "Don't talk about it, and you will soon forget it. It is over. You have a fine boy child. He needs to be fed."

"But I'm too weak and ill." Fluttering her eyelashes, Wilda wilted against the cushion of sleeping furs.

"You'll feel weak for a while," said Horda, "but tomorrow you must sit up and move around."

"Why?"

"It will help you regain your strength."

"I'm not ready to regain my strength. I told you I was sick," she crowed. "I told you so, but you didn't believe me."

"We believed you, but there was nothing we could do

until the little one came." Horda prayed for patience.

"But I am still sick. I am too sick to care for a child."

"Yes, you probably are," said Horda.

Wilda looked smug.

"But you aren't too sick to feed him. Unna and I will take care of him while you recover if you will just feed him."

"Feed him?" Wilda squawked. "I'm much too sick to do any of that stuff. See how swollen I am."

"You should have seen how swollen you were. We've told you it's over. Once the little one is born, the sickness goes away," said Unna. And no matter how many more times you breed, that sickness won't come back again — at least I've never seen a woman have it more than once."

"I'm never going to breed again as long as I live," declared Wilda. "Thuro promised me."

The little one tired of the elusive nipple teasing his lips and nose. He let out a full-throated scream. Startled, Wilda almost dropped him.

"What's wrong?" she yelled.

Unna said, "I told you he's hungry."

"Hungry?"

"Oh, for the Mother's sake, Wilda," snapped Horda. "You do know the meaning of the word hungry. Don't you?"

"Of course, but I told you I am still much too ill to care for a little one." She pushed the screaming baby toward Horda's arms.

Horda bit her lip and swallowed her tears. *Some people don't realize when they are blessed.* Horda's fingers opened and closed on the emptiness left by the death of her own little one. "You only have to feed him. We'll care for him until you're stronger."

"But —"

"Aiyana is the only nursing mother. She hardly has enough milk for her own child," said Horda. "You must feed him yourself."

Wilda pouted.

Horda coaxed, "I'll care for him if you feed him."

Some of Horda's longing must have shown in her voice or her face. Wilda stared at her before she tucked the little one into her bosom. "I won't need your help for many turnings of the sun," she declared.

"I'm sure you won't." Horda moved away before Wilda saw the tears filling her eyes. She clamped her teeth into her lower lip. *Oh, Mother Life. Please, please let me have a little one of my own.*

The evening shadows lengthened on the fifth day after the birth of Thuro and Wilda's little one. Thuro carried on a one-sided conversation with the infant while Wilda primped and preened over a shallow water basket trying various hairstyles for the Naming Ceremony. Suddenly she frowned. "Thuro, did you bring my new tunic?"

"You are going to be a big warrior one day." The baby blinked and waved his hand causing Thuro to chuckle. "Yes, I know it's hard to imagine, but you will be. I'm sure of it."

Wilda stamped her foot. "Thuro, are you listening to me?"

"No." He looked at her. "I was talking to the little one. I didn't know you were talking to me."

"Well, I was."

"What did you say?"

She sighed. "I asked if you brought my ceremonial tunic."

"Nope. I couldn't find it."

"You couldn't find it?" Her voice rose. "I told you it was packed in the big basket beside the sleeping furs."

"There wasn't a big basket by the sleeping furs." Thuro smiled at the baby who appeared to be frightened by his mother's loud voice.

"Yes, there is." She glared. "I put it there when we finally moved into this cave after Gathering."

Thuro raised the little one to his shoulder and crooned comforting sounds to his frightened son. His displeasure was plain on his face. "No, Wilda, the basket of clothes is not beside the sleeping furs. I looked all over the shelter, and I didn't find it."

"Where can it be?" Wilda's eyes filled with tears, and her lower lip began to quiver. "What's happened to it?"

"I have no idea. Neither of us was very careful with our possessions during the last few moons."

"I have to have my ceremonial tunic," wailed Wilda.

"Horda and Unna are cleaning the shelter. Horda said she would look for it."

Wilda screeched causing the baby to cry out. "Horda and Unna are cleaning our shelter?"

"Yep." Thuro jiggled the crying baby on his shoulder. "Shh, don't cry, little one," he whispered. "Your ma's just sounding off a little bit. You're going to have to get used to it. It's a little bit like thunder. It sounds bad, but it doesn't mean anything."

Wilda glared. "How could you?"

He jumped. "How could I what?"

"Ask them to clean our shelter." Wilda sobbed.

"They volunteered."

She sobbed harder. "What will I do? They already think I'm useless."

"Wilda, you were very ill. They know because they told me."

She sniffed. "No one believed I was sick. They kept telling me I was all right."

"We were wrong." He shook his head. "You are getting well, but you haven't completely recovered. Horda told me you would still need more help than usual for a while."

"She did?" Wilda sniffed and smeared her tears.

"Yes, she did. And they volunteered to clean the shelter for us." He frowned. "Didn't you all clean Aiyana's shelter for her when Zakon was born?"

"They did." Her lower lip quivered and tears pooled in her eyes. "I intended to help, but I was busy."

Thuro refrained from asking what she had been busy doing.

"How long?"

"How long what?" asked Thuro.

"How long will I need help?"

"Oh, ahum, ah, I don't remember. I think she said about a moon and maybe longer."

"A whole moon." Wilda's eyes glistened, but Thuro didn't think it was because of tears.

Then Horda called from outside the birthing shelter. "Wilda, may I enter?"

Wilda sniffed and scrubbed the tear stains off her face. "Enter, please."

Horda brought a pale blue tunic embroidered with tiny agates, bird bone beads, and eaglet feathers into the shelter. In her hands she carried matching moccasins and a small leather bag. "Is this what I was looking for?"

"Yes." Wilda snatched the tunic and moccasins out of Horda's hands and began smoothing them.

Horda pretended not to notice Wilda's rudeness. "Someone turned the basket over. You know how men are. If what they're looking for doesn't bite them on the nose, they never find it."

Thuro's eyes silently thanked Horda for her diplomacy. Horda opened the leather bag and took out a tiny tunic of dark green fawn skin decorated with feather fuzz and tiny quills. "I didn't know if you needed something for your little one to wear to the Naming Ceremony tomorrow or not."

Wilda's mouth rounded, and she reached out to touch the exquisite outfit. "That's beautiful, Horda. I — ah — intended to — ah — make a decorated tunic for the little one, but — ahm — I — ah — didn't get to."

"You may have this one for my birthing gift." Horda drew tiny leggings and moccasins dyed to match the tunic from the bag.

"It's too fine." said Wilda though she already held the tunic in her hands.

Horda shook her head. "I made it to pass the time during the cold winter moons."

Thuro asked, "Weren't you making it for your own little one?"

Tears filled Horda's eyes, but she blinked them away. "No, not really." She swallowed the hot lump in her throat. "I was hoping, but ..." She shrugged and shook her head. "No, I didn't plan who would wear it when I made it." She turned on her heel and left the birthing shelter. "I have to go."

"Thank you, Horda," said Thuro.

Wilda frowned. "We really shouldn't take this."

Thuro's eyes speared his wife. "Do you have anything for the little one to wear?"

Wilda shook her head. "She likes to make me look inadequate."

"What do you mean?"

"It's not fair. She wants to take my little one away from me."

"I don't think so." Thuro attempted to follow his mate's disconnected thoughts.

"I've been pregnant and given birth. She's never even been pregnant."

"But she ..." Thuro caught himself before he finished the sentence.

"She what?"

"She's just being nice. She's trying to help you out."

"Oh, yeah. She has all these clothes for little ones, and she keeps giving things to my little one." She complained, "It just doesn't seem right."

"You don't have any clothes for the little one," he reminded her.

"Take her side," Wilda screeched. "Just like at the first Naming Ceremony. Well, this time you will take a major part."

"I'm not taking anyone's side," said Thuro. "I'm simply saying you should thank her instead of griping and whining, because without her help, our little one would have no clothes."

"I was sick."

"I know you were sick."

"But none of you believed me."

Thuro said, "My fa told me the story of a small girl who liked to walk outside the shelters, but she hated to walk alone. She grew bored and lonely and called her friends to walk with her. Everyone else was busy so they ignored her. Then she had an idea. She cried, 'Help! Help! A big-toothed cat is chasing me. Help me!'

"Everyone in the band ran to help her. They were angry and dismayed to find the little girl had just pretended there was a big-toothed cat. She pouted and said, 'Now, someone must stay and walk with me.' But no one did.

"Not many turnings of the sun passed before she walked alone and became bored and lonely once more. Once more the People ignored her call for company. Once more she cried, 'Help! Help! a big-toothed cat is chasing me. Help me!' Once more the People of the band ran to help her and found she had tricked them. They had hardly returned to their tasks when a big-toothed cat really did attack the little girl. She screamed and cried for help, but the People shook their heads and told each other they would not be fooled again. They continued their work while the big-toothed cat filled the little girl's vessel of time."

Thuro watched the dull red of anger tint Wilda's cheeks. She sniffed and glared. She huffed and glowered. "Are you saying I wasn't sick?"

Thuro shrugged. "No, Wilda, I realize you were very sick toward the end."

Tears quivered on the bottom lashes of Wilda's eyes. "But not at first. You thought I was pretending." Her lower lip trembled.

Thuro fought to keep from wrapping his arms around her. "I didn't say that. I knew you suffered the illness of early breeding."

"Yes, I did. Terribly." Wilda fluffed her hair and jingled the beads and shells adorning her braids. She looked up at her husband. "I did suffer — more than most women."

"Wilda, with you everything is more than most people." Thuro tucked the sleeping little one into his cradle. "I will see you at sunrise for the naming ceremony." He leaned down to touch his lips to hers, but she turned away.

Without another word, he was gone. She glared after him stamping her foot and cursing under her breath so she wouldn't awaken the little one.

He doesn't understand me. I am not like other women. I am special, and he just doesn't understand me. I will make him understand. I will, she vowed.

Chapter 29

AT A SIGNAL FROM Mach, the soft cadence of the small drums signaled the beginning of the second Naming Ceremony of the new band. The willow and antelope bone flutes sang the lilting melody and called the People to assemble in the frosty air for the procession up the hill to the Circle of Light.

Mach missed the full rich sound of Thunder Eagle's flute. He would not mention the missing man, but he imagined everyone was as aware of his absence he was.

As was traditional, the parents and their little one were the last to take their places at the head of the procession. Then the instruments echoed across the early morning air. Wilda and Thuro led the members of the band up the trail to the high sacred place Mach and Thuro had marked and purified before baby Zakon's Naming Ceremony.

Mach stood alone waiting to greet Wilda and Thuro and escort them to their places. The others stood in the smudgy shadows around him and waited for the return of the sun.

When the sun's first ray lifted the gloomy shadows and touched the baby's dark head, Mach began the chants and prayers welcoming another new life into the band.

"Thank you, Mother Life, for your bounty and goodness," the People replied when Mach had completed the first prayer.

Without a pause, he went to the next. ". . . Babies are the greatest gift the Mother gives us."

Horda's heart ached as she watched Mach touch the little one's straight black hair. She swallowed against the tears burning her throat. *Oh, please Mother Life, have mercy on us. Haven't we suffered enough? Let us have a little one of our own.*

"Thank you, Mother Life." She forced herself to concentrate as the People joined together in a song of thanksgiving.

"Who brings this child to the Mother?"

Thuro held the infant up to the sun. "Mother Life, I thank you for this fine little one. I promise to educate him in the ways of the People of the Frozen Earth. To teach him our values and beliefs. To show him that I revere you and treasure our ways. I will protect him with my life."

When Thuro's words were finished, he handed the baby back to his mother. Wilda looked uncomfortable, and her voice wavered as she held the little one up and made the same solemn pledges.

Thuro placed his hands over Wilda's on the baby and waited. The sun rose above the horizon and together the parents held the child up to its gentle rays. In a quivering voice, Wilda said, "Mother Life, our first-born son Byrne."

The parents turned to the west where the dying sun would set in the shadowy mountains and raised the baby high.

This time, she spoke more clearly. "Father Death, our first-born son Byrne." They turned to the waiting People, and once more Wilda's voice quivered. "Our first-born son

Byrne."

The soft heartbeat of the drums sounded in the background, and the willow flutes' notes soared and dipped while Mach led chants and performed the dances of thanksgiving for the new life. The People spoke the words of welcome and offered gifts to Wilda, Thuro, and baby Byrne. Then they danced the dances of welcome.

Mach took baby Byrne and held him high over his head. "Mother Life and Father Death, we thank you for Byrne, another new member of our new band. We ask you to smooth the paths of his life. Please, give him your wisdom to share with the People of the Frozen Earth. We beg you to fill his horn of time slowly so he may watch his children's children's children play around cook fires not yet kindled before he walks the Frozen Wilds and becomes a memory like smoke of cook fires long grown cold. We plead these things for Byrne if they be your will."

"Please, Mother Life and Father Death," whispered the People with the soft sibilant voice of the wind.

Horda's mouth curved in a semblance of a smile, but tears burned her eyes and tried to choke her. A sob filled her throat, and the salty tears turned into a tickle. She had to cough. She followed Mach and the others down the path to the waiting feast. *Please, Mother Life, grant us our own little ones.*

The feast would take the place of the morning eat. The women and some of the men had risen early to prepare their special dishes. The crisp scents of burning cedar and sage mixed with the odors of roasting meat and vegetables to perfume the cool air. Talk and laughter filled the morning as the People waited for the call to eat. Some of the little ones pulled awake earlier than usual fretted until they were fed samples from their mother's or some other mother's cooking bag.

Soon the call came to join for the blessing. Silence fell over the area as Thuro called on Mother Life to hear their praises and grant them many turnings of the sun with full cooking bags.

Wilda, Thuro, and Byrne were seated in the place of honor in the light of the morning sun. One by one each man and his family walked to them and presented their own blessing. Each of the wives had some gift for the baby — a small shirt, leggings, tiny moccasins, leather bottoms, a sack of the cedar shavings and wood moss used for padding the baby's bottom to protect it from urine and feces.

Thuro reached out to the People thanking them and exclaiming over the gifts they bore. Baby Byrne even woke long enough to gurgle and whimper a little before he cried. The People laughed and talked to him. Despite Thuro's efforts, Wilda once more managed to alienate the People by her disdainful looks and her insincere thanks.

Realizing what was happening, Thuro whispered, "Behave."

"I am behaving."

"No, you're not."

With a gusty sigh, she pasted a fake smile on her face. "Thank you so much for your gift. I'm sure we will find some use for it." She crinkled her eyes and pointed with her chin. "Just lay it over there with the other stuff."

Thuro's fingers tightened on her shoulder. Anger flashed in her eyes, but she did not speak to him nor did she change her attitude toward the gifts.

Finally everyone had spoken. Then the feast began.

Roaming among the three hands of cook fires, the People ate and visited until the sun was high in the sky. When the feasting was finished, the fires were banked, and the men cleared the area for the games. First were races to see who was the fastest runner with the best endurance. Then there were contests to measure strength, agility, voices, and all the other qualities the band needed to survive.

Though the games were fun and filled with laughter and good-natured teasing, they served a serious purpose. These contests showed the children all the qualities needed for the survival of the band, and they showed the adults which children were naturally talented and who needed help to learn the skills necessary for survival.

A cold wind whistled across the playing area, and the sun disappeared behind a high mountain of boiling storm clouds. Surprised and more than a little frightened, the People watched the sunny day become grey, windy, and cold. The blowing wind carried the smell of snow and tiny shards of sharp ice as the People hurried to return everything to the winter cave.

Wilda frowned and stamped her tiny foot while baby Byrne twisted in his cradle board and squeaked his displeasure. "I cannot believe it is coming a blizzard on my little one's naming day!" She stomped around the sleeping area like an angry child.

Thuro laughed at her. "What? Do you think the spring storms will wait for you to celebrate?"

She whirled on him and glared. "They would certainly wait if it were her and Mach's celebration. None of the real world dares intrude on them."

"You know nothing about it, Wilda," he said sadly.

Wilda screeched, "You tell me I don't, but you never share with me. Everyone who was kidnapped acts like they have a secret. They act like Horda is something special, but I'll tell you, she is not. She acts superior, but I am her equal. No, I am better than she. I have a son, and she does not. So there!" Little flecks of spit flew from her mouth while angry sparks shot from her eyes.

"You have a son only because she knew what to do to keep you and him from walking the Frozen Wilds." Thuro picked up his screaming son and crooned senseless words of comfort to calm him.

"Oh, yes, I knew you would find some way to raise her above me. You think she is wonderful, but you can't see her faults. Her hair and eyes are too light, and her nose is too little. She is almost as tall as you, and her feet are as big as a buffalo's."

Thuro closed his eyes and mentally counted the fingers of each hand before he spoke. He held Byrne out to his mate. "Your son, Wilda."

Stupidly she looked at him. He thrust the screaming infant into her arms. She wrinkled her nose and gagged. "He needs changing."

"Yes, he does," agreed Thuro.

Holding the infant as far from her as she could, she looked

around in dismay. "I don't know h... I mean I can't ch... ah, I haven't ever because someone else always changed him while I was in the birthing shelter."

"Then since you are so much better than Horda because you have a son, perhaps it's time you started to take care of him." Thuro turned on his heel. He strode out of the shelter leaving Wilda holding the angry, wet, dirty infant. Stopping at the door, he said, "And anyway, buffalo don't have big feet."

Thuro realized many of the People had heard his mate's furious voice just as they could hear his son's angry cries. He wondered what he was going to say to them as he stepped into the open area. Not one person was out of their family areas.

Taking a deep breath, he breathed a prayer. *Thank you, Mother Life, for helping everybody be busy somewhere else while Wilda threw her tantrum. Please, Mother Life, I beg of you, help her grow up and be the woman you want her to be. And, please, give me the strength and knowledge to deal with her. Help me to help her because I don't know how or what to do.*

In their family area, Mach looked at Horda. "What are we going to do?" he mouthed.

She shrugged her shoulders and shook her head. Motioning toward the open area, she whispered. "Go help him."

"Me? What do you want me to do?"

"I don't know."

"Well, neither do I."

"He's your friend."

"Your father and Suka said you could help him with her."

"I told you and them I don't know what to do with her," she whispered and pointed with her chin. "Go, Mach. He needs you. He would be embarrassed if I were out there now."

"And you don't think he's going to be embarrassed by my being out there?"

"No."

"Why not?"

"If you are quiet, he's not going to know we know anything about what's going on."

Baby Byrne's screams were becoming frantic.

"I don't have to be quiet. Byrne is making enough noise no one will hear us."

"Go, help him."

"Will you go help the baby?"

"You heard her. She resents me."

"Are you just going to let the baby cry?" Mach looked at his mate as Rain Drop ran into the sleeping area.

Gasping for breath, she said, "You have to go help Wilda, Horda."

"Go find Unna," said Horda. "Ask her to help Wilda."

"I don't know where she is. It's snowing."

"Do you think she's still outside?" Mach looked up in alarm.

Rain Drop grinned. "No, she's with Reeme and Zeek. They been talking about Bran. He learned some new words today."

"Good," said Horda. "Now, you go ask Unna to go help Wilda calm Byrne, but don't yell. Don't let Wilda or anyone else know I sent you for Unna. Do you understand me?"

"Yes, I un'nerstand."

"Good, I'll see to it there is rose tea with camas molasses tonight after the evening eat."

"Okay." The little girl raced across the shelter.

"Now, Mach, please, go talk to Thuro. He needs a friend right now, and I am not it."

"Oh, I don't know," he said. "You know more about how to treat recently pregnant women than I do."

She shook her head. "I don't know anything about his mate."

"And you think I do?"

She had to smile. "No, I don't think anyone knows how to deal with her. But I do know Thuro is beside himself. He doesn't know what to do with her or the new baby."

The baby's screams intensified, and Mach looked frightened. "I don't have any idea, Horda."

"No, but you and Thuro have been friends for most of your lives. You have a long history together. He trusts you. He can tell you how he feels." She gave him a gentle shove.

Mach looked doubtful. "I'm afraid he won't want me there."

"Of course, he does. He doesn't have to pretend with you. Go. Help him. Unna and I will see the baby doesn't suffer too much."

Mach frowned, "It sounds to me like she might be pulling his hair out by the roots."

"It sounds like he is angry right now, but I don't think he is hurting."

"How can you tell?"

"I can't. I'm just guessing since the cries are so loud and insistent." She shook her head at the noise. "Go, Mach, and help Thuro so we can help Wilda."

"But you said she doesn't want your help."

"By now she will be willing to accept anybody's help, I think."

Chapter 30

MACH AND THURO HAD walked to the back of the winter cave when Unna joined Horda.

"Eiyee! That little one has a fine set of lungs." Unna put her hands over her ears.

"I don't think I've ever heard better on any new one."

Unna looked around the deserted open area. "Shall we go see if the new mother will accept some help?"

"She said she didn't want me around," said Horda nervous in spite of her brave words to Mach.

"By now she probably would take help from Father Death himself."

"You go first."

Unna toddled over to Thuro and Wilda's area. She leaned down to the door covering and called, "Greetings, Wilda. Do you need assistance with the little one?"

Byrne continued to scream at the top of his lungs, but there was no answer to Unna's call.

"Maybe she can't hear you," whispered Horda. "Call louder.

"Greetings, Wilda. Do you need assistance with the little

one?" This time Unna screamed her words.

Still there was no reply other than the little one's howls of anger. Unna raised the hide door covering. Wilda sat on the sleeping furs with Byrne's soiled moss and cedar shavings in a messy heap at her feet. Her infant lay beside her stark naked and screaming at the top of his lungs.

"Wilda, may we come in?" Unna asked in a normal tone. "Horda and I will help you with the little one."

After a time, Wilda raised her eyes to meet Unna's. "Of course, you may come in. It doesn't matter. I am the useless one. I can't even give birth without being extremely ill. No one believed me, but I was. And, now, I certainly can't take care of my own child. Look at him." She turned her tear-stained face toward the angry infant. "Even he hates me. Hear him howl?"

"Babies howl." Unna walked into the shelter and picked up the baby. "He does not hate his mother. He is cold." Unna moved closer to the shelter fire. "Have you fed him lately?"

"Not since we came inside."

Unna stopped herself from rolling her eyes. "Besides being cold, he is hungry, Wilda. That is all that's wrong."

"And dirty and wet and mad and ..." Wilda's words trailed off, and tears trickled down her cheeks. "I really want to be a good mother to him, but this is like everything else I try to do. I make a mess of it."

"Nonsense." Unna handed Byrne to Horda who shared her warmth by cuddling him against her chest. Stopping howling, he snuffled and rooted against her.

"Where is the pouch of shavings and moss?" asked Unna.

Wilda was watching Byrne who was sucking noisily on his fist and nestling against Horda. Tears filled her eyes and she shook her head. "I don't know where it is. I was looking for it before he started crying. Thuro brought it in, but I don't know where he put it." Her shoulders shook. "I really want to be a good mother, but I don't know how."

Horda almost felt sorry for Wilda. She had been a pain and cried and whined for no reason except she was pregnant, and she had insisted she couldn't possibly be pregnant because she didn't want to be, but now ... The little one burrowed into Horda's shoulder, and she instinctively cuddled him.

"See," said Wilda, "already my own child prefers Horda to me." Though tears were running down her cheeks and her eyes were huge, dark pools of sorrow, her lips curled, and she managed to look defeated, scornful, and angry at the same time. She snarled, "He knows you will take care of him because you know what to do. Just like you always know what to do. While I," she sighed, "I, never seem to know what to do — about anything."

Anger bubbled in Horda's chest. "You are mistaken."

"What?" snapped Wilda.

"You have quite a talent, Wilda," Horda said pleasantly. Unna clicked her tongue and frowned, but Horda ignored her and continued. "No, Wilda, I'd say you don't need to know how to do anything. All you have to do is bat your eyelashes and whine. Then someone will jump in and do whatever it is you need to have done. You are very good at batting your eyelashes and whining."

Tension and anger crackled in the air like lightning sparks in a summer thunderstorm. Byrne whimpered, and Horda patted his back.

"That's cruel," Wilda said.

"Yes, it is," agreed Horda, "but sometimes the truth is cruel and painful."

"What do you mean?"

"I mean that there are hands of things I have no idea how to do, but it seems I am always faced with one or more of them. No one else knows much better than I what to do or how to do it. Unfortunately, I seem to be in charge. There is no one else to do these things so I take a deep breath and do the best I can. I cannot sit back and whine and wring my hands and say, 'I don't know how to do that.'"

Wilda's anger straightened her back and sharpened her tone. "Are you saying I don't try?"

Baby Byrne yowled his protest.

Horda's anger roared in her ears more loudly than Byrne's cries. She refused to look at Unna whom she knew would be trying to calm her with her eyes. She hadn't given in to her temper in a long time. She sighed and comforted Byrne. "No, I'm not saying you do or do not try."

Looking smug, Wilda nodded her head and set the shells and ornaments in her hair to jangling. "I do try to do whatever needs to be done even though I have been ill."

"Oh, yes, I know how hard you try." Horda felt something snap inside herself. "You try to whine and make us all miserable so someone will do whatever you need done to make you shut up."

"How dare y..." Wilda's hands curved into claws.

Byrne's yowls turned to screams.

"Tsk. Tsk. Tsk. Girls." Even though Unna's admonishing voice was soft, both Horda and Wilda turned.

"Now look what you've done," accused Wilda reaching

for the angry infant. Horda handed him to her. He screamed louder and turned red. He kicked and squirmed. Wilda looked frightened as a small rabbit caught in one of the women's snares. Byrne screamed more loudly and kicked so frantically Wilda almost dropped him.

Two fat tears leaked from his eyes. She tried to cuddle him against her shoulder as she had seen Horda do, but he would have none of it. His arms and legs were stiff, and now his face had the purple tinge of furious children everywhere. Wilda tried once more to cuddle her son. His screams grew louder.

"Take him!" She thrust him toward Horda. "You're so smart. You make him be quiet."

Horda shook her head and backed away. She knew if the baby quit howling, Wilda would hate her even more.

"For the love of the Mother." Unna reached out and took Byrne in her arms. She made gentle shushing noises and rocked him against her chest. His enormous blue/brown eyes fastened on Unna's face as she talked to him. His screams turned to shuddering sniffles, and he stuffed his fist into his mouth.

"You're hungry, aren't you, little one," said Unna.

The baby smacked and sucked on his hand and blinked. Then his chin quivered.

Unna leveled her gaze on Wilda and Horda. "You, girls, can continue your disagreements later." She smiled almost sweetly. "This baby is cold, and he is hungry. Horda, get me the moss and cedar shavings or flax or whatever you have for his bottom and a sacque."

"I don't know where the pack is," protested Horda.

"Then find it," said Unna. "Wilda, I want you to sit by

the fire and think calming thoughts while we get everything ready."

"What?" sputtered Wilda. "I don't know any calming thoughts."

"You'd better come up with some soon. This baby is hungry. You are the one who is equipped to feed him, but you have to make yourself ready."

"I can't feed him," she cried. "I don't know what to do."

Unna snorted. "You have been feeding him for a hand of days since he was born."

"But this is different."

Unna's bushy eyebrows almost met as her dark eyes stabbed Wilda. "Would you like to explain exactly how it is different?"

"Well, I, 'ah, umm, ah, I, ah, don't know how it's different, but it is."

"Nonsense," said Unna. "Anyway, we will help you. The baby is wet or dirty. He cries. You change him. He is happy. He is hungry. He cries. You feed him. He is happy. He is bored or lonely. He cries. You hold him. He is happy." Unna shrugged.

She made it sound so simple. Horda wanted to laugh at Wilda's skeptical expression.

Horda found a fresh supply of cedar shavings and moss as well as one of the rabbit skin sacques the People had given the baby at his naming ceremony. She wanted to take the little boy and attend to his needs, but she forced herself to hand the supplies to Wilda.

"I don't think this is going to work for me." Wilda looked doubtfully at the supplies.

"You haven't tried it," chided Unna. She handed the baby to his mother.

"Yes, I did." Wilda looked at the supplies that had somehow found their ways into her hands. "Didn't you hear him screaming?"

"I believe everyone in the camp heard him screaming," Unna said. "It was the first time, but it won't be the last."

Wilda looked frightened.

Unna laughed. "Oh, no, you don't, Wilda. Sit down and I will show you how to swaddle Byrne."

"He's cold," said Wilda.

"And hungry. So you need to get him dressed so you can feed him."

Wilda sat down and tried to swaddle her newborn's behind with the moss and cedar shavings. He wiggled, squirmed, and pumped his legs, then his face turned red.

Horda chewed her lip to keep from laughing when the baby's bowels opened, and he soiled the front of his mother's ceremonial dress. As if to add insult to injury, he immediately urinated.

Wilda squawked and began to gag. "Help me!" she screeched. "This child has destroyed my tunic!"

Unna took Byrne. "Lesson number one," she said, "leaving the little one's bottom uncovered just asks to have your bottom covered." Unna laughed at her own joke.

"You did that on purpose," said Wilda.

Still laughing, Unna said, "No, I didn't. Like I said, it is a chance you take when you leave the little one without covering."

Wilda gagged again. "I cannot do this."

"Yes, you can," soothed Unna.

Horda brought a woven basket full of warm water from the cook fire. She took Byrne and washed his bottom.

Wilda howled. "My dress is ruined."

"Probably not," said Horda looking at it. "Most likely you can clean it and then re-stretch it so it doesn't show."

"Ooh! As if I would ever wear it again. He shat on it." Wilda wrinkled her nose and gagged again.

"Welcome to motherhood." Unna continued to laugh. "Babies do that regularly. If they don't then, they are stopped up and that is even worse. They also pee a lot, and many of them spit up four times as much as they eat." Her eyes almost disappeared into the wrinkles of her cheeks. "Babies are a messy lot, but they are worth it."

"I don't think so," said Wilda. "I don't want anything more to do with this child."

"Sssht! Sssht," cautioned Unna. "You don't mean that."

Wilda looked at the little one gurgling at Horda and at the mess that used to be her ceremonial tunic. "I'm afraid I do." She burst into tears.

After cleaning Byrne, Horda swaddled and dressed him while Unna used some more of the moss and shavings to clean Wilda's dress.

Unna comforted Wilda. "If it's any consolation, I felt much the same way when my first little one was new."

Though she cuddled the infant against her chest, her attention was focused on the conversation. Unna had never before spoken of her family. Though the older woman showed much skill as a healer and in her work with the children of the band, Horda had never questioned how she had learned her skills. It was too rude, but if Unna wanted to share, she would, and Horda would listen — carefully.

"My first little one was a dandy. Such a set of lungs." Unna nodded, and her eyes looked back into the time long ago. "He sounded much like Byrne when he really got to going." Her hands stroked the air as if she were caressing a child. "He was beautiful, but I couldn't tell him that. My mate was a fierce warrior. He hated it when I reminded the boy of his babyhood. He pushed him to become a man almost from the time he took his first steps. I never had another boy child though I did have two girls. It was almost four hands turning of the seasons before my mate went to walk the Great Beyond."

Tears glistened in Unna's eyes, "Then Growling Bear became Chief of the People of the Tall Grass before my people fought the People of the Mountains." She sighed. "Sometimes I wonder how different our lives would have been if I had insisted on teaching Growling Bear compassion. He was a hard man even though he was young when he went to walk the Great Beyond."

She wiped a tear from her cheek. "My sister's son Bear Claw became the chief when Growling Bear was killed."

Bear Claw? Horda almost gasped aloud. Bear Claw had been Unna's nephew, and he had tried to kill her, his own aunt, when she grew old. Compassion? Horda fought the urge to spit. He had needed more than compassion.

All the People of the Tall Grass had been cruel and slovenly. All except Unna. Tears of understanding and sympathy clogged Horda's throat. She looked beyond the small sleeping area back to the Land of the Tall Grass and saw her own broken and blood-stained body. The remembered pain was so real she clenched her teeth to stop her cries.

The Men of the Frozen Earth had attacked the People of

the Tall Grass because of what Bear Claw and his warriors had done to her and the other Women of the Frozen Earth. All the People of the Tall Grass except Unna, Rain Drop, and Storm Cloud had been killed.

Unna was good to her — so good to her. Unna had saved her life when Bear Claw tried to kill her. Unna had seen her tribe wiped out, but still she loved and worked with the People of the Frozen Earth.

Wilda cried, “You are just saying that.”

Unna’s laughter called Horda back from the past.

“No, I’m not. I made many mistakes in the raising of both my little one and my sister’s. I often ask myself if I could have changed the courses they took.” Unna took a deep breath. “The Great Mystery tells us there are many paths for us to choose. Unfortunately he will not allow us to go back and take another if we choose a bad one.”

Horda wondered at Unna’s words. Never before had she heard her speak of her religion.

Baby Byrne tired of sucking his fist and howled to remind them of his presence. Unna took him and cuddled him for a brief span of time.

“Wilda, you will need some slit tunics to make it easier for you to nurse this boy.”

Wilda looked horror stricken. “Slit my tunics?”

“It is easier than trying to pull it up to nurse. Did you not realize you will need to feed him for at least two turnings of the seasons?”

“I didn’t think about it,” she admitted. “I didn’t believe I was pregnant.”

Byrne screamed and Unna said, “Strip off your tunic and wrap in your sleeping furs so you can feed him.”

Wilda did as she was told. Unna placed him to Wilda's engorged breast, and he latched on and began to make loud sucking noises. Wilda held him as far away from herself as she could.

Unna shook her head. "Hold him against your body, Wilda. He will get cold."

"I'm cold."

"His body will help warm you." Horda stirred up the fire.

Wilda looked at the noisy infant. "Couldn't someone else feed him?"

"No," said Horda.

"Why not?" whined Wilda. "I'm not well. I don't want to do this. Please, Unna. Why can't Aiyana feed him? I don't have milk."

Horda looked at her other breast, which was leaking milk. "You have plenty of milk."

"How do you know?" asked Wilda. "You don't know anything about little ones. Anyway, I was talking to Unna."

"Wilda," said Unna softly. "Aiyana can hardly feed her own child. You know her milk supply is not large. Already her little one has to eat some food because she doesn't have enough milk for him."

"I hate this. It is wrong. It feels bad. I hate this." Wilda's face crumpled, and she wailed. "It wasn't supposed to happen. I don't want to be a mother."

Horda's fingers itched to slap Wilda. "You do not know when you are lucky," she hissed.

"Lucky? Lucky?" In one of her lightning quick mood changes, Wilda's eyes flashed. "Do you call it lucky to grow so fat I could not walk? I swelled until I thought I would burst, and then when the little one was born, the pain was almost beyond bearing. You know absolutely nothing of such things, Horda. I will forgive you for your ignorance."

"Huh!"

"Now, Wilda, the pain is gone. You have a wonderful little one entrusted to your care." Unna cast a warning look at Horda.

"Well, I told you, I don't want him. At least not today." She yawned and tried to pass the baby back to Horda. "I'm tired and need to sleep."

Byrne protested his mother's rude treatment. Horda watched Unna's eyes sharpen to arrow points. "The mother entrusted you with this life. You are the only woman in the band with the ability to feed him. You will take care of him now." She thrust the squalling infant into his surprised mother's arms. Unna turned on her heel and gestured to Horda.

Almost as shocked as Wilda, Horda turned and followed Unna out of the sleeping area.

"Phew. I do not know what we are going to do with that one," Unna growled.

Horda hated the tears she felt pooling in her eyes. Biting her lips, she fought them down before she tried to speak. Byrne's angry cries suddenly stopped as he snuffled. "Do you think ...?"

Unna shook her head and cocked her ear. She mouthed, "Shhh! She's feeding him."

Horda listened to the baby's contented smacking. Then she nodded and breathed a sigh of relief.

Unna motioned with her head, and Horda followed her to the assembly fire. Rubbing their hands together, they warmed them before they were seated.

"What are we going to do if she refuses to care for her son?" asked Horda.

Unna took a deep breath before she spoke. "I cannot say for sure what she will do, or what I will do."

"I can't believe she would be so selfish."

"I can."

"A baby is a gift from the Mother. We are obligated to take care of them. They are precious. Doesn't she know how lucky she is? Doesn't she have any idea what I would give for a little one?"

"No, she doesn't," Unna murmured.

"Wilda doesn't know anything about loss. Does she?"

"No."

"What do you think is going to happen?"

Unna smiled. "I think she is going to bond with this little one. She will learn to care for him and then she will 'forget' all her fussing and behave as if he is the greatest little one ever born, and probably, she will think she is the greatest new mother in the band."

Horda giggled. "She is the only new mother in the band."

"Then she will be correct. Won't she?"

"While the seasons turn before Gathering, she will be right." Horda closed her eyes and breathed deeply. "Oh, Unna," she whispered, "I do so want to have a little one." She rubbed her hands over her flat stomach.

Unna's eyes sharpened. "Do you suppose ..."

Sadly Horda shook her head. "I don't think so, but I hope. Oh, how I hope."

Chapter 31

A FULL TURNING OF THE seasons had passed since the birth of baby Byrne. He was a sturdy toddler, speaking words and phrases, and following Thuro everywhere he could. His ma, Wilda, seemed to have grown up. She took adequate, if uninspired, care of the boy. She did her work though she did not volunteer or seem to take particular pleasure in any of it — no one could fault either her performance or her attitude. No one knew whether she was happy or sad.

Thuro had grown in stature. The slender, shy young man named co-leader of the Band had matured into a thoughtful, well-spoken leader. His muscles had thickened and grown to match his height. No longer afraid to speak before his People, he still thought through his ideas before giving voice to them.

Thuro and Mach realized their time as co-leaders was drawing to an end. Ready for new challenges, the two young men faced the next Gathering with bittersweet anticipation.

The sparse snow cover melted long before the end of the Moon of the Melting Snows; the River which had begun other spring seasons full to its banks was not. Two arms lengths of dry, discolored soil showed where the deep silver water usually ran level with the top of the bank. The shallow areas that before ran knee to waist deep on the adults were ankle to knee deep. The tender grasses, leaves, and foodstuffs of the Moon of the Early Green soon thickened, toughened, and dried.

Though drought was not unknown to the People of the Frozen Earth, it generally was little more than an inconvenience. Dry conditions would last two or three turnings of the seasons. Seldom was there a shortage of both snow and rain so the People were able to survive with minor adaptations. This time, however, the winter had produced only a fraction of the normal snowfall, and only a few sparse rains fell in the spring.

During the Moon of the Growing Food, the People recognized the problems they would soon face. Thuro and Mach called for an assembly.

When everyone had gathered, Thuro spoke. "The snows were scanty. The rains have not come. The Big River grows little. The growing food is not."

A buzz like angry bees went through the assembly. Some of the People had made the same observations as their leaders. Others were not so observant. "What can we do? What will happen to us?" the People cried.

Thuro stood silently through the tumult. Mach watched with pride while his friend, once so shy, waited until the People were ready to hear the plan the co-leaders and their mates had devised.

When the noise faded, Thuro raised his hands and silence reigned. "We cannot see what Mother Life and Father Death have planned for us so we must plan to survive the unknown."

Once more the buzz raced through the assembly. Fear. Anger. Anxiety. Worry. Dread. Alarm. All these emotions and more flooded the People who lived their lives facing the unknown and unexpected and now were standing above a chasm that could lead them to the Frozen Wilds. Thuro waited until the noise faded before he again raised his hands for silence.

"I understand your feelings. We understand your feelings." He gestured to Mach, Horda, Wilda, and Byrne who stood with him to show the People that they were People like them who would hunger and thirst if the rains and snows did not come.

"What are we going to do?" cried Zeek.

"Yes, what?" shouted others.

"First, we are planning for something that may not happen," said Thuro. "The rains may come tomorrow or the day after. The animals may return, and the Big River may overflow its banks. We may have more than plenty again this year."

"But you don't think that's going to happen," shouted Premo. "Do you?"

"I don't know," said Thuro. "As I said, it may happen, but we just don't know. We do know, however, if we go on as if it is going to happen and it doesn't, we will be in major trouble. We will have shortages of both water and food, and when the shortages are here, they will be hard to overcome."

"Hard," snorted Zeek. "How about impossible?"

"Yes, Zeek," said Thuro, "the shortages will be impossible if we haven't planned for them before they become critical."

"So what are we going to do?" asked Urscia.

"We have a plan. My mate Wilda is going to tell you about the caches we already have."

Wilda handed Byrne to Reeme to hold as she stepped up to speak to the assembly. She took a deep breath and tossed her hair over her shoulders jingling the shells and beads. She fidgeted and blinked a hand of times, but then she swallowed and said, "We all have food caches that we prepared when we first came here. I don't imagine most of yours are like mine, but I'm learning. Last growing season, I added new stores on top of what I had left from the season before.

"I know now that is not the best way to preserve food, but I did it that way. I didn't think I would ever need that food again so it didn't matter if I didn't use it. This season and next — it may matter.

"My first job is to clean any spoiled foods out of our cache, count what we already have, and put the oldest stores first so they will be eaten before they spoil. I believe in my cache I already have almost enough food to feed my family for this turning of the seasons. Now, I'm not saying it is exactly what anyone wants to eat nor is it the best tasting, but I believe I could keep my family from starving if we were able to find no new foodstuffs this whole season.

"Then we are going to count what everyone has. No, we aren't going to take foods away from families, but we do know if anyone is starving, we will do whatever we can to help them." She gave her hair a small toss as she returned to her place.

A murmur of approval rippled through the assembled People. Horda watched Wilda's smile transform her face. As bad as the drought would be, it might be a good thing for Thuro and his mate.

Thuro said, "Horda will explain her part in our preparations to you."

Taking a deep breath and squaring her shoulders, Horda stepped forward. "Normally we spend the early part of the growing season eating and enjoying the fresh foodstuffs we find before we begin to preserve them for the winter. As you can see by the way the plants are already turning brown, we will not be able to do that. We will need to water the plants as much as we are able to keep them growing to provide us food to preserve.

"We are going to work in groups and range farther away than the area we gathered in the last growing season because I believe we will not have nearly the amount of foodstuffs we had then. And perhaps the most difficult, we will need to eat sparingly of the fresh foods we do gather so we will have food for the winter moons." She bowed her head and stood while the People thought about her words. Then she returned to her place.

"Thank you, Horda," said Thuro. "Now, Mach will explain our part in this plan." Mach smiled and raised an eyebrow at Thuro who said, "Yes, I know you think I should do all the talking at this assembly."

The People laughed, and some of the tension drained away. If the leaders could still joke about speaking before the People, the situation must not be as grave as it seemed. All four of the leaders relaxed a little. The People were correct. The situation was not grave — yet. They hoped by taking steps early they could keep it from becoming dangerous.

Mach stepped to the front. "I have two things I'm supposed to tell you. First, you all know we do not usually hunt except for fresh meat this early in the season. That practice no longer exists. We will hunt for meat to preserve from this day forward because as water and food become less plentiful so do the animals we eat.

"Second, you know many of us will be busy searching for foodstuffs and meat sometimes far from our camp, so it will be necessary that we all take part in preserving our food. We will be working like in the old days when the People who gathered the food preserved it. This will, in our opinion, be easier and less wasteful than allowing food to wait for someone else to have time to preserve it." Mach bowed his head and waited for the People to think about his words. Then he stepped back.

Thuro stepped forward and smiled. "I have one more thing to say."

The People laughed at his relieved expression.

He shrugged and continued. "We are all aware of places in the mountains where water comes out of the ground. Some bubble up and make streams that run down the mountain, but some are only small muddy spots. These may be the difference between us living and dying in the coming seasons.

"If the Big River dries up, we must have water. We cannot live without it. The plants and animals we depend on for food must have water. They cannot live without it. We cannot live without them."

A worried hum ran through the assembly, and tension rose once more.

Thuro said, "I do not mean to scare you, I mean to enlist your help. Probably every person in this band knows at least one place where there is water. Some people don't realize what the little muddy spots are; others do, but we need to find as many as we can. We must be sure at least a hand of people in the band know where each of the water places is. If the water place is a stream or a muddy spot, we need to take steps to preserve water at its source." He stopped and bowed his head. Then he said, "Are there questions?"

Urscia raised her hand. "Why are you scaring us?"

"We don't mean to scare you. We mean to help you develop a respect for what may happen."

"Yes, but you don't know. Why are you scaring us with maybes?" Urscia persisted.

Unna raised her hand. "May I speak?"

"Please, come up here."

The wizened old medicine woman walked to the front of the assembly. Mach and Thuro stepped down to lift her up so she could be seen. Once in place Unna surveyed the People. Some were whispering and moving around, but Unna stood until the area was silent.

"My people," she said, "did not plan ahead. They were more like grasshoppers that live for a season and die because they do not have the food and shelter needed to survive. Your people, however, are more like the ants that plan and collect food for the long cold winter's months.

"I have watched you do this and marveled at the ease with which you accomplish so much while my people live only in the smoke of long forgotten fires. Now you are faced with a problem. Even I can see that there is not as much water as there was last year. I can see that the plants are already dying. The animals are not as plentiful as they usually are nor are they as fat." She shook her head and looked sad.

"I agree it is possible the rain will start tomorrow, but what if it doesn't? Your leaders have worked together to come up with plans that will help our band meet this challenge if it comes. The work is not really harder, but it is different. It can be done.

"If we follow this plan, we will be prepared if the drought does come. If — thank you, Mother Life — the drought doesn't come, we will have more food than we need. I say 'thank you to our leaders,' and let's get started because I know one thing for sure, you cannot plan for a drought in the middle of it."

Whispers and comments of agreement went through the assembly. Then she muttered to Mach and Thuro, "Now, get me down off here."

Unna went back to her place amid laughter and talking. The general feeling was the leaders' plan was a good one in case they needed it. Horda breathed a sigh of relief. Unna had helped them once more.

"Are there any other questions?" asked Thuro

Zeek asked, "Is there going to be one central food cache?"

Thuro looked at Wilda who stepped forward. "No, Zeek, there won't be one central cache because we all know how easy it is for one to get water in it or to be raided by wild animals or some such. For those reasons, there will be many caches like we have always used. The only difference will be that we will share the contents a little more freely than we do now."

Zeek nodded and smiled at Wilda. "That makes sense. Thanks."

"Any other questions?" asked Thuro.

"Yes." Aiyana raised her hand. "We have talked about the hunting and the foodstuffs. What about the fish from the river?"

Thuro looked stricken. He stammered a little before he said, "I guess we forgot about them."

Wilda laughed as she stepped forward and said, "Most of you know Thuro doesn't like fish. I think he probably did that on purpose because he'd rather starve than eat 'those things.'" She waited for the laughter to die down before she said, "I know we need to harvest fish, but we don't want to take too many from the river. Perhaps you, Aiyana, could help us with that part of the preparation."

Thuro smiled at Wilda who glowed under his approval. Horda and Mach exchanged speaking looks. The brat was growing up.

"Other questions?" said Thuro. No one spoke, and he said, "I'm sure we will have more questions and concerns as we go along so I suggest we are finished now so we can get to work."

"Wait, stop," called Lucza. "I must not have been listening as well as I should have, but I don't understand. Are we all going to clean out our caches and count them before we start to hunt and gather?"

Wilda's face showed her unhappiness so Horda said, "I'm sorry. I don't think we made that as clear as we could have. Wilda, didn't we decide to have the caches cleaned out and counted before we began searching for new food in earnest?"

Wilda nodded. "I think the men can be searching for the water and maybe doing some hunting close to the shelter while we take care of this part. I don't think the cleaning will take too long. Do you?"

Lucza shook her head. "I'm sorry, but we really don't have

too much left."

Horda held her breath waiting for Urscia tc comment about Lucza's incompetence, but she didn't.

CHAPTER 32

THE WOMEN HAD BEEN working in the food caches in the winter cave since the assembly when Wilda screeched. Sure she was being attacked, everyone dropped everything, grabbed whatever weapons they could find, and ran through the gloom to her assistance.

"What's wrong? What's wrong?" they all called.

At the same time everyone realized she was crying — hysterically.

"What's wrong?" asked Dita. "Are you hurt?"

Between her sobs, Wilda said, "I'm worthless. I can't do anything right."

"What?" asked Horda. "What are you talking about?"

"Look at this mess!" shouted Wilda. "It's all ruined, and it's all my fault." She sobbed.

Horda and Dita looked at the wet, gummy mess that was the bottom of Wilda's cache.

Dita shook her head. "It is pretty nasty," she said.

"Yes, it's awful," agreed Horda holding out a handful of the gunk.

"You don't have to agree with me," snorted Wilda. "As I

recall, you were the ones teaching me to preserve food."

"Oh, this mess doesn't have anything to do with the way you preserved the food," said Urscia. "It's because water got into your cache."

All of the women stopped and looked at each other. "Water in a food cache is a bad thing," said Lucza.

"Yes, it is," agreed all the rest.

"But water in a winter shelter in a drought is a good thing," said Horda.

"Yes, it is," they all agreed.

Wilda was now all smiles. "I found the first water place." She dragged out the last of the spoiled food. "Well, maybe it is more accurate to say the water place found me."

"Doesn't matter," said Horda. "We are all glad to have it."

"Now, I just have to decide where to make my new food cache," said Wilda.

While the women were cleaning and counting the food caches, the men had decided to learn about the water places. There were two hands plus one that at least a hand of the men knew, but each man knew at least one water place no one else seemed to recognize.

The men divided into groups of five and started off. Mach, Zhrul, Dyson, Premo, and Zeek made up one group, and they started out toward the mountains up the course of the Big River.

"Hey, look," called Dyson. "Here is a huge bed of water lily tubers. We haven't had any of those since we've been here."

"I've always liked those roasted with antelope or bison. They really catch the flavor, and they are delicious." Zeek smacked his lips.

"I wonder where Thunder Eagle is," said Premo. "I wish we had some salt. I can't think of anything we eat that doesn't taste better with salt on it."

"I hope he's at Gathering this year," said Zeek. "His stories are about the best I've heard, and I like his flute. He can make that thing speak to my spirit, but like you, Premo, I love his salt. It is wonderful."

Mach joined the conversation. "I like the pictures he paints. I wonder if he could paint a rain scene and keep the drought away."

The men walked on in silence until Zhrul called, "Would you look at that?"

"What?" asked all the rest.

"It's the biggest willow tree I've seen lately."

Mach clapped his friend on the shoulder. "That is wonderful. Horda was worrying because she didn't know where to get good willow bark because the trees near the shelter are too small to have the mature bark she needs for some things. This is perfect."

"Yep, it is." Zhrul made a mental note of the location of the tree as well as the water lily tubers. The men turned away from the Big River and trudged up one of the small tributaries still looking for water places. Zhrul called again, "Would you look at this?"

The other men stopped and stared. They had stumbled onto the largest bed of wild onions any of them had ever seen. Not only were there many green shoots of the young plants, there were many plants gone to seed. "Well, we aren't having much luck finding water places," said Zeek.

"No," agreed Dyson, "but we are certainly finding lots of fresh foodstuffs."

"But that's not what we are looking for," argued Premo.

"Do you really think any one is going to care if we come home with lots of fresh food?" asked Mach.

"I — ah — wouldn't go taking all this stuff home today," said Zeek. "Aren't our mates busy cleaning out and counting the caches?"

Dyson grinned. "They'd probably tell us we found it, we'd have to be the ones to preserve it — all of it."

"I'm not sure my mates would be that kind." Zhrul chuckled. "They'd probably feed me as much as I could swallow and then suggest I wear the rest."

All the men laughed at the thought of crusty Zhrul wearing water lily pads, onion shoots, and willow bark. Then they became quiet.

Mach said, "We are finding food we didn't know we had."

"Yes, we are," agreed Zeek. "We are not in nearly as bad a shape as we thought we might be food-wise."

"No, we aren't," agreed Mach, "but we haven't found any water places."

Zeek looked at the tributary. "Not exactly, but do you see how this little branch of the river is still flowing?"

Mach nodded.

"That probably means it is being fed by a water place instead of runoff."

"So?" said Mach.

"So its water is coming out of the ground like the water

places instead of off the ground. That water doesn't go away when it doesn't rain or snow like surface water does." Zeek reached down and scooped a handful of the sparkling water and tasted it.

"Can you tell if it's from a water place by tasting it?" asked Mach.

"No," said Zeek, "I'm just thirsty."

All the other men including Mach laughed.

Zeek looked at the little stream. "But I do think this will be likely to help us in a drought."

Dyson pointed up a slight incline. "The water place I knew about used to be up there."

The men followed the incline and soon found it — a boggy area saturated with muddy water. They all clapped Dyson on the back and congratulated him.

"We will dig out a basin to collect the water so the mud can settle. Then we can dip it up to use if we need it." Zeek walked around the water place looking at the mud and poking it. "Looks like there may be two or three sources," he said. "That should provide a pretty good supply if we have to have it."

Then Premo asked, "How are we going to use this area if the drought comes?"

Dyson looked shocked then perplexed.

Mach said, "It's really not far from the winter shelter. Is it?"

"No," said Dyson, "the shelter is almost in a straight line over there." He pointed to the southwest. "I've hunted antelope and deer over here. It takes only a short span of time to walk it."

"Then why did we come the long way by the Big River?"

demanded Zhrul.

"Ahh, I, ahh." Dyson stuttered and stammered under the older man's anger.

"We came this way," said Mach, "because we were by the river checking other water places we already knew."

"And anyway," said Zeek, "if we hadn't come this way, we wouldn't have found the water lily tubers, the wild onions, or the willow bark."

"No, said Premo, "and we wouldn't have learned about ground water and under the ground water either."

Zhrul took a deep breath. "Forgive me, Dyson. This appears to have been a valuable trip. When we go to the water place I know, I hope we have as much success."

Dyson blushed. "I can't take credit because I didn't know about any of the things except the water place."

Zeek looked at Zhrul and Mach and laughed. "That boy's going to have to learn. Isn't he?"

"Yep," said Zhrul.

"Learn what?" asked the confused Dyson.

"To say 'thank you' and shut up," said Mach. "It's safer that way."

All five of the men chuckled as they returned to the winter shelter.

The morning sun pushed pink fingers above the horizon to drive away the shadows before it touched the scant dew on grasses already browning in the dry weather. A single eagle soared in the early light casting its shadow on the earth below. The caches were cleaned and counted. A hand's hand plus four fingers water places had been identified, and the People had made plans for how to best use the water each provided. The women were taking turns ranging wide looking for foodstuffs to be preserved. The men had divided themselves into two groups and were hunting and preserving their kills and roughly preparing the hides and pelts for use by the People.

Urscia's legs suffered from the walking and carrying. She hated to admit it, but she had to stop. No one had begun to harvest the fish in the river so she said, "I'm sorry. I can't walk anymore, but I have more sinew than I need. I'm going to make a net to use in the river." She sat and knotted the sinew for two turnings of the sun. Some of the People looked at her and shook their heads thinking she had lost her mind, but no one said anything.

On the morning of the third day, Urscia called Lucza and Horda to come and help her. She handed each one side of the thing she had made. It covered an area about the same as two armspans square and was made of knotted sinew with small stones on two sides and a piece of braided leather about an arm's length on the sides with the stones. Every one looked at it and told Urscia that thing was very nice, but no one quite understood what it was.

Instead of being angry, Urscia who had been resting took her crutches and called them to follow her to the Big River.

Everyone did. Men, women, and children — they all wanted to see what she had made.

Once there, she said, "Okay, Horda and Lucza, I want you to wade out in the river. Stretch the thing between you and hold it as open as you can."

Though they shivered when they climbed into the river,

Horda and Lucza did as they were told.

"Now, grab the braided leather and drop the thing into the water," directed Urscia.

They did, but they almost lost their balance and nearly fell to be washed down stream.

"Dig in your feet," shouted Urscia. "Now, pull back and lift it out of the water."

All the People yelled and cheered as Horda and Lucza pulled out several fish that had become entangled in the thing.

"It works. It works," shouted Urscia. "I wasn't sure if it would, but it does."

Willing hands took the thing and helped the shivering women from the river.

"It's a great idea," said Horda when she could talk. "But I think it needs to be a little bigger."

"I think you need to figure out some way it can be used without having to stand in the river," said Lucza.

"I'm working on it." Urscia watched Thuro take the thing in his hands and drop one side in the river.

A short time later, he pulled up several fish including a trout as long as his forearm.

"Hey, Urscia," he called. "This is a good idea, and it works, but I'd still rather not eat these things."

All the People laughed as they walked back to the shelter with the first fish they had caught with the sinew net.

Mach and Thuro's band had worked hard all through the spring and summer moons. As there had been little snow the previous winter, there had been less rain that spring and summer. The hot sun burned the plains and mountains alike. Sharp-edged shadows provided no relief from the relentless heat.

The band's caches were well-filled because they had started early and worked together toward a goal. They did not have nearly the supply of blubber they would have liked because many of the animals simply had not found enough to eat to develop that protective layer of fat. But no matter, they would not have to ration. They had moved plants to the water places they knew so they would have food for the next season. It would be more difficult to hunt, but the Big River was still flowing. Zeek thought it was supplied more by underground water than the surface water they had feared.

All in all the People of this little band were happy and successful. Horda smiled as she thought back over the last turning of the seasons. They had done well. It seemed all their big challenges had been worked out.

She clapped her hand over her mouth and looked to the sky. *Please, Mother Life, forgive me. I didn't mean to brag. Thank you for working out so many of the problems of our lives. Without you, we would have more trouble. Thank you, Father Death, for allowing us to go on. You are merciful. Thank you.*

#

The People were preparing for the trek to Gathering. They had one more turning of the sun before they left. Everyone was excited except Horda. She found herself fretting over all the negative things she could think of. Unna grew frailer with each passing year. Horda wondered if this would be the last time she saw Zaaco. A little voice in her mind whispered she ought to be grateful to have had Unna and her father for so long.

Mach's mother Woda and his sister Saba had gone to walk the Frozen Wilds at the previous Gathering when Saba's long hair had caught fire while she was learning to cook. Woda had covered her with her own body, but instead of smothering the flames, she had caught fire herself. Both the deaths were so unexpected she wondered if Mach had come to terms with the losses. She wondered if she ever would.

And then, as she had for four turnings of the seasons, she longed for a child of her own. Sometimes she thought she would scream if anyone else told her it would happen in the Mother's own time. She knew they were right, but she didn't need any one else to tell her that. She hoped Nuroo would have some new suggestion for her at this Gathering.

The sun rose the next morning barely able to shine through the heavy clouds, which shadowed the day. Thunder grumbled and the earth steamed until the sun stood overhead, and then the sky opened and rain poured down. The band, which had returned to the winter shelter to prepare for Gathering, stood at the opening and peered out.

Before sunset, the Big River was full and roaring louder than they had ever heard it. The prairie looked like a big water, and still the rain poured down from the slate grey sky. They decided to delay leaving for Gathering the next morning because the rain still poured.

"Delaying won't be a problem," said Mach.

"No," said Thuro, "we were leaving a whole hand of days before we had to since we had finished putting by the supplies."

"I don't think we are going to have a big drought this year," said Lija.

"Nope, it certainly doesn't look like it," agreed Imal.

"Does that mean we did all that work for nothing?" asked Storm Cloud.

"No," said about three hands of people at once.

Storm Cloud held up his hands. "I wasn't complaining," he said. "I was just asking."

Wilda said, "Storm Cloud, we did a lot of work. Some of it was kind of extra since it rained, but what if it hadn't rained? What would have happened to us if we hadn't prepared?"

Storm Cloud looked at her and said, "We would have starved like we used to when I was a little one."

Gathering passed quietly that year. Mach and Thuro's band had done the most to prepare for the drought that threatened the People. Each person of their band was asked to explain about their preparations to the members of all the other bands including the Inner Band.

"I had no idea we were doing anything unusual," said Wilda.

"Me either," admitted Horda. "Remember how we just figured what we needed to survive?"

"Yeah, and you even listened to me," said Wilda.

"We've all come a long way, haven't we?" Horda grinned. "I never thought I would say this, but I hope they don't separate us yet."

Wilda's eyes were shiny when she said, "Me either."

Chapter 33

AN ANGRY WIND ROARED and moaned outside the cave as the weak sun fought to push back the darkness. Icy drafts puffed around the door covering. Looking disgustedly at the remains of her cook fire and yawning, Horda shivered in the cold morning air. It feels more like the beginning of the Moons of the Long Blizzards than the Moon of the Early Green. She yawned again. Mother Life, I feel like I haven't been asleep in a hand's turnings of the sun.

Rubbing her eyes and stretching her shoulders, she pushed back into the sleeping area and donned a fur parka and leggings over her morning tunic. Even as she fought to keep her eyes open, she took the coals from their sleeping fire and rekindled her cook fire.

Still shivering and fighting to keep her teeth from chattering, she fed the struggling flames grass, twigs, and bark until the fire blazed. More frigid wind whistled around the door covering driving the last vestiges of sleep from her head. She pulled her parka around herself and yawned.

Still cold she went to the assembly fire where she stirred the embers into flames. Then she fed it twigs and kindling until she could add a large log. She warmed herself and looked at Thuro and Wilda's area. All the moons had come and gone twice since Byrne was born, and they were back to his birth moon, the Moon of the Early Green. Horda and Mach pretended not to notice, but even though Wilda was working and doing her part, it seemed Thuro was more mother to the boy than his mother was.

As far as Horda could tell, Wilda fed the little one, but she left almost everything else about his care to his father. Not that Thuro seemed to mind, though hunting season had been difficult for him and the little one last year. He had struggled to take care of his son and do his work. Now that Byrne was more active, it would be almost impossible.

Would Wilda take over then? Who knew? Is there some way I can help my mate's friend without angering his mate? Horda shook her head. She doubted it. Even though Wilda had grown more reasonable in many ways, it sometimes seemed Horda's existence angered Wilda.

Please, Mother Life, help me to keep my mouth shut. Please, help Wilda to see this little one for the wonderful gift he is. Help her to care for him and guide him to grow up to be the man you mean for him to be. And help me not to interfere. Please.

As far as Thuro told anyone, Wilda cared for Byrne and was the kind of mother she should have been. People who watched her closely knew that was not so, but they could not complain as long as her mate did not, and the little one suffered no injuries or illnesses from his mother's carelessness. Wilda had learned, and she performed her fair share of the work adequately if not really well. No one could truly fault her, nor could she be banished.

Horda wished there was some way she could make Wilda

behave as she should toward baby Byrne. But there didn't seem to be any way. Though it hurt her, she tried to avoid trouble by limiting her role in the boy's life.

Still she longed for a little one of her own, and still Mother Life told her to wait. She wrapped her arms around the empty ache of her flat stomach. *Oh, and Mother Life, please, I beg of you, allow me to have a little one. I promise to care for it to the best of my ability and guide it in your ways. Please, oh, please, hear my prayer.*

Dressed in a breech cloth, Mach stepped out of the sleeping area. Horda laughed as she watched his eyes round. "By the Father's teeth," he huddled over the fire, "when did it get so cold?"

"It feels like the beginning of the long blizzards." She ran her fingers down the gooseflesh puckering his arms.

"Stop that." He shivered. "It isn't time for the long blizzards. Is it?"

"No, according to the counting cords, it is the Moon of the Early Green." A strong gust of wind twirled the smoke of their fire and pushed the warmth away. She pulled her parka more securely around her cold body. "I don't think I could stand it if winter was just beginning."

The Moon of Melting Snow had not yet come, but the little snow had already melted.

"I'm afraid it is going to be really bad this hot season," said Mach. "Remember how little snow and rain we had most of last season? Then all of a sudden enough came so we made it."

"Listen to the wind. It's just drying out the land even more," said Horda. "I kept hoping the snows would come, but they didn't. We didn't even have enough snow to cover the ground. It's scary."

"Why is it scary?" asked Mach. "We all worked together last year, and we could have survived well even if the rains hadn't come."

"I know, but what if we can't find what we need this season?" She sniffed as tears ran down her face.

Mach took her in his arms. "Hey, I know it's scary, but it is going to be okay. I remember one time before it was so dry. I had about four winters. The Green River just barely gave us enough water to drink. The animals disappeared, and the plants didn't grow.

"The long dry lasted for almost three turnings of the seasons. It was bad. Not only were we thirsty, we were hungry. The men were looking for water, but there wasn't much to find."

She sobbed. "I don't remember, but I remember the stories, and I don't see how this is reassuring me."

He held her close and made soft wordless sounds of comfort. "Of course, you wouldn't remember it. You were little more than a baby, but my point is we were so much better prepared last season. And we will be this season. You should not worry."

"Humph. Says you." She touched her mouth to his and turned back to the cook fire. "Should I start to save food?" she asked between sobs.

Mach listened to the storm's howl. "I don't think so yet. We don't want to waste, but, Horda, you know we still have almost half in the caches. Perhaps the Mother will send us snow and rain. I think we will be all right."

"Why?"

He took a deep breath. "I don't know why. I guess I'm

just hoping it comes a deep blizzard today."

"What do you know?" Horda snapped. "I don't believe one blizzard will be enough."

He gave his normally even-tempered wife a perplexed look. "Okay, then I'm praying to Mother Life to send us water and to Father Death to spare us."

"Well, I am too," she barked. "The storm's sharp teeth are sucking the water from the earth and gnawing away at the covering."

Rubbing his hands together, Mach glared toward the front of the cave just as a violent gust of wind lifted the corner of the hide curtain and shook it. "I will have to secure that as soon as we finish the eat."

Another wind gust lifted the hides even higher and caused the smoke to boil around the shelter. "Why don't you secure it now so we don't choke to death?" whined Horda.

Coughing, Mach said, "Okay. I'll dress and get right to it."

"Wise idea. I'll give you just a little time before I fix the morning eat."

Clapping her hand over her mouth, she stood very still and looked at Mach with big frightened eyes.

He watched a definite green tinge crawl up her face. "What's wrong?" In one step, he was beside her holding her against his chest. "What's the matter? What is happening? Are you ill?" She leaned against him and took a shaky breath. He leaned back so he could see her face. "Are you going to answer me?"

She swallowed hard. He watched the sickly shade of green crawl back down her face to her neck. He frowned.

Then she pushed away from him and ran for the opening

of the cave. "What's the matter with you? Where are you going?" demanded the frightened Mach as Horda charged out the opening. He had taken three steps to follow her when she pushed aside the hide covering, and he was hit by a blast of cold air. "By the Father's dirty teeth!" he muttered before he waded outside into the cold weather.

Jumping around in the cold, he found Horda not far from the shelter opening. He shook his head and spewed questions. "Where did you go? What is the matter with you, woman? Are you ill? Have you lost your mind? Are you trying to freeze yourself to death? Is it something you ate? Do you need me to call Unna? Don't you realize it is cold out here?"

Horda's eyes sparkled, and she smiled at her nearly naked mate. Grabbing his arms she hugged him before she laughed out loud. Her laughter stopped the flow of his questions.

He held her and stared into her eyes. "By the name of the Mother, Woman. If you don't tell me what is the matter, I am going to ..." He sputtered as he tried to decide on a fitting punishment though such punishments were completely foreign to the People of the Frozen Earth so he jumped up and down in place trying not to freeze.

When she laughed again and hugged him once more, he threatened to share her breath.

She turned her head. "I have no mint to chew, and I'm sure my breath is sour."

He frowned and tried to wrap himself and the bouncing Horda in her parka. "Did you throw up? What is wrong with you?"

She giggled again and hugged him even tighter. "Think, Mach. Think."

His teeth chattered. "I'm trying to think, but I am freezing."

"Then go inside." She broke away from him and spun around. "Thank you, Mother Life. Thank you, thank you, thank you! I promise to do the best I can. Thank you."

Mach caught her hand and pulled her back inside the shelter where the smells of the cook fires stopped her laughter. He watched her turn green again and run outside. This time he was right behind her and held her head.

"What is going on?" he demanded.

"I really wish I had some fresh snow to wash my mouth," she said.

He glared at her and found a bit of almost clean snow from a sheltered area.

Her eyes danced, and she said, "You really have no idea what's wrong. Do you?" She chewed on the snow and rinsed her mouth.

Mach shook his head. "I'm assuming you know and are delighted, but I personally do not find vomiting a cause for excitement."

"Think about it," she said. "I was sick once before, and you helped me."

He still looked puzzled.

"What is the one thing I want more than anything?"

"A little one, but ..." His eyes rounded. "Are you trying to tell me ..."

Suddenly shy, she ducked her head and nodded. He reached out and wrapped her in an embrace. "Did you know?"

"I didn't know for sure, but I was hoping."

He pulled her closer. "Why didn't you tell me?"

"I have hoped before. I was afraid I was just imagining things, but now I'm sick too. I'm pretty sure." Her eyes sparkled, and she laughed out loud. "Oh, thank you, Mother Life. Thank you."

"You must take care of yourself." He realized once again that he was cold. "Come inside. It's cold out here." He pushed aside the hide covering and led her into the shelter.

The heat and smells assaulted her nose, and the sickly shade of green tinted her face and neck before she ran outside once more. She fought to control her breathing and stop the awful nausea, but she lost.

Mach ran in and grabbed his own parka and an armload of sleeping furs before he went outside after her again. "Horda, this will not do." He draped a sleeping fur around her. "It's much too cold for you to stand out here."

Echoes of Bear Claw's words and the nausea finally overcame her happiness. She glared at Mach. "Do you think I'm choosing to stand out here? Do you think I am choosing to throw up? Do you think this is something I want to do?"

Mother Life, I'm just making a point to him. I do want to do this. Oh, I do. So very much. Thank you.

"Well, every time I take you inside you run out."

She sighed. "Why do I run out?"

"Because you don't like the smells. Why do you turn that funny shade of green? I've never seen anyone actually turn green before."

"Sometimes, Mach, you make me understand what Suka said about Elko at the Mating Classes."

"What?"

"She said Elko was the smartest man on earth when

he wasn't the dumbest thing on two legs." Horda smiled sweetly.

"What does that mean?"

"That right now you are as dumb as anyone I have ever known. And I daresay a whole lot dumber than most." She touched his face. "I'd say you are as dumb as a tree, but I don't want to insult the tree."

He snorted. "I don't understand." He caught her hand. "Just come inside before we freeze out here."

"Go get Unna." She pulled her hand out of his and shivered as the wind whistled.

"Why?"

Horda rolled her eyes. "Just do as I ask, please." She took another fur from him and wrapped it around herself. "Hurry, if you don't mind. I'm getting cold."

"Then why don't you come inside with me?"

She took a deep breath and swallowed against the nausea boiling in her stomach. "Have you noticed that being inside makes me vomit?"

He blinked. "Yes, I've noticed, but can't you just stop it?"

"Stop it? Stop it? Just like that, wave a magic stick and stop vomiting. Hunh. I'm sure."

"Don't get angry, Horda. I just thought you could breathe more slowly or something and keep from throwing up."

"Mach." Her teeth chattered, and she looked angry and terrified at the same time. "I really want to see Unna. Now! I need her. Will you please hurry? We can discuss this later." She shivered and pulled the furs more closely.

He turned to go.

"Don't you frighten her to death either," Horda called.

"Just ask her to come outside. And be sure to help her bundle up. This wind is cold."

Chapter 34

PULLING HORDA OUT OF the shadows into the cold sunshine, Unna handed her dried mint leaves. "Chew these. When the smell of them is strong in your nose and the taste is in your mouth, try to come inside. I'm too old to stand out here. I'm freezing."

Unna glared at Mach who tried to look innocent while he hovered around them.

"What did he do?" asked Horda. She obediently chewed and breathed deeply.

"Oh, nothing much except try to bundle me into half the furs in the shelter and tell me you were probably going to freeze to death if I didn't get here in the next beating of my heart."

"Well, you were shivering, and your teeth were chattering." Mach was also shivering violently though he had on a parka and was wrapped in a bison robe.

Horda looked accusingly. "I told you not to scare her to death." She chewed more mint.

"I didn't scare her," said Mach. "I'm the one who is scared. She is as cool as can be."

"Of course, I am," said Unna. "I have been expecting this call."

"Am I the only one who doesn't know what is happening?" Mach glared at Unna and Horda in turn. "When I told her you needed her, she got up, picked up her bag and said, 'Where is she?' Just like she expected you to need her."

Unna laughed. "I hoped."

"You hoped?" squawked Mach. "You hoped Horda would be ill?"

"Yes, I did. I have been praying to Mother Life for a long, long time." She smiled at two of her favorite people in the whole world. "I have asked her to let me see your first little one."

Horda felt tears fill her eyes and threaten to run down her cheeks. She bit her lips, and she was freezing and shivering. "Do you really think this is happening?"

Unna nodded. "I've seen the early signs. I was pretty sure this was going to be the time we have been waiting for. I'll need to check you, but I'm certain I'm correct."

Mach frowned and closed his eyes. Unna looked at him and then at Horda. "Wipe those tears off your cheeks before they freeze," she grumbled.

"Oh, Unna, I had almost given up hope." Horda scrubbed her cold face on the edge of the robe.

"Nuroo told you not to worry, child."

"But this is the fourth winter since we were kidnapped."

"In the Mother's own time," said Unna. "In the Mother's own time."

Suddenly those were the sweetest words Horda had ever heard.

Mach looked from Unna to Horda and back. "Are we

really standing out here in the snow talking about a little one?"

Giggling Horda took his hand. "Not a little one, Mach. Our little one."

A look of wonder infused his face. "Mother Life, we are talking about our little one."

"That's right, Mach. We're talking about your little one," said Unna. "Your little one."

He hugged Horda and leaned down to share her breath. "We are going to have a little one." He laughed and squeezed her. "You are going to have my little one."

Echoes of Bear Claw's excitement rang through Horda's memory.

Unna heard them too. Catching Horda's eye, she shook her head. Then she patted Mach's arm. "Why don't you go inside and get dressed? I imagine Horda is going to need to lie down for a little while. See if you can fix her sleeping place so it is warm but doesn't smell too much of the cooking odors. I'll bring her in as soon as I can."

Taking a deep breath, Mach wrapped his bison robe around Horda and put his parka on Unna before he ran inside. Unna drew the coat around herself and breathed deeply. Horda snuggled into to the robe, but she avoided breathing as much as possible.

"He sounds much like Bear Claw sounded when he discovered I was breeding," Horda murmured.

Unna stood silently for a span of time before she spoke. "Yes, he does, Horda. It is a normal reaction."

"I know." She looked across the snow to the yesterdays so long ago.

"He is not Bear Claw," said Unna.

"I know."

"How do you feel?" asked Unna. "Besides being nauseated, I mean."

"Wonderful."

"Are you tired?"

"Tired?"

"You know. Do you wake up wishing you could go back to sleep?"

"Now that you mention it, I do. Sometimes it feels like my eyes are too heavy to stay open by themselves. I thought I was getting lazy."

Unna chuckled. "There are many words I would use to describe you, but lazy is not one of them."

"But it's barely morning and I'm ready to go back to sleep."

"That's normal. Don't you remember when Wilda was first breeding?"

Horda frowned. "Wilda doesn't like to work anytime."

"I know, but do you remember how bad she was when we came back from the Inner Band? That's the way some of us are when we are breeding. I don't know what causes it, but even women who normally do their share of the work find themselves so exhausted all they want to do is sleep."

"The first time I could hardly lift my feet even in the mornings, and I was so sick. I felt hollow." Horda wiped a tear off her face. "But I had to keep pretending because I didn't want to admit —"

"Don't speak of that time." Unna put her fingers on Horda's lips. "It is over."

"No, Unna, I'm sorry, but it is not over. That time is with me every step I take." Tears swam in Horda's eyes, and she took a deep breath. "I told myself it was over. I have tried to forget it, but I can't. It haunts me. I thought it was over, but I wonder if it will ever be over."

"Yes, Little One, it is over. It has been over for a long time, but you wouldn't allow yourself to believe it was really over." Unna hugged Horda with all the strength in her fragile body. "You couldn't let go until you finally had a little one of your own. Now —"

"I am thankful to Mother Life for this chance to have a little one."

"Horda, I, too, am thankful to the Great Mystery for allowing me the opportunity to see that not all people are as selfish and worthless as my People had become. I am thankful He allowed me to survive with your People who have hope for the future." Unna handed Horda more dried mint leaves. "Just think by the Moon of the Long Blizzards, you will have a little one in your arms."

"Oh, my," Horda frowned. "Think how I will look at this Gathering."

Unna laughed out loud. "You will look like you swallowed the moon."

"I can't go."

"Don't be a silly goose. Of course, you will go. We will make you a new ceremonial tunic."

"We will?"

"Are you coming inside?" Mach called from the opening. "Or do you plan to stay out there until you freeze?"

"We're coming inside." Unna handed Horda the last of the mint leaves. "How do you feel?"

"Better." Horda smiled and rubbed her stomach. It was still flat, but she almost believed she could feel the little one growing there.

"A little better or much better?"

Horda watched a single sunbeam break through the cloud covering and drive away the grey shadows. Smiling she blinked and sniffed the cold wind before she hugged Unna tightly. "Much, much better."

Scott Monroe

GRACE ANNE SCHAEFER

Grace Anne Schaefer, a retired English teacher, lives in central Texas and has been married to her first husband Kenn, a transplanted Hoosier saint, since 1969. Their daughter Anja, an independent spirit like her mother, teaches high school English.

Her daughter is a leukemia survivor, her husband is a bladder cancer survivor, and Grace Anne is a ten-year breast cancer survivor—all three are testimonies to early detection and the best possible care.

In early 2006, Grace Anne was almost felled by a congenitally malformed aortic valve. Her heart surgery has given her a new lease on life by finally allowing her to finish this book and get back to doing what she loves most: traveling and meeting friends—old and new—at pow wows, festivals, and book signings. She is currently at work on the third book in the ***People of the Frozen Earth*** series—***To Walk Above the Clouds***.

People of the Frozen Earth – Book Three

To Walk Above the Clouds

To Walk Above the Clouds, the third book in the *People of the Frozen Earth* Series continues the saga. Mach and Horda are finally parents of a baby girl whom they name Lara. The little one brings happiness to everyone in the band Mach and Thuro led. Then disease and death cause Lara and her parents to be moved to Emol's band where Mach and Horda soon learn Emol's laziness was not the cause of all his people's problems.